CHANGE MANAGEMENT

CONCEPTS, TECHNIQUES, STRATEGIES & EXECUTION

2ND EDITION

MOID SIDDIQUI
R.H. KHWAJA

ATLANTIC
PUBLISHERS & DISTRIBUTORS (P) LTD

ATLANTIC
PUBLISHERS & DISTRIBUTORS (P) LTD

7/22, Ansari Road, Darya Ganj, New Delhi
Tel.: +91-11-4077 5252, 2327 3880
E-mail: orders@atlanticbooks.com
Web: www.atlanticbooks.com

Published by Atlantic Publishers & Distributors (P) Ltd 2024

Previously Published by SAGE Publications in 2014

Printed & bound in India by Atlantic Print Services

Praise for the First Edition

'The book is of enormous relevance today as in the age of globalisation we are under constant pressure of being ahead of others to survive.'

—Dr R.K. Pachauri
Chairman, The Energy and Resources Institute
(Quoted in *The Asian Age*)

'Here is a book not just for the library book shelf but one with nuggets of wisdom that can be applied to change management companies, in personal lives and at the work place.'

—Livemint.com and *The Wall Street Journal*

'This is a fresh approach adapted on the subject of change management where the book is a treat to the reader. The lucid style to convey powerful thoughts is a definite plus of this book. The book leaves a sense of excitement and the satisfaction of having read a good book for the reader, where the authors deserve kudos.'

—Prajnan

'*Change Management: Concepts, Techniques, Strategies and Execution* by Moid Siddiqui and R.H. Khwaja is a classic in the area of managing change. There are several books on "managing change", but what sets this book apart is its different tone and tenor, its "storytelling" technique and its critical, in-depth and practical treatment of the subject matter. Throughout, the reader finds a blend of philosophy and pragmatism, which makes the book all the more exclusive of its kind ... The book could be considered as a path-breaking contribution in the area of organisational dynamics which is so crucial for effective governance in organisations and society. It is a must for the policy makers, business leaders and researchers in public administration, business management and public service.'

—Journal of Administrative and Governance

'A striking feature of this book is that it examines change as a natural corollary of life. Hence, it impresses upon the fact that change is not just a mantra for growth, rather improvising and adapting to change is the only way for survival.'

—The Times of India

'[This book is] a good blend of theories, concepts and practical techniques.'

—Mail Today

'There are several books on managing change but what sets this book apart is its different tone and tenor, its storytelling technique and its critical and in-depth treatment of the subject matter.'

—Asian Age

'It will be an invaluable source of information for all professional managers ... The book is encapsulated with practical wisdom. The book has takeaways relevant to any individual or enterprise embarking on the process of change management ... *The Change Management* is a useful and engaging book on change management.'

—Management and Labour Studies

'*Change Management: Concepts, Techniques, Strategies and Execution* is refreshing in its perspective and commentary ... Easy to grasp business lingo ... uncomplicated yet in-depth analyses and creative scenarios coupled with relevant quotes by masters mark this matter of facts musing by Moid Siddiqui and R.H. Khwaja ... CEOs, entrepreneurs, business consultants, professionals in all fields and students of management should make a dig at this worthy investment.'

—Delhi Mid Day

I dedicate this book to
my son Feroz Siddiqui, my heart;
to
my daughter Fairina Siddiqui, my soul;
and to
my wife Ruquiya Siddiqui, my heart and soul

Moid Siddiqui

I dedicate this book to
All Singarenians, past and present!
May the spirit of Singarenism continue to prosper and
may all Singarenians continue to work with
perennial zeal in serving
Mother Singareni.

This book is also dedicated to
My wife, Naazneen, and my children. Naazneen
is my eternal source of strength and inspiration.

Amreen, my daughter, and my son, Fazal, have
constantly encouraged me to convey my message
on the philosophy of
Singarenism.

R.H. Khwaja

Contents

PART II: THE SINGARENI LOVE STORY: TURNAROUND FROM THE HEART (LEADERSHIP, STRATEGIES AND EXECUTION)

List of Figures

Foreword to the First Edition

'Managing Change' has always been fascinating and exciting, though it is a tough and delicate activity for any executive. However, 'Managing Change' is not by choice; it is an essential activity. I have believed: 'Change when you are still strong and when change appears unnecessary—do not wait for the day when you have no option but to change.'

The mantra that I followed all through in my life is 'to lead the change process personally'. In any process of change management, the leader must lead from the front and take ownership of the process. This responsibility cannot be delegated. Though it is easy to give sanctions and allocate budgets, the chief executive officer (CEO) must lead the process by his personal involvement.

There are three reasons why I have appreciated this book and believe it will create a good ripple effect. First, its title *Change Management* is realistic, depictive and expressive of both, *anxiety* and *excitement*. If 'anxiety' overtakes 'excitement', you lose; if 'excitement' overtakes 'anxiety', you win. Second, it is a unique blend of 'concepts' and 'practice'. Moid Siddiqui shares concepts and techniques of change management, and R.H. Khwaja the turn-around story of Singareni Collieries, revealing the first-hand experiences about leadership, strategies and execution. And third, it inspires hope—when a company that was referred to Board for Industrial and Financial Reconstruction (BIFR) twice can be turned around, why not those other companies suffering from minor (and major also) ailments? A book must provide solutions—*Change Management* does this neatly, soberly and well.

I do not know Moid personally, but know of him distantly as the person who is doing good for Corporate India through his books and his workshops. I know Khwaja very well—a bright and dynamic bureaucrat who proved his entrepreneurial acumen and leadership skills not only by turning around a sick company and restoring it to great heights of profitability but also leaving the impress of his signature—The Khwaja Way—wherever he worked. When I started writing the Foreword for the book, co-authored by him with Moid, my dilemma was, 'How can his "supporter" brag on the "supported one" and still be judicious!' So, I have decided to keep focus on the book rather than the authors, yet I would say that they have done a great job.

This book tells us, *not only the leader but also those led are equally responsible and partners in managing change*. It is not a one-man show. The change must impact everyone, and everyone must become a change agent. It reminds me that in the tsunami (a few years ago), fishermen found themselves in a situation where there was no leadership. So they took up the challenge and went out of their way to rescue people. Everyone can, in his or her own sphere, be a leader. Leadership operates at all levels and it emerges differently in different situations. I don't think leadership is an inborn trait; it's not in one's genes. Rather, the environment plays a vital role. Everyone should have opportunities to think and plan and then develop the acumen to use these opportunities to their advantage.

Change is not all about the change in structure, processes, and enterprise resource planning (ERP) through technology. Change means change of mindset and approach at micro levels and change of culture and work ethos at macro levels. If I have to list the achievements of Tata Steel, I would start with the change in mindset. The company has, of course, undergone a structural change and we have modernised our machinery as well, but the most important change is that our people have been thrust out of the comfort zone they were living in before 1990. They were made to realise that they would have to fight for their survival. That has been our most significant achievement. 'Fire in the belly' and the 'will to succeed' have also been crucial factors towards the positive changes in Tata Steel. I find all these factors, with immense clarity and forceful depiction, when the authors talk about the 'hard track' and 'soft track' of change. 'Never forget the fact that corporations do not transform, people do,' says Moid.

> For the real success of transformation it is necessary that you must hold the ethical and human values steadfast so that the 'belief system' becomes persuasive throughout the organization. Let the *espoused values* seep into the bloodstream of the organization ... Managing change is managing transition, both *hard track* and *soft track*.

My experiences in managing change are not much different.

With technology advancing at the rate that it is, we are likely to lose touch with the human side of business. So, 'hard track' must be balanced with 'soft track', what John Naisbitt calls 'hi-tech' and 'hi-touch'. These are certain ground realities which are ignored by most of the companies in today's turbulent business scenario. I think the traditional 'birth to grave' system that Tata Steel had has been shaken to a certain extent by the advent of new technologies and new ways to do business. But, at the same time, a balance has to be struck between the two. Good old values cannot be totally abandoned; they have to be amended to a certain extent to make allowance for rapid technological change.

I find a good *jugalbandhi* between Moid and Khwaja—an absolute harmony of thoughts and approach. 'The uniqueness of the saga of the Singareni was bringing change with a human touch,' writes Khwaja. 'The essence of *Soft Track* is in giving primacy to human aspects and man management. Our emphasis was to avoid, to the maximum extent possible, human suffering while undertaking reforms. Our slogan was 'Reforms with Human Touch—Management from the Heart.' No wonder he could perform such a Herculean task successfully by genuine consideration to the *human factor*. The love story of Singareni turnaround is no fairytale or fantasy—it is a reality in flesh and bones. The success story is not only revealing but also inspiring for other entrepreneurs.

As a wise man once said, 'Change is hard because people overestimate the value of what they have—and underestimate the value of what they may gain by giving up'. 'Giving up' is a challenge—easy to say and understand but difficult to practise. 'Let go' and 'sense of direction' are two significant attributes that contribute to the prosperity of a business. It should be agile and fleet-footed, it should have the ability to reassess the path it has taken, and it must have the courage to mend paths and decisions if they are found to be out of place. The important thing is that change should be welcomed, not resisted. The 'let go' mindset helps reduce resistance. One must have confidence in self and one must trust the future. 'Optimism' is always good if it is properly balanced with capabilities.

One must know the disadvantages and discomforts of the so-called comfort zones. It takes enormous courage to get out of a comfort zone. Such decisions are courageous decisions, and they determine your destiny and that of many others. The decision I took to come back to India at the invitation of Mr JRD Tata was, I think, the most significant. I was comfortably settled in Britain when I got a letter from JRD saying that I should come back to India and that there was a job waiting for me at Tata Steel. I took him up on the offer, and that changed the course of my life. Breaking the 'comfort zone' is of great significance in change management—both in personal and corporate contexts.

'Communicate, communicate, and communicate—the vision and objectives of the business to all personnel for effective change management' are the mantra that I have followed religiously. I am happy the book on change management contains a chapter—'The Magic of Communication'. 'Sarma decided to introduce new method of communication,' shares Khwaja giving credit to his predecessor, which is a rare gesture in today's corporate world.

He further writes,

> Sarma started writing letters separately addressed to the executives and to the workers at periodic intervals. The content of the letters was simple. He shared the serious problems and issues facing the company and the efforts of the management to resolve them. This was a masterstroke by him.

When communication fails, *rumours* float to fill the void. This phenomenon is as certain and true as the sunshine—fail to communicate, be ready to spend your time, money and energies in countering grapevine.

Resistance to change is an important issue in change management that has been articulated proficiently in the chapter 'The Boiled Frog …'. 'People don't resist change. They resist being changed,' says Peter Senge. Taking the masterly cue from the management guru, Moid adds:

> The first action is to decide what can be done to minimize the hindrances before looking at how to increase the *driving forces* for managing change. It is because there is tendency that for every new force introduced into a system an equal and opposite force tends to oppose it.

Many books have been written on change management. But *Change Management* is different. This book is pragmatic with an 'Indian flavour', full of anecdotal and personal experiences of both the authors, which are rich in content and absolutely contextual to Indian situations.

I hope you enjoy and benefit from the read. I know I did.

Jamshed J. Irani
Director, TATA

Preface to the First Edition

'Change or Perish!' is a catchphrase that sums up all one needs to say about change. Change is a corporate need, not just for thriving but also for a simple survival.

It assumes more importance because if change is managed without understanding the 'genetics of change' and 'change dynamics' the chances are quite bright for, what is said, 'changed and perished'. In 30 years of my corporate experience, the toughest task that I have found is managing change. I sympathise with those delegates who pay and listen to the so-called change experts from academics, who themselves have never managed change. I pity the readers who buy and try to collect change recipes from the cookbooks authored by theoreticians, who themselves have never taken a single change initiative, let alone managing change!

'Change Management' is a serious subject. It should be dealt with utmost care and seriousness. Change is not a dance—dance is rhythmical. In dance, steps are predicted and predetermined. So book titles like *Dance of Change* do not appeal to me. Change is a thrill, excitement and adventure, which involves a high degree of risk and danger, where chances of failure are almost 50 per cent, if not more. Managing change is a game of trapeze or a feat of acrobats. Hence the title of this book, *Change Management*, is well thought out.

Most of the publishers publish books written by world-renowned personalities and which are huge money earners. The books like *The GE Way* (The Jack Welch Way) and *The Apple Way* (The Steve Jobs Way) belong to this category. But, why hasn't a single publisher gone for a book, *The V K Way*—the contribution of Dr V. Krishnamurthy to Corporate India is no way less than what these two American chief executive officers (CEOs) have contributed. When I compare them, I keep the difficult Indian conditions in mind. Managing companies in India is entirely a different ball game. Indian publishers must realise that Indian managers can learn more with Indian examples, understanding the ground realities of this soul.

I know Singareni Collieries Company Limited (SCCL) and its working culture for the past one decade; SCCL was one of our prestigious clients when I was the director (HR) in Bharat Earth Movers Limited (BEML).

It is one of the toughest places to work in. Once I had selected a guy as the general manager (Industrial Relations [IR]) only because of his track record in Singareni Collieries. I wanted a man with good experience in industrial relations, who could afford to be tough with trade unions. HR managers with a stiff spine, if not extinct, are scarce. The Singareni guy did well in BEML; any place is heaven for those who have worked in the toughest situations. One can deal with trade unions, even the rebellious ones, because dealing with them is a part of the curriculum—you are taught in the institutions and later you learn in organisations with experience. But I have yet to see a curriculum of any professional course in which they would teach how to manage the Naxalites, terrorists or militants! In Singareni you need to deal with such outside elements! I cannot forget one of my visits to Ramagundam complex of SCCL where I was ambushed in the dead of the night and my car was stopped by blocking the road with a huge tree. I was lucky that a few trucks appeared on time and their plans failed. A tough place needs a tough leader.

My meeting with Khwaja—the co-author of this book—was accidental. Once I received a call from Chandrakant Sharma, Group General Manager Human Resource (HR), SCCL. He wanted me to conduct a retreat in which his chairman, directors and top team would participate. He wanted me to keep the 'balanced scorecard' as the central theme. By that time I had resigned from my active lucrative corporate assignment and had started my own consulting firm 'Intellects Biz'. When Sharmaji told me that his CEO is an

Indian Administrative Service (IAS) officer, I gave a few convincing excuses to avoid the assignment. Bureaucracy and I do not go together. Even as the Director HR of a public sector company, I could never have a heart-to-heart relationship with my government bosses—the bureaucrats. I used to protest strongly when sometimes a *babu* from the ministry represented a joint secretary in the board meetings. But for my other colleagues, even an attendant from the ministry mattered a lot.

Somehow, Sharmaji was very persistent, and I could not find an escape route. I met Khwaja for the first time at the resort where the retreat was conducted. The whole day he remained on my mental scanner. I was watching him from all angles. He seemed tough but was an extremely humble person—a highly disciplined person with great humility! I found him hard as a coconut shell on the outside and soft as its kernel in the inside. Those were the days when he had recently taken charge of Singareni as chairman and managing director (CMD). Later, after a couple of years, he changed even his exterior—he became the semblance of humility and modesty. In the very first meeting we fell for each other.

Those who know Khwaja well say that in the skin of a bureaucrat he is a sharp entrepreneur. Above all, he is an extremely fine human being, who demonstrates values in his actions.

Later, I met Khwaja many times. The last retreat that I conducted for his team was on the theme of 'Pygmalion Manager'. During those sessions I shared some of the facts, based on the survey as well as some studies conducted by my 'Intellects' team at SCCL. Everyone was zapped when they discovered that the top team of Singareni under the leadership of Khwaja, quite unwittingly, followed the 'Pygmalion Leadership'. I told them that whom they call chairman was a passionate Pygmalion, who not only turned around the company but also brought the highest ever glory to SCCL in terms of productivity, profitability, ecology-friendliness, healthy IR and above all, corporate bonding. In this meeting, I had declared that my book on 'Pygmalion' would not be complete unless a chapter on 'Singareni Turnaround' is included (the Pygmalion project is progressing well). During that retreat, Khwaja shared with me that he would leave SCCL soon. I promptly decided to feed my greed and took a promise from him that he would be the co-author of my next book on Change Management in which he would share his experiences of turning around SCCL. He agreed but corrected me that the turnaround was started by his predecessor, A.P.V.N. Sarma, and that, later he relentlessly completed it. Giving credit to others is a rare quality of leadership. People like Khwaja are not often seen in today's corporate sector. Contrarily, you will find many CEOs claiming success only during their tenures—'The company has been doing extremely well for the past three years, two months, and 21 days!' types of claims are very common in Corporate India.

It was a Herculean task for me to sell the idea of writing the Singareni story by using the pronoun 'I'. He was very hesitant. More than hesitation, he was feeling shy to say, 'I have done this … I have done that …' The second thing about which I was a bit persistent was the story format of the book. Being a practising manager I know people are not interested in theory; people are interested in hearing the story, 'How did you turnaround, or how did you transform the company?' I was lucky; he agreed to both the requests, which became the unique selling proposition (USP) of this book—*Change Management* is different!

Many are learning from his 'Singareni Love Story'—each chapter contains many techniques, concepts and practical tips on change management. But one thing I want you to etch on a stone is his advice, 'Never hire a consultant for managing change.' He did not hire; he and his team performed the miracles. You must understand the simple fact that in life there are certain activities that cannot be performed by anyone other than you; engaging a consultant for managing change would reflect on one's professional impotency.

This book, *Change Management*, has two parts: (a) Genetics of Change and (b) The Singareni Love Story. Again, the first part has two sub-sections (i) Change Dynamics and (ii) Change Techniques. In the first part of the book you will find concepts and techniques and three true stories on transformation, whereas in the second part you will find the stunning turnaround story of Singareni. SCCL was referred to the Board for Industrial and Financial Reconstruction (BIFR) not once but twice, yet not only did it survive but also thrived. The Singareni leadership and Singarenians played such a miracle that this turnaround deserves another exclusive book with the title, *The Singareni Way* or *The Khwaja Way*.

I am a lone writer—I always acknowledge my thanks to my Apple iBook and Apple iMac-5 who are my close companions besides my loving wife, Ruquiya Siddiqui. The time that I devote on writing books is grabbed from Ruquiya's share of time. It is a great sacrifice that she has been making for my sake. She is the first fan of my books. Of late she has been engaging herself in translating some of the spiritual books written by me in Urdu and Hindi. The habit of writing is highly infectious, I swear!

No book can be conceived (honestly speaking) without having been inspired from some other books and authors. I acknowledge my thanks to all of them whose names I have mentioned in Annexure IV.

Finally, I am indebted to R.H. Khwaja, former Secretary, Ministry of Mines, Government of India, and the former CMD of SCCL for his good gesture to be my co-author and for the many good words that he wrote for me.

I acknowledge my thanks to Intellects Biz's team, Vishalakshi, Shravani and Prasad for rendering their wholehearted assistance in conducting the survey on 'Pygmalion Effect in Singareni'. Mr Chandrakant Sharma, Group General Manager (HR) and Mr S. Chandrasekhar, General Manager (Co-ordination) of SCCL, were also very helpful and cooperative; they rendered support for timely completion of the studies and survey at his complexes.

'One friend, one person who is truly understanding, who takes the trouble to listen to us as we consider an issue, can change our whole outlook on the world', says Dr E.H. Mayo. Dr Sugata Ghosh, the former Vice-President Commissioning of SAGE Publications, is that one friend and one person who gave a very positive response and support when I shared the idea about this unique project with him, which kept my enthusiasm vibrant all through. I also acknowledge my sincere thanks to Mr Vivek Mehra, Managing Director & CEO, Mr R. Chandra Sekhar, Associate Vice President

Commissioning, and Mr Sachin Sharma, Commissioning Editor, and other professionals, technicians and staff members of SAGE Publications and Response Books whose invisible contribution is immeasurable.

Moid Siddiqui

In my opinion, it has become a fashion for civil servants to write about their experiences. When my co-author, Moid Siddiqui, suggested that I must write a story on Singareni Collieries Company Limited (SCCL), I was a bit reluctant. I was wondering why someone would be interested in my experiences in SCCL. Moid pointed out that the remarkable turnaround of SCCL from a loss-making public sector undertaking (PSU) to a successful company with highest ever productivity and profitability, within a short period of seven to eight years, is a rare success story in the annals of Corporate India. Moreover, the uniqueness of the saga of Singareni was in bringing change with a human touch. He also emphasised that the Singareni story had some dimensions, which strongly reinforce the concept of 'soft track' in change management. The essence of soft track is in giving primacy to human aspects and people management. As a consultant, Moid was convinced that it was imperative to share how the company had taken certain daring initiatives and implemented novel innovative schemes which do not have many parallels in the management of PSUs in India.

Moid's persuasive charm was irresistible. Soon I was struggling to pen my thoughts on paper. I found the going very tough. Civil servants find it very easy to talk and lecture, but writing a passionate story was an entirely different proposition. On a few occasions, when I expressed my distress in my struggles with writing, Moid was unrelenting. He kept pushing me, and that is how I have been able to complete my portion of the book.

I have completed more than three decades in the Indian Administrative Service (IAS). I consider my half-a-decade stay in SCCL as perhaps the most satisfying assignment I have ever worked on. The origin of SCCL goes back to 1886. When I assumed charge in October 2001, the workforce was over 100,000. The company was in a net loss regime. The accumulated losses were over ₹570 crores. Extremism was rampant in the coal belt. Although my illustrious and distinguished predecessor, A.P.V.N. Sarma, had done outstandingly well as the chief executive officer (CEO) of this company, the challenges were still daunting.

Human beings always respond to challenges—the power of resilience is put to test only during adversities. I was quietly determined to do my very best. I promised myself that I would not let down Singareni and Singarenians. I started evolving the concept of teamwork and team spirit from my initial days itself. Slowly and steadily this blossomed and flowered into a mighty force. In 2002, we coined the term 'Singarenians' and then moved to 'Singarenism', developing a full-fledged human philosophy. By the time I left the company in September 2006, we had a Singareni song, Singareni flag, Singareni badge, Singareni day celebrations, and above all, bonding as one family, symbolised by the logo of the company 'One Family, One Vision, One Mission'.

I hope readers will find this brief sharing of my experiences useful. Our country has to fully utilise the vast potential of our PSUs, which are either grossly neglected or micro-managed with bureaucratic interference and rustling losses. It is time that our political executives display visionary leadership with an iron-will for turning around PSUs, which are making losses. I hope the Singareni turnaround story will inspire others. No matter how adverse the circumstances, success is possible if we have a clear vision and well-planned strategies for execution. No mission can succeed unless it is carried out passionately with human care and concern for people and their families. Let more PSUs in the country rise from ashes like the Phoenix—SCCL attained glory from the gloom.

The 'turnaround', as they call it, was my romance with nature and the people of Singareni, who have now got an identity as 'Singarenians'.

R.H. Khwaja

Acknowledgements to the First Edition

There are so many individuals who have guided me, motivated me and helped me in completing this challenging task. I hope some of my friends and colleagues who helped me will not mind if they find their names missing in this list. I can assure them that it may be due to simple oversight but not due to lack of appreciation on my part.

I must first thank all Singarenians—82,000 plus family. All my colleagues, directors and other senior officers in the company were teachers to me at some stage or the other. But I would be failing in my duty if I do not acknowledge P. Vasudeva Rao, J.V. Dattatreyulu, G. Srinivasa Ayyangar, Sriram Taranikanti, D. Madhusudana Rao and K. Ramakrishna. My other colleagues who were great motivators include D.L.R. Prasad, Surendra Pandey, T.R.K. Rao and S. Chandrasekhar. Other Singarenians whom I would like to acknowledge are Dr M. Mukunda Rao, P. Chandrakanta Sharma, N.V. Rajasekhar and V.S.R. Murthy.

I acknowledge with deep gratitude the constant guidance and encouragement of my distinguished co-author, Moid Siddiqui.

My father, Prof. Jamal Khwaja, has always been an abiding source of strength, guidance and inspiration to me. He provided me with invaluable insights in attaining a flow in my writing whenever I encountered road-blocks. As a distinguished writer and an intellectual himself, he was instrumental in my carrying on this work to its logical conclusion with grit and determination.

I am extremely grateful to D.V. Prasad and T. Ravindranath, my former colleagues in SCCL, who helped me in processing the book in Microsoft Word. I owe special thanks to P.V. Subba Rao, my personal secretary in Public Enterprises Department, who cheerfully and willingly did the bulk of the work. If not for their dedicated efforts, this part of the book would have remained only in the realm of my thoughts.

Various colleagues provided data and inputs, which have been used in this book. I would like to thank them all.

R.H. Khwaja

Preface to the Second Edition

'You cannot step into the same river twice,' said Heraclitus, a great Greek philosopher more than 2,500 years ago. *The sun is new each day*. Each morning when we get up we see a new world. Change is constant—it moves seamlessly. What is new today antiquates tomorrow. *Change Management*, a book authored almost a decade ago cannot escape from the process of change either. As time passed we felt the need to revisit and revise some chapters. What you hold in your hands is a new sun.

We are indeed deeply overwhelmed by the tremendous response the first edition of *AoC* received from a very wide spectrum of discerning readers. Taking into consideration the feedback received from you the readers, our publishers, and reviewers of the first edition, we are encouraged to make its appeal more contemporary for the management of change. The book received good international and national coverage as reviews were published in prestigious journals.

They say 'Change or Perish'. But we are witness to many a company, which changed and perished. *Cause?* They did not realize that Change Management is not a dance where you take robotic predetermined steps that one has rehearsed well before the actual performance. Managing change is managing the unpredictable variable. Change is acrobatics—a risky feat that warrants both *courage* and *conviction*. Managing change is like riding the tiger—the fall is fatal. For this reason *envisioning* is prerequisite to managing change. To our mind, Change Management is the most challenging task in leadership, where *excitement* not *anxiety* must dominate. Readers will find true stories of success and failures. The success and failure experiences provide guidance for managing change confidently without reinventing the wheel.

It is easy to say, 'Bell the cat'! But *How to bell the cat* is crucial. Strategies, though essential, cannot convert into success by themselves. Many a brilliant strategy fails because they are conceived much ahead of their time. An idea, whose time has come, can alone get you the dividends. In 'Change Management' both *timing* and *execution* are but the two sides of the same coin—if one side defaces, its value is lost. It is pertinent to note that the concepts, techniques and strategies of management are ultimately dependent upon execution of decisions. Failure is the ultimate outcome if good decisions are badly executed or not properly timed. As an old saying goes, 'The Path to Hell is paved with noble intentions.' No matter how meticulous one is in planning and strategizing, defective execution with bad timing is the cause of death.

Whether you are an entrepreneur seeking a competitive edge, a practising manager assisting the CEO in managing change, a student in a management institute, a research scholar, a faculty, a politician contemplating to change the country, or a bureaucrat looking forward, we think you will find creative and workable ideas for bringing about change in your respective spheres. As a manager your orb is the *Future*. Learn to live in the future. As Mahatma Gandhi said, 'Be the change that you wish to see in the world'. This is the takeaway from *AoC*.

Things change. And friends leave. New friends join. But time doesn't stop. Change changes yet remains changeless. Like time, change is eternal in this temporal world. Change will not occur if we wait for someone's help or an auspicious time. You cannot stop the future—You cannot rewind the past. So just learn from the Past but don't dwell in the Past. Live in the Present for the future, gaining benefits from the riches of past.

This book is the product of a *jugalbandi* between the two of us. You will find both, the concepts, techniques, processes and strategies in Part I, and leadership, turnaround strategies and execution in Part II. Providing you theory laced with real-life hands-on experiences is the objective of this book.

Behind every success stand some invisible people. Among them are Mr Vivek Mehra—Managing Director and CEO, R. Chandrasekhar—Associate Vice President, Commissioning, Sachin Sharma—Commissioning Editor, Ms Aarti David—Marketing Head, SAGE Publications (Response Books). We find in Mr Vivek Mehra a very vibrant and dynamic personality with ingenuity and creativity. His sobriety and humility has won our hearts. He gives us comfort as well as thoughtful guidance. He is the charming gardener who takes care of every plant in the garden of SAGE. As James Allen says, 'No duty is more urgent than that of returning thanks.' We hasten to thank all of them and also those who worked behind the curtain.

While we express our gratitude to our readers, whose interest in the book inspired us as well as the publishers to go for the revised edition, we are aware that the quality of words is insignificant in explaining the emotions that flow from the heart. We say thanks *Dil Se*.

Moid Siddiqui
R.H. Khwaja

PART I

Genetics of Change

Everybody has accepted by now that change is unavoidable. But that still implies that change is like death and taxes; it should be postponed as long as possible and no change would be vastly preferable. But in a period of upheaval, such as the one we are living in, change is the norm.

—Peter F. Drucker

(A famous management guru)

Source: Management Challenges for the 21st Century

SECTION I

Change Dynamics

If you always do what you've always done, you'll always get what you've always got.

—Anthony Robbins

(Author of *Giant Steps: Small Changes to Make a Big Difference*)

Source: http://thinkexist.com/quotation/if_you_do_what_you-ve_always_done-you-ll

Scarecrow Does Not Scare Crows 1

In my school days we were taught a poem—'The Scarecrow'. It was the story about a gardener who was disgusted with the crows who used to spoil his crops. The gardener would run around the entire day throwing stones and cursing the crows. It was a very tiring exercise, but he had no other option than to continue with this exercise. By the end of the day he would be very tired. One day his friend suggested him a trick and he made a scarecrow. It was so nicely made that it looked like a real man. Once it was erected the problem was solved. The crows were scared and did not come anywhere near it. The gardener heaved a sigh of relief and decided to take a break and went to his village with his family. But when he returned after a week, he found that his vegetable garden was completely spoiled by the crows. The crows had eaten the seeds and spoiled the vegetables by poking at them with their beaks. What amazed him most was that the crows were sitting on the head and shoulders of the scarecrow. He also found a nest under the hat, which was earlier worn by the scarecrow. 'So, the trick failed! Trickery doesn't work long,' explained the teacher.

I understood the moral of the poem and our teacher explained it to us verse by verse. But what my young mind was not ready to accept was the twist of the story—when the scarecrow scared the crows earlier, why could not it do so later? After all, they were birds; no one can explain the trick and guide them to work smart. Either the crows shouldn't have got scared in the first place but if they were fooled once, how could they outsmart the gardener later? I thought, I argued but refused to accept. Finally, I consoled myself by treating it as only a work of fiction and left it at that.

Today, when I look back I just laugh at my innocence. What did not appeal to my logic then is clear to me now. Trickery alone or any new thing or device is effective for a short time. It loses charm after some time. What worked yesterday may or may not work today. The reason is simple: What was applicable yesterday may not be appropriate today and, for sure, will not be relevant tomorrow. This mantra is the seed of change. This explains the need of change for change.

In the context of business, change is necessary because it relates to the future, where the managers shall live forever during their corporate life. It is easy to advise managers, 'Look into the "Future" because that is your constituency!' But when it comes to reality, managers do not find any crystal ball. They always look for one. Tell them, we do not have crystal balls, but we do have some mantras: The most reliable way to look into the future is by understanding the present! But unfortunately we tend to look into the future while still living in the past, without even wanting to know the present!

Change and future are twins. They resemble each other so much that one is mistaken for the other. Sometimes it is difficult to make a distinction between the two. To understand the need for change one must understand fully the cut of time, what we call future. What leads us to the future can also guide us in managing change.

There is another mantra—I call it Gayatri Mantra of change—the 'Bellwether Approach'. It is simple: In the corporate world, corporate America's yesterday is the today of the advanced European and ASEAN countries, and shall be the tomorrow in the context of the developing countries like India. Hence, Indian entrepreneurs and managers are lucky. They can always learn their lesson, good and bad, and make midcourse corrections keeping an eye on those who are ahead of them.

Yet, another golden mantra! There are two ways to manage change: (a) Inside Out and (b) Outside In. They are not buzzwords; they are the untold reality in change management.

INSIDE OUT

This mantra begins with a simple query: 'Why do I exist?' or 'Why does my organisation exist?' The answer you get becomes the purpose of your being. So, first you must try to locate the meaning or purpose of your life or corporate life and then find means to accomplish the purpose.

Ask another question, 'What do I stand for?' or 'What does my organisation stand for?' The answer you get is your set of 'values'—ethical and human. Purpose and values make your vision. Purpose gives you meaning and values measure the righteousness of the path that you have chosen to achieve your vision. This way you first decide as to what you want to achieve and then work out the means to manage the external environment—tapping into resources, building networks, honing up the skills and broadening their influence. In the end, you meet the goals. This way the journey begins from within. The external factors are only supportive. If the purpose is profound and powerful, one needs to exert little. The power of purpose makes things happen. Vision, purpose and values are the major constituents of this mantra. I will discuss them in detail in Chapter 4.

OUTSIDE IN

This mantra suggests that first you should take all the external factors into account—the available skills, competencies and capabilities of your subordinates and peers, salary structure, role profiles, material resources such as building, machinery, finances and so on. Then, you need to ensure optimal utilisation of the available resources. The Outside In mantra, thus, helps you to create the future by taking into account the available resources. In this approach, the focus is kept on resources—pushing meaning or purpose to the backseat. Changing technology, changing customers' profiles, removing various barriers and coping up with statutory changes are the external factors, which find focus here.

Both these mantras have their benefits—it really is not a toss-up between the two. You could just as well blend these two mantras! The underlying truth is that there is no surefire remedy or a one-size-fits-all strategy to deal with tough situations, either in life or in organisations.

Despite knowing this we grow pumpkins on the pathways and plant scarecrows at our workplace expecting miracles to occur! When you sow seeds of jackfruits it is foolhardy to expect apples to grow.

Have we ever thought, 'Why we continue to do things the way we were doing earlier, even when it does not work?' The reason is simple—we have lost the sense to distinguish between the dead and the alive. Most of the concepts that we are practising, preaching and pleading are already dead, and nobody has bothered to bury them.

If you do not challenge the existing practices, then there will be two potential dangers. First is that you can get locked into one approach, method or strategy without even considering other alternatives, which might be more appropriate. As a result, you may approach your problems with preconceptions; hence, you will solve them only in one way. This syndrome is known as the Aslan Phenomenon. The second syndrome is known as Swami's Cat.

Aslan Phenomenon

The Aslan phenomenon unfolds in the following sequence:

1. We make rules based on a reason that makes a lot of sense.
2. We follow these rules scrupulously.
3. Time passes, and things change.
4. The original reasons for the generation of these rules may no longer exist, but because the rules are still in place we continue to follow them.

How the Aslan Principle came about is an interesting story. A man liked to run every morning. There were five or six routes that he could take. But he used to take the longest one as he used to stop for some gossip and fun at his friend's house in the neighbourhood. His friend's name was Aslan. So stopping at Aslan's house became the rule for having some fun, but things changed. Aslan moved from the neighbourhood. Nevertheless, the man continued to take the longest route and stopped at the same place—even when Aslan no longer lived there.

This happened to him, it happens to you and me, and it happens to most of us. The name 'Aslan' became a metaphor thence. Thus, the cardinal principle of change is creating realisation that there is no particular virtue in doing things the way they have always been done. Have you ever thought, why do we still say 'dial the number' knowing well that no dialling device exists anymore in our telephones? We still refer to 'clockwise' and 'anti-clockwise' directions taken by the hour's needle while wearing a digital watch. Until recently our cars used to have two keys, one for ignition and the other for the boot.

Swami's Cat

Swami's cat has become another metaphor for change management! Whenever Swamiji, the chief priest of an ashram, prayed he used to ask his disciples to tie his pet cat to a chair. This ensured tranquillity in meditation, as the cat used to disturb him. Swamiji died but the disciples never forgot to tie a cat to a chair before performing meditation. The practice continued in the ashram for centuries!

Most of the organisational practices are the result of either 'Aslan Principle' or 'Swami's Cat'. It is time to locate and discard most of these routine practices, which worked yesterday but are no more relevant to the present context. Such dead practices are still alive because no one cared or dared to bury them. Hurry up, let us do it right now!

Let us pledge that we shall not plant any scarecrows anymore! *Remember*: There is no permanent reality except the reality of change.

You cannot step into the same river twice.

Man cannot discover new oceans unless he has the courage to lose sight of the shore.

—André Gide
(A French writer)
Source: http://www.quotedb.com/quotes/1420

2 Why can't You Step into the Same River Twice?

In 500 BC, Heraclitus observed that one cannot step into the same river twice. No one questioned him. Some did not question because they very well understood what the great philosopher of Greece meant by the phrase! But many did not question because they understood a naught! The 'Emperor's New Clothes' syndrome does work, rather strongly. People prefer to be silent on the thoughts of such lofty personalities, and never dare question them, even if they understand little. They think, 'Why to get exposed?' The guy was great and he must have surely thought before saying. So, by default, the sayings of great people become great. People may or may not understand them. But it is a fact that no other guru, sage or monk ever explained the genetics of change so clearly and that too in such few words.

Those who understand the meaning of these simple words with bottomless depth understand the genetics of change. I have seen many quoting this phrase without actually understanding its meaning. I have seen many teaching on 'how to manage change?' little understanding the genetics of change. One must understand the inheritance of change first. A clear understanding of the inheriting forces that govern change will make the job of managing change very easy.

So, we begin with Heraclitus' ancient wisdom on change. 'Change is constant' is an ancient thought, not a new discovery. In the BC era, Heraclitus of Ephesus conceived the great idea 'You cannot step into the same river twice'. A flowing river constantly changes its content and shape. It may look the same from moment to moment, but actually it is never the same. So also it is with the cosmos: New things come into being, few others die and everything changes. The world which existed yesterday is not quite the same as the one today. What worked yesterday may not work today, and what is unlikely today could be the sure thing of tomorrow.

Change is constant! Nothing (except God) is as permanent as change. Even the river changes in a fraction of a second. When you take a second dip, it is not the same water, though the river remains the same. Similarly, the world is not the same as yesterday. It is a changed world though it remains the same for most of us. Today we may experience similar things as yesterday, but they are never exactly the same. To remain adaptive in this changing world one must constantly ask the question, 'What assumptions should I update?' The question, 'what is no longer true' will help one in discarding certain unwanted obsolete thoughts and practices. Asking, 'what is now possible?' enables one to think creatively about matching solutions. 'If every situation is different, how can one improvise?' is a brilliant question that keeps one vibrant and agile with the changing time. Once you understand the art of changing with the current of time, you know the trick of stepping twice into the same river. When you take a second dip into the river, neither the river is the same nor are you the old 'you'. You are now a 'changed you'!

Change is constant, continuous, dynamic and seamless. Life is not the sum-total of 'snapshots'—it is a continuum. Gautam Buddha realised it 2,500 years ago and for this reason he said that there are no absolute events in life—life is a seamless flow. We cut life and slice out events. We cut time and slice out hours, minutes, seconds, milliseconds, microseconds, nanoseconds, picoseconds, femtoseconds and attoseconds! Scientists are trying to divide time into further fractions. What they do not appreciate is that time is indivisible—the infinite cannot be segmented into finite. Time is a continuum; continuum is indivisible! Today time is finite because we link it with the speed of light, which is finite. But our understanding of time in terms of the 'speed of light' simply reflects our limitations. Since we do not know about anything faster than the 'speed of light' we have accepted this as the parameter, which, even the scientists know, suffers from its own limitations.

Neither time nor change can be sliced down or segmented—they are in continuum. Like time change flows. Change does not follow a uniform pattern. For this reason we say future is unpredictable. Managing change is managing uncertainty and unpredictability. Some authors have written books like *Dance of Change*. Change is not a dance! Dance is always rhythmical—the steps are predetermined and the performance is predictable whereas the process of change is more like acrobatics. In dance, there is no risk involved; gymnasts, trapeze and acrobats take risk.

Reality rarely presents itself to us with clearly defined boundaries, it is always hazy at its corners. For this reason, ambiguity and vagueness are of much greater importance in change management as they can help us in understanding the pattern of change. In order to be able to figure out the pattern of change, it is better to try and prevent yourself from searching for logic or finding reasons. What we call 'vision' is mostly the reflection of one's 'intuitive wisdom'.

Yet, sometimes, 'cosmos' in a very subtle way speaks to us in patterns. The occurrence of an event once could be an incidence, twice could be a coincidence, but when the event occurs three times or more, normally it forms a pattern. The only way to understand these patterns is to fine-tune our mind to 'pattern-seeking' and 'pattern-finding' mode. Once we develop this sensitive ability, despite uncertainty we can understand the patterns of change better. These patterns are given the name 'cycle of change'—if an event occurs many times in a certain sequence, it becomes 'cyclic'! These cycles make future predictable.

It was Heraclitus who first discovered the continuity in change. No wonder, some management gurus consider him to be the 'father of change management'. He created his own approach to understand reality. He was very sensitive and observant. He paid close attention to what was happening around him and then thought about it until it made sense to him. He felt that consulting one's own intuition was the appropriate method to understand change. As he had put it, 'Things love to conceal their true nature.' He felt that one can discover reality through one's intuition.

Heraclitus overviewed, everything is continually changing, and it often takes less energy to move on to the next phase of a process than to fight to stay in the current one. Heraclitus held that all things—including those that we think are quite stable—are changing, developing and transforming continuously. He further observed that this 'flow of change' is not taking place at an even or a uniform rate. The only way to understand the flow of change is to change your point of view.

Every time we take a dip into the river, it is not the same river—it is a changed river. The sun is new each day! Every day is different. Every day is a challenge. Every day when we wake up there is another basket of opportunities. What did not work yesterday has a chance of working today.

Just flex your risk-taking muscles and dare to change the crossbars while swinging high in the arena as a trapeze artist!

To conquer fear is the beginning of wisdom.

—*Bertrand Russell*

(A philosopher, historian, logician and mathematician)

Source: http://thinkexist.com/quotation/to_conquer_fear_is_the_beginning_ of_wisdom/199727.html

3 Change Management—A Trapeze Feat

There are some events you just cannot forget. One such event, which is etched deep in my mind, is a trapeze feat that I witnessed when I was a child (Figure 3.1). Like any other child I was very fond of the circus. I had heard so much about the circus shows in our town from my classmates that I insisted my parents to take me to one, and they obliged.

Figure 3.1 Acrobats

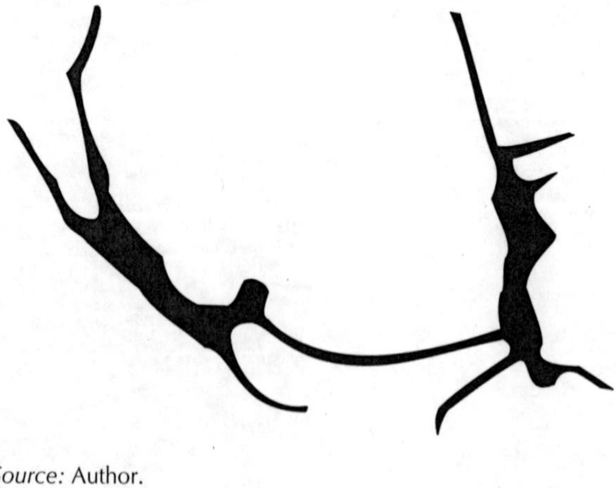

Source: Author.

It was a frosty night. I was enjoying the circus feasts along with my parents. Watching gymnasts, acrobats and trapeze artists was exciting, but it was the little Brownie—the clown—who stole the hearts of the spectators. He was making all sorts of funny gestures pretending as if he was unable to perform, but he was a real expert. He climbed one of the hanging ladders and landed on a hanging platform at a great height and stood beside the circus girl who was ready for a game of trapeze. Once the feat began the girls swung from one end to the other changing crossbars swinging from different directions. After leaving one swinging crossbar they used to somersault in space, flip their bodies and then hold on to a second crossbar, which would take them to the other end. It was a great show. The clown continued to make all sorts of gestures standing on the platform at great height. All of a sudden one circus girl pushed him and the clown pretended as if he was falling but he immediately caught hold of one of the swinging crossbars and then, changing from one crossbar to the other, landed at the other end. The trapeze girls started another fun game by tossing the clown from one crossbar to another, as if they were playing throw ball using the clown as a big ball! The clown's funny gestures made the crowd laugh and clap.

After a great deal of struggle, somehow, the clown escaped and landed onto a hanging platform where no girl was there to tease or torture him. Before he could heave a sigh of relief, he saw a big bear approaching him. As the bear approached nearer, the clown made funny faces as if he was scared of the bear as well as of the swinging crossbars. Through his gestures and body language he was telling the crowd that he was caught between the devil and the deep sea—if he stayed, the big bear would swallow him; if he caught one of the swinging crossbars, he might fall! When the danger became inevitable, just before the big bear could grab him, he jumped and caught one of the swinging crossbars, which took him to the middle. He looked at the crossbar, which was approaching him from the other end. Now, once again the clown was in a dilemma! If he caught the second crossbar, it would take him to the other side of the platform but he would have to leave the bar that he was holding. It was risky. If he left the hold and, by chance, could not catch the other one immediately, he would fall. On the other hand, if he did not change the crossbar, he would swing back and land on the same platform where the big bear was waiting for his prey. He was supposed to take a decision, on an important issue of life and death, in a fraction of a second. He immediately caught the other crossbar but did not dare loosen the grip over the first one. This gave him a deadly jerk—holding two crossbars, which were swinging in opposite directions, was a terrible mistake. Due to this jerk he lost his grip over both the crossbars and had a big fall. He continued to be funny while falling amidst thunderous claps from the jubilant audience. Obviously he was safe, as he had fallen into the safety net.

It was great fun!

Today, I take the same trapeze feat as a great lesson. After serving corporate India in five public sector undertakings (PSUs) and two private sector organisations on senior and board level positions for over three decades, where I was instrumental to many change management initiatives and organisational restructuring programmes, I have understood the trapeze feat better and have taken it as a great lesson. Change management is a trapeze feat—nothing less—nothing more!

Swinging from one crossbar to another is not a matter of ease. When an acrobat swings forward she expects to hold the other crossbar, but she can only do so when she loosens the grip over the first crossbar, which she was holding tight. Finally when she does leave this crossbar in anticipation of holding the other one, for a moment she remains anchorless! This situation of hovering in space without any support or anchor is what we call transition in change management—a situation where both morale and self-esteem are at their lowest ebb. Managing change is managing transition which by itself is a trapeze feat. Managing this 'anchorlessness'—transition—is the real challenge in change management.

I find that many organisations are not sensitive to the need of change. They think of change only when a piece of their cheese smells horrible, or when they see the deadly bear approaching them threatening their survival. They hire a consultant in a hurry—an academician who has never managed change. Now, this fellow who has never fought a battle is supposed to teach them 'how they must fight the battle?' So, the so-called expert goes back to the basics, reads some 'cookbooks' and goes through a few case studies of organisations that have managed (or mismanaged) change. He then comes out with a final 'game plan', absolutely clear in his mind; whether it succeeds or fails he is going to get an exciting case study for his next thesis. He conducts retreats to explain his plans dramatically, and to enhance the saleability of his 'recipes' he uses all sorts of modern technology. An article in *Fortune* magazine entitled, 'In Search of Suckers' puts it quite accurately: 'Quietly, without fanfare, the advice business has been hijacked. New gurus armed with nothing more than pens, podiums and tremendous shamelessness have co-opted what used to be a nice, wholesome calling: dishing out good advice to business-men and business-women.' One should not blame them, but those who hire them should be blamed. Tom Peters explains how he makes money availing the 'ignorance-laced' mercy of his clients: 'We are the only society that believes it can keep getting better and better. So we keep on getting suckered in by people like me.'

'Much has been written about the good, the bad, and the ugly of consultancy,' writes Jack Trout in his book entitled *The Power of Simplicity*, co-authored with Jack Trout. 'You should realize that complexity is at the heart of a bad consultant's business. If it were simple, companies would do it themselves. So, the trick is to constantly invent new complex concepts.' These consultants can be called 'modern-day Robin Hoods'. They rob from the rich and keep the wealth with them. But instead of bows and arrows, these Robin Hoods are armed with complex buzzwords and ideas that they use to nail their prey. They make simple, complex and persistently invent new catchphrases, making simple complex and more complex!

Such 'cookbook recipes' are the major cause of failures. Research studies reveal that most organisations do not handle change well. 'Less than 30 per cent of the organizations that implement large-scale change are successful,' observe Ramnarayan and Nilakant in their prize-winning book *Change Management*.

Once the thesis on 'change management' is handed over, the consultant disappears leaving the owner clueless and wondering, 'Where do I go from here?' So, he now relies on people within his organisation which in turn proves to be a golden opportunity for these 'young talents' inducted from Indian Institute of Management (IIMs), Xavier Labour Relations Institute (XLRI), Indian School of Business (ISB), Massachusetts Institute of Technology (MIT) or Harvard Business School (HBS) to hit-and-try what was taught to them in the classrooms. They conduct 'brainstorming' or 'brain stilling', 'triggering' and 'wild-idea generating' meetings, though the focus remains on proving an important point, that is, 'See, how much I know'! They demonstrate their technology skills using buzzwords. Ross Perot, in a visit to the HBS, rightly commented, 'The trouble with you people is that what you call "environment scanning", I call it "looking out the window".' John Rock, General Manager, Oldsmobile vividly describes the attitude of these guys, 'A bunch of guys take off their ties and coats—go into a motel room for three days—and put a bunch of words on a piece of paper—and then go back to business as usual.' What people do not understand is that a mere 'mission statement' is not execution of change just as a map is not the state territory. A mission statement constitutes only 1 per cent of change management activities. It is execution that constitutes the remaining 99 per cent.

This way, these swollen heads work out some colourful plans on the paper using the 'cut and paste' technique. While consultants refer to some cookbooks and make their own recipes of change, these mavericks refer to some textbooks and professional journals like *Harvard Business Review* (HBR) or *Training and Development* (T&D) and prepare their project report by using the 'cut and paste' technique. Now, the poor owner of the company does not know how to proceed further. By this time he is successfully confused! So, in disgust overlaid by confusion, he shows the green signal with one hand while simultaneously holding the engine driver by his collar with the other. The 'engine drivers' are smart enough to get the right signal from the big boss as to whether he wants him to follow the new track or the old beaten track! When confusion becomes the goddess of worship, it is better to hold all guards tight and firm. So, while following the change process, the big boss or the owner covertly gives support to the legacy system. While adopting new practices, he does not discard the old ones. In a way he does the same mistake as the clown—holding both the crossbars, each pulling in opposite directions! No wonder he has a big fall.

It does not mean that change management fails; what fails is the ill-conceived and mismanaged change execution. Therefore, a clear understanding of change genetics and change dynamics is absolutely necessary. Clarity in perception makes the process of execution right.

Managing change is like managing two opposite forces—two crossbars each swinging in opposite directions. What are these two forces? They are 'desire for stability' and 'desire for change'. The former provides comfort and complacence, and the latter creates anxiety and fear. Obviously, most people choose the easy option and continue to follow the beaten track. Likewise, an acrobat feels safe and comfortable holding tight the crossbar that brought her to the middle of the arena. Now in order to catch the second one, which will take her to the other end, first she has to let go of the one which she finds safe and protected. The very idea, 'what if I lose the grip over this and can't catch that?' is more fatal than the fatal fall. If she continues to hold the first crossbar, after awhile it will swing back and she will never reach the other end. So, to reach the other end, she has to take the risk of changing the crossbars. While doing so, she will remain anchorless for a while in space. But, when she catches the second crossbar, she will reach the other end.

To understand the acrobatics of change, let me explain the metaphors. The first crossbar brings the acrobat from the past to the present. If she does not catch the second one, she goes back to the past and remains there for rest of the time. However, if she dares to catch the second crossbar, she faces a moment whereby she hangs in space 'anchorless'. This anchorless moment is the acrobat's 'present'—the 'Now'! The second crossbar is the future.

Once she catches it she lands on the platform at the other end. Now you must have realised which is the most crucial moment in the entire process. Obviously, it is the anchorless moment, where she is just hovering in space hoping for the best or the worst. And if she catches the second one without leaving the first, surely she will get a jolt of her life, which could be unbearable and may even cause a fatal fall.

Leaders trying to bring about change must understand clearly that in a real change game there is no safety net like in a circus. If this reality is well understood with a positive mind, the change agents will rehearse properly and take all extra precautions, which might be necessary for keeping the show on. Too much brooding may be bad but taking abundant precautions is a sign of professional maturity. Everyone cannot be Jack Welch who most of the time managed through his intuitive reflexes. One need not wait for a fatal accident to introduce the practice of wearing helmets at the shop floor! To start digging a well when you are thirsty is foolish.

I have tried to make the complex phenomenon simple. Once you understand the trapeze game, you understand change management, although it is a simple process, it is risky. The game of change warrants clarity in decision making, good deal of practice, rehearsal, courage, spontaneity, and above all a positive bent of mind, what we call 'positive attitude' in management vocabulary. Those who manage the anchorless moments succeed and others fail. People of strong willpower and decisive mind find those 'moments of suspense' exciting and challenging—they enjoy them and they succeed. Whereas people with a timid mind and a negative approach find the same moments alarming and dreadful—they feel threatened and get nervous. They do not enjoy these 'anchorless moments' because their hearts are not filled with excitement and thrill but with anxiety and apprehension. Yes, you have guessed it right! They fail, they fall and sometimes the fall can be fatal.

As mentioned earlier, managing change is managing the interplay between the two opposite forces—'desire for stability' and 'desire for change'. The desire for stability is a limiting force and the desire for change is a growth process. Thus, a change maker must understand these two forces clearly as well as the dynamics involved in their interplay. Then, he should try to find the ways and means to override the first and support the second. He must ponder upon:

1. What are the 'limiting forces' that impede the process of change?
   How do they hamper progress and growth? What are the specific limits or constraints that come into play? How do they manifest themselves? Who are the guys standing against or opposing change? What are their interests? How far those interests can be taken care to impede the opposing forces? What strategies and initiatives can be planned to override the resistance?
2. What are the 'growth support' forces, which would accelerate the change-making process? Who are the supportive people with positive attitude? How can they be encouraged and supported? How can their support be harnessed and utilised in moving things in the required direction?

Now, let me deal with the first thing first!

LIMITING FORCES

The limiting forces arise due to people's love for stability and security. Obviously, they would not like or welcome any change initiatives because in doing so their 'comfort zones' will be adversely affected. To use the 'trapeze metaphor'—'I feel so secure and safe holding the existing crossbar, why should I take the risk of leaving it? How do I know I will be able to have a firm grip on the other one?'

Stability looks for 'status quo' and once you are obsessed with status quo you cannot dare travel on new tracks. The beaten track then becomes your favourite path. So, how to overcome such an obsession? Create awareness about the danger and hazard of eating rotten cheese. Once people become aware that the existing cheese smells foul, they will try to look for a piece of fresh cheese elsewhere.

This way they come out of their comfort zones. The problem is not that they cannot find fresh cheese but that they cannot get a whiff of the foul smell of the stale cheese.

'GROWTH SUPPORT' FORCES

Having uprooted the cacti and the mushrooms, the ground is now clean and ready to receive manure or fertiliser. The change agent can now create favourable conditions by harnessing the growth-support forces or progressive forces and by taking the support of people with positive attitude. Once you give the needed support and confidence, they will come out with more vigour and enthusiasm than you expected. They will push the organisation towards success and make change happen. To use the trapeze metaphor, once the acrobat gains confidence her anxiety will transform into excitement. She will no more focus on 'how not to fall' but will look for 'how to swing across?' Once her fear is diminished, she will have no anxiety or apprehensions. She will experience sheer thrill, excitement and joy.

Let me share that under normal conditions the 'limiting forces' and the 'growth support' forces are in balance. Unless someone applies force to diminish one and enhance the other, they remain in perfect balance within the comfort zone of status quo and this status is known as 'quasi-stationary equilibrium'—each force pulling the other, thereby maintaining a balance. To make 'change' happen, first you have to break this equilibrium. It is possible both ways. But one is not supposed to follow the 'either/or' formula. On one hand, you are required to weaken the 'stability forces' and on the other, strengthen the 'progressive forces'. Both these forces need to be tackled. Either this or that will not work.

The change agents must understand the dynamics of change. Change is an interplay between two forces—when the 'growth support forces' overtake the 'limiting forces' the process of change begins.

The truth is that our finest moments are most likely to occur when we are feeling deeply uncomfortable, unhappy, or unfulfilled. For it is only in such moments, propelled by our discomfort, that we are likely to step out of our ruts and start searching for different ways of truer answers.

—**M. Scott Peck**, *The Road Less Travelled*

4 If You Do Not Know Where You Are Going Any Road Will Take You There!

About 2,500 years ago Gautam Buddha observed that if you do not know where are you going, any road will take you there! How true! If you do not know where you want to go, you need not ask anyone about the direction. Take any road and it will surely take you somewhere.

Both sagacity of the BC age and the wisdom of fairy tales are gold mines. You can learn a lot from them. Most of the fairy tales are packed with wisdom and passion. *Alice in Wonderland* is one such fairy tale which is full of wisdom. When Alice could not find the way to get out of the maze, she asked the Cheshire Cat, 'Could you tell me, please, which way I ought to go from here?' The Cat replied, 'That depends on where you want to go?' On this Alice replied, 'Really, I don't know!' 'Then it doesn't matter which way you go,' said Cheshire Cat. 'Anywhere you go will be somewhere other than this place.'

Vision is the seed of change management—what you sow, is what you reap! A clear vision gives clarity to your change programme. The only way you can create your future is through your vision. Developing the vision is the job of the founder of the company, or the hired CEO. The leader creates the vision, shares it with people, hones it up, gets support of his or her people and carries it passionately till its completion. The CEO has to play the role of the ring master—overseeing all the events maintaining absolute discipline, without using the whip. A 'culture of discipline' blended with the 'ethics of an entrepreneur' creates miracles. 'When you combine a "Culture of Discipline" with an "Ethic of Entrepreneurship", you get the magical alchemy of great performance', writes Jim Collins in his book *Good to Great*.

Discipline is a prerequisite to any change programme. When you have disciplined people, you do not need hierarchy. When you have disciplined thought, you do not need bureaucracy. When you have disciplined action, you do not need excessive controls. Such simple equations evade the commonsense!

There are three important things without which your change programme cannot succeed—'vision', 'purpose' and 'values'. Vision gives you direction, purpose gives you meaning and values measure the righteousness of the path that you want to follow. If you compromise with any one of these, your company will go astray. Both purpose and values are a part of vision. They maintain the equilibrium of vision. Let me put it in a pictorial form (Figure 4.1).

I have not borrowed James C. Collins and Jerry I. Porras' Vision model—I have adapted it and made it simple, sharp and focused. Their pattern was complex as they tried to put many things together. What they call 'Big Hairy and Audacious Goal' (BHAG) does not belong to the vision community. To my understanding, BHAG is a stand-alone snapshot. Why BHAG alone, there are many other things that can be related, but they do not become an integrated part of the vision pattern. That would only make the simple, complex.

Figure 4.1 Articulating a Vision

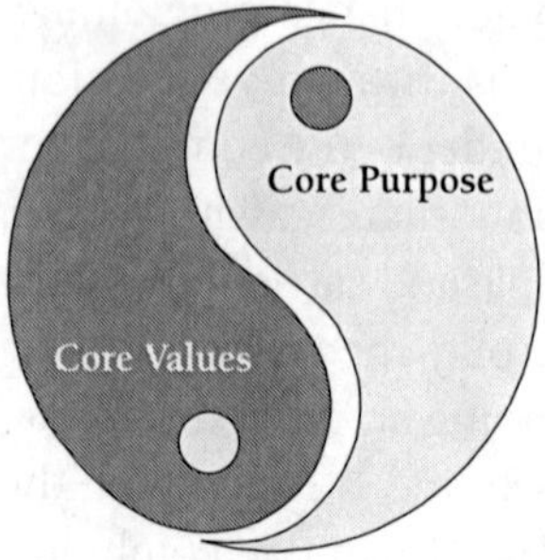

Source: Computed by the author based on the Vision Model by James C. Collins and Jerry I. Porras in their book *Built to Last*.

Vision has two major parts—purpose and values. I will try to explain them through two simple but important questions:

1. 'Why do I exist?' Or 'Why does my organisation exist?'
2. 'What do I stand for?' Or 'What does my organisation stand for?'

'Why do I exist?' This question leads us to the purpose of our being. Why have I come to this mother earth? What am I supposed to do? What am I supposed to leave behind? There could be many such probing questions. Many times such simple questions ring many bells in the mind, but we do not pay any heed to them. We drop them because we cannot afford to hold them long—they are so hot! 'Why do I exist?' Think for a while and you will feel the heat on your forehead! We never try to understand our 'self' and the purpose of our being. 'Only once have I become mute', says Kahlil Gibran, the Sufi of Lebanon, 'When someone asked me, "Who are you?"' A Sufi, who has answers for every question, fails to answer, 'Who I am?' When you ask, 'why does my organisation exist?' the answer that you get is the purpose of your organisation's being. Life is not worth living without a purpose or meaning. This equally applies to the life of an organisation. If your organisation does not have any purpose, create one for its spiritual health. 'Those who long for, live more,' is an age-old saying. Purpose will get you and your organisation longevity. People who believe that money or physical aspects can be the purpose of life are grossly mistaken. Neither can moneymaking be the true purpose of life nor can an organisation exist only for making money, not even a commercial organisation!

Food is necessary, but it cannot become the purpose of life. Likewise, profit is necessary but it should not become the sole purpose of a company's being. People assume quite wrongly that a company exists simply to make money. While profit is an important reason for a company's survival and growth, it cannot be and should not be the real reason for its being. Profit must come as a residue.

Often we refuse to believe in the reality just like an ostrich sticking its head in the sand. One may call it self-seduction or self-deception. This way we digress on purpose and start running after money, but like a mirage it deceives us.

Just like the stupid musk deer, man is also running through an endless maze of sense objects, earning, spending, acquiring, hoarding, wasting all and striving for more, only to get himself exhausted. He ultimately dies due to his own exhaustion, without achieving the joy and satisfaction that he is seeking. Swami Chinmayananda's story of the musk deer is very powerful and revealing. It opens up our mind. Nowadays, many entrepreneurs and CEOs are no different from Chinmayananda's musk deer. Without knowing the direction, they are speeding in a mad rush for gaining the cutting edge and finally burning themselves out. Like the stupid musk deer they are running through an endless maze of glamour and physical lures; they ultimately dry up in greed. It is time to reflect and introspect. Reflect deeply on questions like—'why do I exist' or 'why does my organisation exist'. Such questions are of great importance in change management. Change—what for?

When you ask yourself the question, 'what do I stand for?' think for a while and you will hear your conscience speaking to you: I stand for values—honesty, truthfulness, care, love and a host of such softer aspects of life.

Likewise, an organisation also stands for softer aspects—ethical and human values. It also stands for economic and commercial values. So, organisational values can be divided and discussed in two parts, each part is further divisible as under:

1. Economic and commercial values
   - Value addition
   - Brand value
   - Value innovation
2. Ethical and human values
   - Core values
   - Espoused values

While the economic and commercial values are important from the moneymaking point of view, the ethical and human values are the ones that measure the righteousness of a path. Let me first discuss briefly the segments of economic and commercial values.

Value addition is nothing but the difference between the final sale price and the cost of material of a particular product. Let us assume that a product's material cost is *X*. After you add value to the material and convert it into a particular product, it is sold at the price *Y*. Thus, '*Y* – *X*' is the value addition. Value addition includes all other overheads (wages, rentals, plant and machinery running costs, electricity and so on) and profit. As *X* and *Y* are fixed, you can get better margins by reducing the overheads. It is a very simple equation of business management. Value addition is of greater significance in the manufacturing industry.

Brand value is the customer's perception about a particular product, service or company. The perception is created through a process of image building. Brand value also encompasses organisations and people. James C. Collins and Jerry I. Porras, the authors of *Built to Last*, give a new dimension to brand value. They said, 'We are going to see companies increasingly assume that "What they stand for" in an enduring sense is more important than what they "sell".' Ethical values will build the brand tomorrow.

The term 'value innovation' has been recently coined by Professor W. Chan Kim of Boston Consulting Group. He is the professor of strategic and innovation management at INSEAD Business School. Chan Kim and his business associate, Renee Mauborgne, have recently written a book titled *Blue Ocean Strategies*, in which they have for the first time talked about value innovation. 'Business is not all about gaining the competitive advantage—"do not compare; do not compete," is the sort of bold message you get from their book. They observe, 'Our research for over 15 years finds that competition has come to play a central role in defining Strategy.' 'But business strategies must take us beyond competition', they note. 'High growth companies pay little attention to their rivals. They create the uncontested space', explains W. Chan Kim. We create our own boundaries in a competitive market. But the duo adds, 'Your job is to play with the boundaries rather than the boundaries that we create!' Thus, value innovation is all about innovation of service, delivery, products and the total outlook towards business

With regard to ethical and human values, they can either be core values or espoused values. It is important to understand the difference between the two. The core values are those ethical and human values that exist in the organisation, you do not add them. So after scanning the organisational culture you come to know about certain values, which are prevalent. You accept these existing values (or some of them) as your core values. The espoused values, on the other hand, are those values that you intend to follow; they may not be prevalent in the organisation. Yet, since you believe in them, you decide to espouse them. People make mistakes in understanding this subtle difference and take espoused values as the core values of the organisation. Yes, once you espouse certain values, in the course of time, they may even seep into the bloodstream of the organisation and become its core values.

Without entering into matrimony with values and determining the boundaries of purpose, no company or commercial organisation can survive—I would bet my last penny. Your company may swell—but 'swelling' is not 'growing'!

Both purpose and values are appropriately relevant today and will find more relevance tomorrow. Core purpose is a company's reason for being; core values are the essential and central tenets of a commercial organisation. If you club purpose and values, you get 'core ideology', which provides the glue that holds an organisation together through the test of time.

Like an organism, an organisation too has a life cycle. Few large corporations live even half as long as a person. A survey conducted by Royal Dutch/Shell revealed that one-third of the Fortune 500 firms in the 1970s vanished just in the next decade. Further, a study conducted by James C. Collins and Jerry I. Porras reveals, 'Companies that enjoy enduring success have core values and core purpose that remain focused while their business strategies or practices endlessly adapt to the changing world. Core values are the essential and enduring central tenet; core purpose is the organisation's reason for being.'

Many companies, which start with values but go astray when the harsh reality bites deep into their foundations. When the time of test arrives they forget the basics of value lessons. Even Ford, during bad times, had forgotten its magical formula: 'Putting Profit after People and Product was magical at Ford'. For creating 'what is not there', most of the companies seem to be content with 'what has remained there', letting the purpose of their being as a bygone phenomenon! But those who behold the purpose and proceed with confidence holding the ethical values like a believer who holds the holy scripture of his faith near to his chest come out as champions.

We may or may not believe in values, but they affect us in the long term. As a Zen saying goes, 'When you accumulate virtue with continued practice, you do not see the good of it, but in time it will function; if you abandon right and go against truth, you do not see the evil of it, but in time you will perish.'

Look at Japan. The moving force behind its recovery from ashes after the Second World War was a set of common core values shared by the Japanese. These values are manifested as part of their lives—honesty, caring, responsibility, humility are a few values to quote. They practise these values meticulously.

The societies that do not have values and people who are stiff with unethical attitudes, are prone to death. Likewise, the companies who compromise with values and make money by hook or by crook without following ethical norms are more susceptible to an unanticipated collapse. An age-old adage asserts, 'Stiff and unbending is the disciple of death; the gentle and yielding is the disciple of life.' Values stand for life and vices for death. Unethical practices take away agility and liveliness, which are the first and foremost prerequisites for survival while living in consequences and competitiveness. Agility and liveliness are also prerequisites to a good change programme.

Let me ask you a simple question: Whether a nation's positive image of the future is the consequence of nation's success or whether a nation's success is the consequence of the positive image of the future? The obvious is not answered. All those nations that had a clear image of the future succeeded; all those nations that did not have a clear vision for their future have gone astray.

Now let me ask the same question in the context of business management. 'Whether an organisation's positive image of the future is the consequence of the organisation's success or whether an organisation's success is the consequence of the positive image of future?' Someone may blame me for some sort of 'verbal acrobatics'. No, these are two different and opposite perspectives. In fact, any organisation's success is the consequence of the positive image of future—the purpose of its being. It is the positive, profound and strong vision that grants excellence or world-class status to an organisation.

The pattern of language in Box 4.1 will help you in getting a better understanding about articulation of vision with its two major components—purpose and values.

Most of the world-class companies articulate vision. Vision helps them in managing change, as they know well the direction that they are required to follow. The change pattern does not affect their vision. On the contrary, vision becomes their guiding star for managing change. As already mentioned, vision is the make-up of

Box 4.1 Vision Articulation

Core ideology provides the glue that holds an organisation together through Spacetime!

Core Purpose	**Core Values**
Why does the organisation exist?	What does the organisation stand for?
Core purpose is a company's purpose for being. 'Purpose' is like a guiding star on the horizon—forever pursued but never reached.	Core values are the essential and enduring tenets of an organisation—have only a few, usually four or five ...

Source: Adapted from the book *Built to Last.*

Box 4.2 Value Samples

Wal-Marts	We put customer ahead of everything
P&G	When you cannot make pure goods of full weight, go to something else that is honest, even if it is breaking stone.
3M	Innovation: Thou shall not kill a new product idea ...
HP	Do unto others as you would have them do unto you ...
Ford	People as the source of our strength
Disneyland	Disneyland will never be completed as long as there is imagination left in the world

Source: Adapted from the book Built to Last.

values and purpose. Let me show you some samples of values and purpose as evolved by some of the world-class companies (Box 4.2).

Box 4.3 shows some of the purpose samples of a few Indian and global companies.

A few renowned 'strategic visions' of some of the visionary companies that have changed the corporate world are discussed in the subsequent part of the chapter. The most challenging strategic vision was conceived by John F. Kennedy, former President of

Box 4.3 Purpose Samples

Infosys	Harness Indian intellectual capital
Wal-Marts	Customer is King—give him royal treatment
Amul	Contribute to society through cooperative effort
Boeing	Reach out for tomorrow
Birla	Entrepreneurship in serving a national cause
Sony	Changing the shoddy image of Japanese products
Nagarjuna	Service to society

Source: Author.

the United States, when he asked National Aeronautics and Space Administration (NASA) scientists to put a man on the moon by the end of the decade. The rest is history. Amidst all odds, the NASA scientists fulfilled this strategic vision—a man landed on the moon within a decade's time. Although Kennedy was not alive to see it, the powerful 'strategic vision' remained the driving force. That is the power of purpose!

Now let me quote a famous strategic vision of Akio Morita, the co-founder of Sony. When Morita visited America he realised that the youngsters have a great passion for music. So he asked his engineers to produce a palm-sized tape recorder at the price to suit a young person's pocket. Walkman is the product of this great strategic vision. It has become such a powerful brand that every palm-sized tape recorder is called a 'walkman'.

Soichiro Honda of Honda Motors wanted to go for an eco-friendly car. He puts his strategic vision in these words: 'You eat and drink, you leave your waste behind, and someone has to clean it up … Well! What we need to do with these vehicles is not to produce any waste in the first place!' Even today, Honda cars are unbeaten insofar as their eco-friendliness is concerned.

Today, IBM and Apple are dominating the world laptop market. But, it was Toshiba, which created this tiny machine. The CEO of Toshiba asked his engineers to produce the impossible! He instructed them to build a product using technology that they do not have. He further added that if his engineers did manage to produce the hardware there wouldn't be any software available for it.

He observed that Toshiba has to compete in a market dominated by IBM and that it must beat other Japanese companies. He challenged them to bring the product to the market in two years.

Miracle did happen.

Boeing's simple vision is to build world-class aircrafts and this has been keeping this company vibrant and the world leader.

Jack Welch's principle to keep it simple stupid (KISS) stands for making the change processes simple. 'Business management is not "rocket science"; we have chosen world's most simple profession', says Jack Welch. He adds, 'So whatever you are doing, keep it simple! Simple vision; simple communication; simple systems; simple processes; simple measures!'

Vision is powerful. It connects the present with the future. A manager's constituency is the future, where he has to live forever. It is vision that takes him there. Vision is the seat of change management.

Create a positive and profound vision. A visionary is a dreamer who dreams through purpose, holding the values steadfast. Quietly create your vision, lucidly articulate it and passionately own it, and untiringly drive your vision towards fulfilment. Vision makes the way. The significance of a person is not in what he attains, but rather in what he longs to attain. Live your values holding on to your dreams and not your nightmares.

A powerful vision is like a strong rope, which helps you in crossing a river. Just like a rope that connects the two banks of a river, a vision connects you with the future—the other side of the river.

A vision without action is like a dream. So, for supporting your vision with action you must understand the ground realities. Robert Fritz in his book, *The Path of Least Resistance*, articulated the power that visionaries create for themselves by balancing a powerful vision with a clear view of current realities. For this reason, a great visionary, Jack Welch, always pleaded, 'See the reality as it is, and not as you wish it should be.' A good visionary leader is always a practical man. He not only sees dreams but also knows the art of turning them into reality.

Action without a vision will lead you astray. Goals have a tremendous pulling power—like the propeller of an aircraft it pulls the entire organisation towards the required direction. Understanding of reality no doubt makes you pragmatic in approach, but it is not enough. The leader must spend some time thinking about the goals and aspirations of the group engaged in managing change. You must find the answers of some simple but important questions like, 'What do I really want to create, in business terms'; 'do our quality norms meet the industry's required standards, or are we required to raise the bar'; 'is cycle time reasonable', 'how broad is the customer base' and a host of such probing questions. They provide clarity to our 'goals' and 'standards'. Yet, another important question, 'Would your current actions, responses, systems, processes and mental models lead to your desired vision?' If the answer is 'yes', you can carry on. But, if the answer is 'no', be clear in your mind that all your efforts are but a 'pass-time'.

When you do not know where to go, any road will take you there. It is only vision with action that changes the world. Each one of us is gifted with the ability to make a difference. This ability is your intuitive wisdom.

It is the power of vision that shapes the future and gives direction. Purpose fills your heart with positive emotions that charge your actions. Mission takes you there. Values pave the righteous path. Virtue cleans your heart and soothes the soul. Wisdom provides the required sense to make the right decision. All these softer aspects matter a lot in change management.

You can live in the universe either as an observer or as an actor. Do not remain as an observer in the universe. Choose to be an actor in the universe. And remember, you cannot play the role of an actor in the universe unless you become a good acrobat who knows the art of managing change.

First decide where you want to go …

People don't resist change. They resist being changed.

—Peter Senge

(The author of the famous book *The Fifth Discipline*.
The quotation is sourced from the same book.)

5 A Boiled Frog Never Jumps Out of the Frying Pan

If you place a frog in a pot of boiling water, it will immediately try to scramble out. But if you place the frog in water, which is at room temperature and do not scare it then it will stay put. If the pot is now placed on a heat source and you gradually turn up the temperature, something very interesting happens. As the temperature rises from 70°F to 80°F, the frog will do nothing. In fact, he will show every sign of enjoying himself. As the temperature gradually increases, the frog will become groggier until he is unable to climb out of the pot. Although there is nothing restraining him, the frog will remain in the pot and boil. Why? Because the frog's internal apparatus for sensing threats to survival is geared to sudden changes in his environment, not to slow, gradual changes.

Many authors have written the parable of the 'boiled frog' in different ways. But the lucid way in which Peter Senge, the author of *The Fifth Discipline*, has put it in, has no parallels. Most of us become 'boiled frogs' and lose sensitivity to the required changes in the environment. Like the boiled frog we prefer death to a fresh lease of life—change and resistance go together. They are parallel forces. When such resistive forces become a part of the system, process and culture they cause disability in the change process. What Peter Senge calls 'learning disabilities' are in fact the organisation's inherent resistance mechanism that impedes the change process. He observes, 'In most companies that fail, there is abundant evidence in advance that the firm is in trouble. This evidence goes unheeded though, the individual managers are aware of it'. Such profound observations by Peter Senge got him a place as a management guru.

There are many organisational disabilities (a few of them were explained by Peter Senge), which make people 'boiled frogs'. They are as follows:

1. *'Arrived at'*: The 'arrived at' syndrome is disastrous in change management. It takes away the sensitivity for change. This syndrome is the cause of many ailments such as complacency, overconfidence, 'we are the best', 'best cannot be bettered'. This syndrome is the sole cause for creating comfort zones. The 'arrived at' complex also leads to 'narcissism' syndrome in which the victim starts loving his or her own self and thinks 'I am the best' or 'my organisation is the best'. Thus, such people lose sensitivity to change requirements. Even if someone suggests, the 'arrived at' syndrome does not allow a person to respond positively.
2 *Mine is better than yours*: When does a boy say 'My toy is better than yours'? He says it when he likes someone else's toy and finds it surely better than his. So, to overcome these inner sufferings and to console himself he immediately makes a tall claim. I have seen many CEOs suffering from such a complex. This complex never allows them to go for a change. Each practice—even a stone-age one—is considered better than the others. So they prefer to compromise with the stinking cheese. If someone says that your cheese smells foul, they will say, 'No, better check up your nose. There seems to be something terribly wrong with it!'
3. *I'm perfectly OK*: People create their own invisible boundaries and prefer to live within them undisturbed. If any initiative for change is taken up, they oppose it and say, 'Everything is fine, better you affect change in others' areas.' We are trained to be loyal to our job, profession, rank and discipline, and

to everything that belongs to us, including space. We do not tolerate any intrusion. This disability is so strong that people refuse to learn new things, thinking 'it does not belong to me or my area of expertise!' The famous parable of an American car manufacturing company speaks volumes. This American company found that as against three different bolts they use as per their standards, the Japanese car manufacturing company uses only one standard bolt for multipurpose use. They realised that they were losing time and money. Investigations revealed that three different components were the responsibility of three different groups of engineers, each responsible for 'their component only'. Thus, everyone was content with his own position and responsibility—'I'm perfectly OK'—without bothering for the larger cause. On the other hand, the Japanese had one designer responsible for the entire engine mounting. This 'I'm perfectly OK' syndrome encourages what is known as 'Uni-functionalism'. When people in organisations focus only on their position, they have little sense of reasonability for the results. Even if the overall results are disappointing, each one appears to be fully satisfied in his or her area. They feel 'someone else has spoiled the broth'. The victims of this syndrome always assign failures to external factors.

4. *Experience*: 'Experience' no doubt matters most. But when it becomes a syndrome it causes disability and hinders the change programmes. Anything you suggest will be overridden by the person on the plea of his or her long experience in dealing with that particular issue or situation. 'Don't bother, I know well how to do—I have been doing this for the last 20 years,' will be a common response from such people. The 'experience syndrome' hardens attitudes and robs flexibility. People having such a syndrome prefer to work in a closed environment in which all windows and doors are shut and there is no inflow of fresh air. As a wise man once said, 'We learn best from experience but we never directly experience the consequence of many of our most important

decisions.' We hardly know whether all through we managed or mismanaged!

5. *Snapshots*: Mostly we try to understand business in snapshots. This creates a myopic approach and we see everything like a horse— with blinkers on. We start counting trees losing the beautiful sight of the forest. We try to see everything in close-ups. We develop an obsession for precision—we tend to accept 'precisely wrong' than 'vaguely correct' solutions. What we forget is that neither life nor corporate life is the accumulation of some stand-alone events. Once we are conditioned to see life as a series of events, we start searching a separate cause for each event.
6. *Illusion of someone*: 'Someone' is an illusion. There is no someone in real life. Everyone has to bear his or her own Cross. Everyone has to face his or her own death and no one will come as a substitute. We must develop the habit to face the charge squarely. During my childhood, my elder brother used to tell me a story about baby sparrows. Every evening they would get frightened hearing that the farmer will call someone and get the tree cut. But the parent sparrows were sure that no one would ever come, so they consoled their babies not to bother. But one day when they got the news that the farmer himself would get an axe and cut the tree the next day, the parent sparrows told their babies, 'Now time has come to fly away.' Do not wait for a Messiah to come; manage change yourself.
7. *You can't do that here*: 'You can't do that here' is one of the biggest barriers in change management. It is one of the most common disabilities. When I first heard Peter Block in one of the international conventions in India, people were hooting against his newly developed 'empowerment' management practice. They shouted, 'Peter go back and try "empowerment" in America; all that will not work here in India.' He laughed and said, 'It doesn't work even in America.' What he made loud and clear was that it was not a question of India or America; it was a question of not accepting any new idea

with the syndrome, 'it can't work here!' What we condemned yesterday, today we practise it with a sense of pride. The famous 'You can't do that here' syndrome is described as a consequence of the following five anxieties:

- *We*—they are worried about their identity.
- *Cannot*—they are worried about their beliefs and values.
- *Do*—they are worried about their sets of skills.
- *That*—they are worried about their behaviour.
- *Here*—they are worried about the environment.

8. *I have already tried this many times*: Any change suggestion is spontaneously countered by, 'I have already tried this many times, but it didn't work.' If you ask him what he or she tried that had not worked, you would know that he or she did not even hear what you suggested to him. Barriers work spontaneously like autosuggestions.
9. *Ostrich approach*: No one is more blind than the one who refuses to see. Wilful blindness is very common in change management. Like an ostrich, people bury their heads in the sand and refuse to see. What they do not realise is that the ostrich has a bigger problem than a limited vision; his rear end is an enormous target for the hunters. They are the people who become victims and make the organisation suffer due to their wilful blindness. They always turn the Nelson's eye and say, 'I can't see.' Peter Drucker is very right when he says in the context of change management, 'The problem is not that we can't solve the problem; the problem is that we cannot see the problem.'
10. *Environment mismatch*: Lastly, 'environment mismatch' stands as the biggest barrier and disrupts the change process. Judith Petts, former Professor of Environment Risk Management and Pro-vice Chancellor Director, Centre for Environment Research and Training, examining management and non-management employee attitudes in England and Wales, found that people respond well to environment-matching

suggestions and oppose strongly to environment-mismatch changes. Change process is impeded when a strong mismatch exists between a personal belief and a corporate philosophy. Life cycle assessment (LCA) measures the environmental impacts on the entire life cycle of an organisation from cradle to grave. Such techniques are extremely useful for managing resistance arising out of mismatch of beliefs.

Kurt Lewin developed a tool—force-field analysis—to help understand the existing position within a system and to identify those forces that may help or hinder the introduction of change. If the driving forces of change (helpers) are greater than the resisting forces (hindrances), then progress can occur. A list of various forces operating in the system is drawn through a brainstorming exercise. Having made a list of these hindering and supportive forces, a decision on the relative strength of each force is made to construct a diagram using different sized arrows to represent the magnitude of each force. This plotter is used for change-making process.

The first action is to decide what can be done to minimise the hindrances before looking at how to increase the driving forces. This may seem odd. It is because there is a tendency that for every new force introduced into the system an equal and opposite force tends to oppose it. Indeed, some hindrances may appear simply as a consequence of trying to push through change and, paradoxically, removing that driving force may help overall. Pushing too hard can actually prove to be an obstacle to change. According to a parable, a boy began to give large doses of cod-liver oil to his pet dog because he had been told that the stuff was good for the ailing dog. Each day he would hold the head of the protesting dog between his knees, force its jaws open and pour the oil down its throat. One day the dog broke loose and spilt the oil on the floor. Then to the boy's greatest surprise the dog not only lapped up the oil that had spilled but came back to lick the spoon. That is when he discovered that what the dog had been fighting was not the oil but the way it was being given.

Realism in change is a necessity. We cannot afford to lose or waste our resources only to discover later that the mission for change has become another casualty, as it could not override the resistance. Since the resources are finite it may so happen that the desired change is impossible to introduce due to powerful negative forces. 'Force-field analysis' helps us taking a decision whether to proceed with the change or the resources would be better deployed elsewhere.

The other technique to monitor the plan for change is 'change audit'. No matter how carefully the plan has been drawn, something unexpected can happen. 'If anything can go wrong, it will', is Murphy's Law. It is impossible to plan for all eventualities but if the audit is closely monitored, you will be able to take remedial action as soon as a problem occurs. You will need to ensure that all the action points are followed through. The following checklist will serve a good purpose:

1. Have the action points been implemented?
2. If they could not be implemented, has something else been planned or implemented?
3. Are all the deadlines being met?
4. Has the goal been achieved?
5. Has there been any noticeable difference?

Barriers to change can frustrate your change programme. Studies reveal that because of the difficulties involved in implementing change programmes—with employees presenting more formidable barriers—there is a good chance that change efforts will be frustrated. According to a survey conducted by International Overseas Consultants, a recruitment organisation, 60–70 per cent of corporate change programmes are regarded as having 'failed'. The *CFO Journal* points out that only 16 per cent of senior corporate executives were fully satisfied with their re-engineering programmes, in contrast to the 68 per cent who were experiencing problems. The biggest barrier is usually the people in the organisation. Resisting a 'forced change' of the status quo seems to be a normal natural human response. People put skids under change, points out one consultant. The initial response of people in an organisation undergoing change is absolute denial of the issues needing to be addressed.

As changes move on, people enter a period of fear, they start to resist the changes and try to isolate themselves from the restructuring. As the changes continue, resistance grows and attitudes harden even further.

'The trick in managing barriers to change is not just to recognise them, but because we know them, to bring them to the surface early, so that the inevitable resistance to change can be managed and redirected,' says Ms Debbie Rynda, a consultant who represents the Stellar Team. Leadership is crucial to change. Although leaders do not need to be charismatic, they need to make a persuasive and convincing case for change.

Good leaders are normally good communicators. Good communication is vital in the process of change to allay fears and promote the right amount of enthusiasm. 'Failure to manage communication has the strongest correlation to unexpected change program costs—both direct and indirect,' says Ms Rynda.

When creating a new structure, organisations frequently neglect the fact that restructuring will alter the lives of the employees. Therefore, there is a need to involve employees in the restructuring and to communicate to them why these changes are being made, both on a conceptual and a practical level. Those whose lives are affected must be actively associated in change programmes.

Another method to overcome adversities is to go for 'reverse brainstorming'. Such an exercise not only generates excitement but also provides a forum for involvement. A manager shared the following experience:

> I had gone through a team meeting for planning a new project. The plan was more or less ready, but I did not see much excitement about the change programme. It seemed as if the members had reservations, but they were not expressing them. Then I tried what I like to call a 'reverse brainstorming' session. After we prepared the project plan I got my group together and we brainstormed the reasons. Why the plan would fail? Though the

> group initially thought that it was a strange assignment, they warmed up to the task. In an hour's time, we came up with 62 reasons why our change plan would not work. At that stage, I informed the group that there was another important part to the exercise. We had to prioritise the concerns and do action planning. The group then looked at the 62 items carefully and identified eight significant factors, which posed major threats. We then worked out a detailed plan to ensure that those factors were taken care of. This exercise helped us not only in identifying and avoiding a number of potential problems but also in providing a platform where people felt involved.

One can learn many things from the above experience. 'Employee-involvement' is the best weapon to counter adversities.

The boiled frog syndrome is one extreme tendency, which takes away the sensitivity for change. Forcing change without consultation is another extreme approach where people whose life is going to be affected by change are denied participation in the process of change. A good change-maker understands these extreme sharp edges well and knows the art of mending them moderately to make the change flow smooth and effortless.

If the shoe doesn't fit, must we change the foot?

—Gloria Steinem

(A famous American feminist icon and journalist)

Source: http://www.brainyquote.com/quotes/authors/ g/gloria_steinem.html

SECTION II

Change Techniques

The reasonable man adapts himself to the world; the unreasonable one persists in trying to adapt the world to himself. Therefore, all progress depends on the unreasonable man.

—George Bernard Shaw

(An Irish playwright and a great scholar)

Source: http://www.quotationspage.com/quote/692.html

6 Managing Creative Change—Five Actors

Creative change—how stupid! Someone may say. Change is always creative. The answer is both—'yes' and 'no'—it may be or it may not be. If you consider the word 'creative' as an extension to the verb 'create', then you are right. But when you use this word as a contraction to the adjective 'creativity', you are wrong as it stands to say something more. The word 'creative' means both: (a) having power to create or that which creates and (b) pertaining to imagination or originality. When you benchmark and manage change, there is no creativity implied. But when you benchmark and make some value addition, surely you have managed a creative change. Some wise people may find this explanation as superfluous and think that I am trying to explain the obvious. But I am aware that my book will be read not only by wise people but also by those whose first love is to split hair. The extra efforts are for them.

Creative change is no longer a convenience; it has become a necessity in the new age where 'blue oceans' are being created every day. Before I explain in detail the 'blue ocean strategy' let me share an anecdote with you.

A cap seller took shelter under a shady tree, and as he was very tired he fell asleep. When he woke up he saw that all the caps from his bag were stolen by monkeys, who were wearing them and nicely sitting on the branches. He had heard a lot about the habits of the monkey. So, he removed his cap and threw it on the ground. In response the monkeys did the same. He then collected all of his caps and returned home. He narrated this incident to his son to make him wiser. Good learning takes place by sharing one's experience. Next time it was the son's turn to go for trading. On his way he chose the same tree to take shelter and fell asleep. When he woke up, he found that all the monkeys were sitting on the tree wearing the caps, stolen from his bag. It did not upset him as he already knew the trick to get the caps back. So, he removed his own cap and threw it on the ground. One monkey jumped from the branch and picked it and ran away. The trick did not work the second time.

So, if you have to remain in business one-time innovation will do no good. As the cap seller taught his son to make him wiser, some old monkey must have also made the young ones wiser. Do not think that your competitor is sleeping when you are innovating. You have to innovate ceaselessly as an ongoing activity. Business is not all about competing and benchmarking—it is also about creating blue oceans through value innovation. Business is not cloning to look like our competitors—so do not match! Neither is it about fighting a battle with your competitors—so do not compete. Business is creating a new uncontested space.

BLUE OCEAN STRATEGY—A SIMPLE EXPLANATION

Why do some companies achieve sustained high growth in both revenues and profits? In a five-year study of high-growth companies and their less successful competitors, W. Chan Kim and Renee Mauborgne, the authors of *Blue Ocean Strategy* found that the answer lies in the way each group approaches strategy. The difference in approach was not a matter of managers' choosing one analytical tool or planning model over another. The difference was in the companies' fundamental, implicit assumptions about strategy. They found that the less successful companies took a conventional approach: their strategic thinking was dominated by the idea of staying ahead of the competition. In stark contrast, the high-growth companies paid little attention to matching or beating their rivals. Instead, they sought to make their competitors irrelevant through a strategic logic we call 'value innovation'—they made a brilliant observation. They share their research findings in an article titled 'Value Innovation. The Strategic Logic of High Growth' in *Harvard Business Review* as follows:

> When Virgin Atlantic Airways challenged its industry's conventional logic by eliminating first-class service in 1984, the airline was simply following the logic of value innovation. Most of the industry's profitable revenue came from business class, not first class. And first class was a big cost generator. Virgin spotted an opportunity. The airline decided to channel the cost it would save by cutting first-class service into value innovation for business-class passengers. First, Virgin introduced large, reclining sleeper seats, raising seat comfort in business class well above the industry's standard. Second, Virgin offered free transportation to and from the airport—initially in chauffeured limousines and later in specially designed motorcycles called LimoBikes—to speed business-class passengers through snarled city traffic. With those innovations, which were on the product and service platforms, Virgin attracted not only a large share of the industry's business-class customers but also some full-economy-fare and first-class passengers of other airlines. Virgin's value innovation separated the company from the pack for many years.

Stop copying or comparing with your rivals; think for yourself. 'Competition in overcrowded industries is no way to sustain high performance. The real opportunity is to create an uncontested market space', is the latent message that one gets from W. Chan Kim and Renee Mauborgne, who have created good ripples in the corporate world with their new concept of 'Blue Ocean Strategy'. 'How to create uncontested market space and make the competition irrelevant' is a simple explanation to what they call, Blue Ocean Strategy. 'The first principle of Blue Ocean Strategy is to reconstruct market boundaries, to break from the competition and create blue oceans', they explain.

Creativity and change go together. If change is for betterment, it has to be managed using the route of creativity. There is no other route. Both creativity and change need some techniques and capabilities, as well as some inborn traits. If you want to go for a creative change of your business organisation then take the road not travelled—it may be risky but this is the way to discover something new and innovative. Robert Frost is famous for his poem 'The Road Not Taken', which he composed more than 90 years back. This poem is quite contextual to this chapter, as it gives both insight and confidence to those who aspire for managing a creative change.

The Road Not Taken

Two roads diverged in a yellow wood,
And sorry I could not travel both
And be one traveler, long I stood
And looked down one as far as I could
To where it bent in the undergrowth;

Then took the other, as just as fair,
And having perhaps the better claim,
Because it was grassy and wanted wear;
Though as for that the passing there
Had worn them really about the same,

And both that morning equally lay
In leaves no step had trodden black.
Oh, I kept the first for another day!
Yet knowing how way leads on to way,
I doubted if I should ever come back.

I shall be telling this with a sigh
Somewhere ages and ages hence:
Two roads diverged in a wood, and I—
I took the one less traveled by,
And that has made all the difference.

Managers aspire to get an outstanding rating in their appraisals without standing out! How can you expect such rating unless you have contributed something that makes you stand out of the crowd!

Just as status quo is antithesis to change, bureaucratic approach is normally considered as antithesis to creative approach in business management. A bureaucratic approach is inflexible and stiff, as it exercises strong controls. Contrarily, a creative approach is flexible and agile as it does not exercise much control. Should change be managed through strong controls or less control? Should it be managed with fixed ideas and inflexibility or with an open mind and flexibility? The following 'Jobs–Sculley parable' will make you ponder:

When Steve Wozniak the co-founder of Apple—a semblance of maturity—separated from the company, Steve Jobs, his partner, a creative genius, became an unguided missile, as the practical Wozniak complemented Jobs' creativity. Systems were viewed only as obstacles by the whisking Jobs. Managerially, Steve Jobs was speeding over a cliff—he was creating a growth that was too rapid and uncontrolled. So, John Sculley of Pepsi was appointed on Apple's board to outweigh Jobs' whizzing entrepreneurial business practices, which misapplied systems. To have a firm grip over premature ageing, John Sculley, with the support of the board, managed to get Steve Jobs to quit. Was he right? It is a billion-dollar question. To justify his action (or perhaps to console his bleeding conscience) John Sculley came out with his thick book, *Odyssey—Pepsi to Apple*.

The Jobs–Sculley parable is perhaps the best quotable example available in the field of business management to discuss the pros and cons of controls or to make a choice between flexibility and rigidity in approach.

John Sculley, in an anxiety to give sanctity to controls or call it Standard Operating Procedure (SOP), cut out the freewheeling behaviour of the company by ensuring Steve Jobs' exit. Employees of Apple, who were accustomed to Steve Jobs ways of functioning, started facing abnormal problems. It was perhaps not at all warranted to get rid of the 'live wire' of Apple—Steve Jobs. John Sculley and Steve Jobs could have formed a complementary team by counterbalancing controls and flexibility. John Sculley wrongly perceived the problem in terms of either/or. Both flexibility and controls are needed. We must learn from a mother cat who catches her kittens with her sharp teeth without even a mild bite. This is possible only when controls are exercised by applying mother wit with tenable flexibility in change management. Time passed. John Sculley is out and Steve Jobs is in, but now he is a more balanced and matured personality.

Standard operating procedure and systems are good so long as they are open to change and fully aligned to the dynamic business needs, sensitising the external environment. Monitoring growth of companies without systems is a bit risky and could be unmanageable in the long run. Systems are *sine qua non* to business. The lack of both—systems and commonsense—leads to total chaos (south-west quadrant) (Figure 6.1). Again, sheer dependence on commonsense is not enough. Such configuration of business practices is synonymous to 'organised chaos', which can suit small companies in the initial stages (north-west quadrant). Where systems are in place but they are interpreted without using commonsense and with unbending approach, this reflects bureaucratisation of

Figure 6.1 Typical Creative Change Matrix

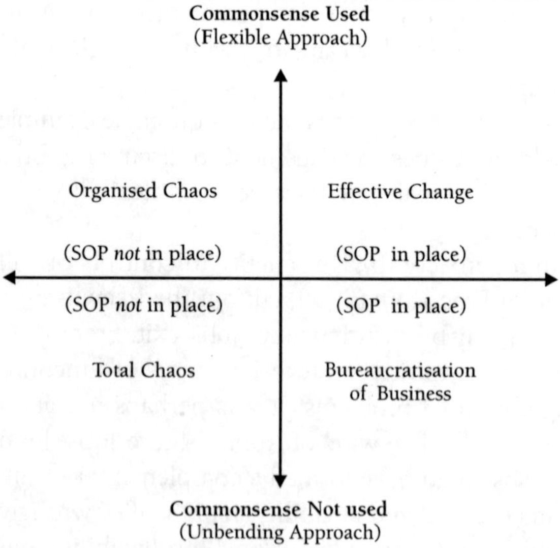

Source: Computed by the author.

business (south-east quadrant). The key to success in managing creative change lies in the existence of dynamic systems and their interpretation with a positive approach and their application with commonsense (north-east quadrant).

Systems and SOP are a boon when applied with commonsense and amenable approach.

Roger von Oech, who wrote many books on creativity, used the word 'actors' for identifying different roles played in unleashing creativity. Likewise, you need some actors for managing change, and each actor plays a specific role. Yes, every change maker is an actor; sometimes he has to play many roles. But the following five roles are most crucial:

1. Columbus
2. Artist
3. Judge
4. Sufi
5. Warrior

This chapter has a specific relevance to creative change management, which is a different cup of tea. There are many books on change management but I can hardly find one that throws some light on this sub-theme of change management. In the new age, creativity and innovation have assumed greater importance. The hallmark of the ability to manage creative change is a leader's mental agility and flexibility.

A creative change maker must either wear five hats or associate five creative people, each playing a different role. But all the five roles are important.

COLUMBUS

Christopher Columbus (1451–1506), a great European, discovered America. In creative change management there has to be someone to play this role. His job is to explore new avenues and business opportunities. Management of business in the new age no longer requires competing with each other in the same puddle of dirty water. W. Chan Kim has come out with a new approach to business, which he calls 'value innovation', that is, creating or discovering 'blue oceans'. Just as research and development (R&D) is important for product development, Columbus is important for business innovation and to make new discoveries so as to create a distinct place for the company. It is your Columbus who will take your company into the future.

The role of Columbus is to collect all possible information that might be relevant for a new expedition such as facts, new concepts, new technologies, new knowledge, variety of experience, and benchmarking data and information. He should be a good net surfer.

How to make Columbus' role effective in creative change management?

1. He must look for ideas in a lot of different places.
2. He must look for second and third right answers.
3. He must be tolerant to ambiguity.
4. He must be a good net surfer.

ARTIST

Once Columbus collects the requisite raw material consisting of information, data and host of other things that can be converted into some good pattern of ideas, the role of the artist begins. A pattern of ideas is like many pieces of coloured glass at the end of a kaleidoscope. When you turn the kaleidoscope a little bit, you can see new patterns in it. The artist must work in close association with Columbus so that the creative ideas can get many patterns.

The artist must be open to many ideas. He should be very smart in converting ideas into clear pictures, with beautiful colours. His art must be depictive—which is an advanced stage of description. He must know how to see both the foreground and the background. He must know how to enhance the background so that the faint picture in foreground becomes clearer! The artist should be able to see the details from many angles, even upside down and must not ridicule any idea or data furnished by Columbus. The artist must fully trust Columbus—even if he fails to discover India, surely he will discover America. Trust your Columbus as he will never disappoint your artist.

The artist must be capable of painting even modern art, which may not make much sense to people but a genius can discover something new from the zig-zag patterns.

How to make your artist more effective?

1. He must be a daydreamer.
2. He must always ask, 'What if?' and, 'Why not like this?'
3. He must have courage to challenge the basic assumptions.
4. He must have courage to override the bureaucratic barriers.
5. He must look at things in different ways.

JUDGE

The judge must understand clearly that both Columbus and the artist are explorers and dreamers. They may not understand the ground realities. They are very emotional, passionate and intuitive people who do not possess a rational or logical mind. They are more like kids who are not much bothered or concerned about the consequences. Against this backdrop, your judge must play the role of a very mature and highly responsible person.

He must ask, 'Is this idea any good?' 'What are the very positive and negative aspects?' 'Is it worth pursuing?' 'Why shouldn't this idea be dropped?' 'Will this idea give the returns that I am looking for?' 'Does it match with my strategic vision and mission?' 'Does it fulfil my business objectives?' 'Do I have the requisite resources to make it happen?' He must ask host of such probing questions. His job is to use a searchlight and trace out all the dark spots, which can create problems.

The judge's job is not to explore but to make a decision after a thread-bare scrutiny and analysis. He must make an evaluation and weigh the advantages and disadvantages in the suggested ideas of Columbus and the messages conveyed by the artist through his or her paintings. He must be a logical person who holds reason steadfast.

While the roles of the first two actors are like that of a child, the role of the judge is of a matured adult. The first two actors are daydreamers, and your judge is a ruthless hardcore realistic and practical person. Not fantasy but reality is his psychic.

How to make the judge more effective?

1. He must be critical but constructive.
2. He must convert most stupid into most creative.
3. He must evaluate standing at a different coordinate system (CS).
4. His job is also to suspect and apprehend—pick holes if needed.
5. 'Foolproof' is his Extra Sensory Perception (ESP).

SUFI

Sufi is your soul searcher. After the judge has made his decision and selected some ideas and strategies for implementation, the sufi will guide you about the righteousness of the path chosen.

While the judge uses his mind, the sufi relies on his heart to make decisions. The judge has a strong logical base whereas the sufi's intuitive wisdom is matchless. The sufi does not believe in politics nor does he know how to formulate strategies. His real asset is his value system. He is a very soft person but when there is a question of values he is the most uncompressing and inflexible person. He will never compromise with his values come what may!

The sufi is highly enlightened. He plays the role of a conscience of an organisation. He is the 'man in the mirror'. The sufi is a person who possesses a tremendous amount of ESP. He is highly intuitive and perceptive. He is also a great visionary who can see the future and make prophesies. His vision is broad and holistic.

How to make your sufi more effective?

1. Allow him to meditate and maintain tranquillity.
2. Let him discover the solutions from within.
3. Never argue with him and try to find out the reason for his saying certain things or giving certain advices as he does not know 'how he knows the truth'.
4. Do not mistake his humility as his weakness—he is humble but not meek.
5. Understand his nature; he is not aggressive or assertive. Therefore, he will not push his opinions or views forcefully.
6. If you trust him he will develop the character of your business.

WARRIOR

It is you who has to play the role of a warrior, he cannot be hired. If you are the change maker you cannot delegate this role to anyone else. Demonstrate courage to do all that is necessary to make your idea a reality. If you want that your ideas should succeed, you have to play an assertive and aggressive role, and if need be, sometimes become offensive.

You have to carry along with your Columbus, artist, judge and sufi, and show equal respect to each. You cannot be biased in favour or against anyone. Your main role is execution. If the idea is good and noble you have no other option but to execute it. Your job is both to initiate and complete the change process.

Your Columbus has made many discoveries; your artist made clear-cut plans and suggested many strategies. After a thorough scrutiny and analysis, the judge has given clearance to certain plans and strategies. The sufi okayed what is righteous. Finally, it is time to execute the ideas. Execution is not all that simple as you think. You have to be ready to face a lot of opposition and override many barriers. If you want good ideas and plans to succeed you may have to be offensive, assertive and at times a bit aggressive.

As a warrior you have to play both the roles—the role of the army general and that of a soldier. You have to maintain discipline and order. Remember, everything that comes from discipline is functional and everything that comes from indiscipline is dysfunctional. You have to slog and motivate your people. But remember, that there is no one who would motivate you. Here, you are the motivator and the motivated, all-in-one!

To summarise all the five roles:

1. Your role as Columbus is to explore new information, resources, ideas and territories. If you cannot play this role directly, you can appoint a Columbus.
2. Your role as an artist is to convert the raw ideas into solid actions and strategies. If you cannot play this role directly, you can associate some good artist—there are no hassles.
3. Your role as a judge is to evaluate, analyse and decide on merits, the final strategies and game plan. It is better you play this role yourself. Nevertheless, you can seek guidance and assistance.
4. Your role as a sufi is to find out the righteousness of your path and game plan. Again this role has to be played only by you. If you wish to seek guidance, seek from your conscience. Your sole guide is your soul and your solitary assistant is your heart.
5. The role of the warrior is your role for translating the dream into a reality.

You are a warrior—you cannot delegate this role.

Once you and your actors have played the roles effectively, the organisation witnesses a creative change. In case you find some hiccups, there could be only two reasons—either all or some of the actors have not played their roles effectively, or the time for creative change was not ripe.

Ineffective roles and bad timings are always the causes for failures in creative change management. There is a saying, 'The most powerful thing on this earth is an IDEA whose time has come.' The latter part of the phrase is more important. There are many bright ideas which die in the mother's wombs as they were prematurely conceived. There are many films that fail on the box office not because they were bad but because they were made ahead of time. They failed because the audience did not acquire the required maturity to understand the subtlety and brilliance of those films.

Unlike in a film or in a drama, the roles of these actors are not defined by strict boundaries. These roles should be viewed holistically for the entire team to generate many creative ideas, analyse them, perfect them and finally to ensure their execution. Here there is a lot of scope for the overlapping of roles. Further, there is also a fair amount of shifting back and forth between roles. For example, though the judge may give clearance, the sufi may put his foot down on ethical grounds or the artist may be very excited with certain ideas, but the judge may reject it because he does not find it a good fit to the current needs.

The second important thing in this role-play is the principle: 'first thing first'. First Columbus and the artist should be allowed to play their roles without any interference from the judge and the sufi. Both of them should be kept away when the first two actors are playing their roles. Unless freewheeling is provided Columbus and the artist cannot play their roles effectively.

Empower the judge to overrule or override any idea or suggestion mooted by Columbus or artist. It is not a question of the best idea; it is a question of the best matching idea. 'Good-fit' is the key thing. There are four sets of possibilities. The same can be best explained through the matrix shown in Figure 6.2.

Let us assume that Columbus and the artist finally give 50 ideas to the judge. The judge has to make the selection on the basis of good-fit? So he plots them as per their quality of creativity (idea attractiveness in general) and the applicability of the idea to creative change programme on a matrix at *X* axis and *Y* axis.

In the above matrix you will find 13 ideas placed in three boxes at south-east, middle-south and middle-east (darkest colour) that are poor on both the parameters. They are neither good creative ideas nor do they suite the current needs. The judge will throw them in the dustbin marked as poor ideas.

Now you find 17 ideas in three boxes at south-west, centre and north-east (moderate dark colour); they are low on both the

Figure 6.2 Portfolio Management Matrix and Strategic Analysis

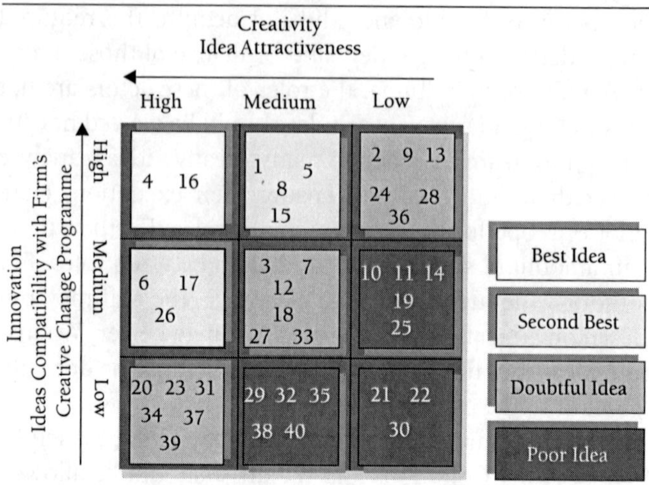

Source: From the author based on a figure in G.K. Chesterton. 1988. 'Problem Solving and Creativity' in *The Creativity Gap*, pp. 121–154.
Note: Each number indicates an idea from the list submitted for screening.

parameters, except the centre one. These ideas are also not very suitable. So, the judge will keep them in a tray marked as 'doubtful ideas'. They are not thrown outright but are kept in abeyance for future use.

Now your judge looks at the two boxes at middle-north and middle-west (medium on both axis). In all there are seven ideas. They are moderate on both the parameters. They are not best yet worthy of consideration. The judge will keep them in the 'select-basket'.

In the north-west box are two ideas—they are the best-fit. They are extremely creative ideas and most suitable to the current creative change programme. So instantly the judge will pick up these two ideas. He will also pick up the other seven ideas from the select-basket. Finally, he will pass on these nine best-fit ideas to the Sufi.

Now the sufi has to play an important role. He will use a different plotter called—value–goals matrix. He is quite aware of the difference between strategic requirements and value requirements—goals are related to business strategies and values to business ideology, or business character. His job is to see and assess these best-fit ideas from the viewpoint of 'value-goals'—what impact we want to create to retain or enhance our image as a value-based company. The sufi will reject all those ideas that do not create the required value–impact. Say, out of nine he rejects four on the basis of value–criteria. So, finally five best ideas—good-fit and value-based—will emerge. Now the role of a warrior begins.

Now will be the need to activate the warrior in you. The following tips and techniques list ways to activate the warrior.

TECHNIQUES TO TRIGGER THE WARRIOR IN YOU

The warrior must possess some capabilities and certain leadership traits. But these are not enough. He must also learn certain techniques to become a good warrior. The purpose of this section of the chapter is to share some traits, techniques and capabilities that can activate the warrior in you.

1. *Appreciative inquiry (AI)*: Although AI is a recent discovery in the area of behavioural science, it is a very powerful technique, which can also be used by the warrior to make creative change effective. A simple way to understand 'AI' technique is to consider the meaning of its two words separately and independently.

Each part of this phraseology is powerful and creates impact even as a stand-alone word. But when combined, it creates synergy par excellence. Both hydrogen and oxygen are two important gases. But when they join in a particular combination they produce water—the most nurturing substance on earth essential for the survival of human beings and life per se. Appreciation stands for recognition—it adds value to one's enthusiasm and boosts up the morale whereas inquiry is four-dimensional—'4D'—discovery, dream, design and destiny. Thus, AI creates four-dimensional awareness and appreciation: (a) what best have I achieved (discovery), (b) what best I might possibly achieve (dream), (c) what best it ought to be for my achieving (design) and (d) what best I will eventually receive (destiny).

Appreciative Inquiry works successfully because it treats people like people, and not like machines. In Bernard Shaw's famous drama *Pygmalion* Eliza Doolittle tells Col. Pickering, 'I shall always be a flower girl to Professor Higgins because he treats me as a flower girl and always will; but I know I can be a lady to you because you treat me as a lady and always will.' What made Eliza say this powerful dialogue? It was Professor Higgins who transformed Eliza from a flower girl to a lady, but he never treated her as a lady. On the other hand, Col. Pickering in no way contributed in converting her from a flower girl to a lady, but always treated the flower girl as a lady. It was not important for Eliza who made her what! What was important to her was 'who treated her as lady'! How she was treated made all the difference! Appreciative Inquiry is all about treating a flower girl as a lady—a respectful human being.

For playing this role you can always seek assistance from the sufi. Listen to your heart and act according to the voice of your conscience.

2. *Create a warrior's heart*: Your job as a warrior is to lead and manage change with a lion's heart. As Talleyrand, a brave and famous military commander said, 'I am more afraid of an army of one thousand sheep led by a lion than an army of one thousand lions led by a sheep.' How true!

What makes you lion hearted? How can you muster enough courage to act on the ideas cleared by your judge and sufi? There is no direct answer to such valid questions. Believe it or not, the following simple tips will fill your heart with a lion's courage.

- A well thought-out plan will get you enormous confidence.
- Encourage your people and boost their morale. In turn, your morale will grow manifold and you will get encouragement.
- Trust your actors, trust their ideas and trust your people who are there with you shoulder-to-shoulder to turn your dreams into reality. Trust and faith perform miracles in change management.

- Share your experiences of success with your people. Recollect and remember the past events of success. Keep them close to your heart. Celebrate the success of your people. Remember, success is a matter of consciousness. When you celebrate others success, in fact you feed your own consciousness and prepare it for greater successes.

3. *Seek support*: Once your vision is created you must share it with your people and get their support. Winning support is important in change management. Always remember the Biblical prescription: 'United you stand; divided you fall!' Success largely depends on the support system that you have created around you in the organisation. 'How to develop a support system?' You can learn from the following:

- *Gypsies*: A sick gypsy never goes to a doctor alone. Five to six gypsies always accompany him. A powerful support system exists in their culture.
- *Wild geese*: Wild geese flock together, honking and encouraging each other. When a goose is hit by a hunter and falls, it does not fall alone—two or three geese also fly down and try to give it all their possible support. It is only when the injured goose is not able to fly that those geese leave it behind and fly away.
- One can learn support culture from the crows too. If you do not believe me then just hit one crow and see how heaven caves in. The other crows will come together and make your life miserable.

4. *No excuses*: 'No excuses please' should be your catchphrase. Neither offer excuses nor accept excuses. Follow the Singaporean phrase 'Die, die, must do!' Unlike the English phrase 'Do or die' the Singaporean phrase does not give you an option of avoiding the task by dying. This reminds me of the Spanish explorer called Cortez who had burnt his ship after reaching an iceland called 'Veracruz'.

The phrase 'burn the boat' was coined from this incident. Once you burn the boat you on purpose destroy available options for retreat.

Retreat does not suit a warrior. Now that you are a warrior, you cannot retreat. So, chain your leg to a log and fight so that even in the worst of situations you are unable to retreat. Do not go by the literal meaning of the words; instead, try to understand the spirit.

5. *Develop your risk-taking muscles*: Change management is all about managing 'uncertainties' and the journey towards an unknown territory. Obviously, it is full of risk. God has gifted 'risk muscles' to every one of us. What we are required to do is just to flex them. Ricardo Semler, the author of *Maverick* says, 'A turtle may live hundred years, but it moves only when it sticks out his head!' As Arthur Koestler, a Jewish–Hungarian polymath author, said, 'If the Creator had a purpose in equipping us with a neck, he certainly would have meant for us to stick it out.' How can you flex your risk muscles? Here are some tips:

- New ideas create excitement. So, invest your energies in new ideas.
- Think about unknown territories and try to tackle the issues outside your field of expertise and experience. Start doing small things and one day you will realise that you have performed a miracle by doing the impossible!
- Cock up your head and stick out your neck—the tall see the farthest!
- 'Playing safe' is risky. Never opt for 'safe play'. Learn to choose the difficult path. What you think is difficult, is the path that leads you to success! Sometimes risking favours; sometimes it is safer to risk.
- When at crossroads choose the untravelled or less-travelled path.
- 'Success comes to those who dare and act', said Pandit Jawaharlal Nehru 50 years ago. So, dare and act. 'Daredevil' is a positive phrase—surely you do not become a devil by daring.

- Begin with minor and incremental changes, what is called Kaizen. This will give you confidence and, in turn, courage to take risk.

6. *Systems architect*: Peter Sange's 'Systems Thinking' is a great *mantra* of change management. First provide the required support to systems, then work for them only until they acquire their own pillars and support systems. As a change maker be a 'systems architect'. One single reason for failure in change management is the change makers' inability or incapability to think and manage change in systematic terms.

7. *Develop sensitivity and cognitive faculties*: Peter Drucker once said that the real problem is not that we do not have solutions, but that we do not see the problem. Unless you see and cognise the problem you cannot solve it. So, develop your cognitive faculties so that you can sensitise the issues.

8. *Be a catalyst*: If your people stand united you gain; if they stand divided you fall. So, if not for any other reason, for your own benefit play the role of a catalyst to make the process of execution smooth. Your role as a warrior is to influence, persuade, unite and lead people towards a common goal. Be a catalyst to be a good and an effective warrior.

9. *Do not break rocks*: Your job is not to break rock; your job is to make the temple. So develop an eye that can see the holistic pattern, and develop a mind that works for efficacy and results. Set high goals, induce and inspire your people, and pursue the change process relentlessly until you get the desired results. The taste of the pudding lies in its eating.

10. *Be discontented*: A warrior must raise his bar of expectations high and try to achieve them. This is possible only when you are not satisfied with your own performance. You have to keep the standards of your performance high. Raise the bar of your expectations and you will be surprised to know that people are capable of delivering more than what you expect from them. Discourage the 'arrive-at' syndrome. Create excitement and convert irritations into inspirations.

An inventor was asked why he spent 16 hours every day thinking about his work-plan and strategies. 'Because I am dissatisfied with everything as it currently exists in its present form', he replied. When Steve Jobs' design engineers created the first motherboard, thinking it was the 'world-best', he raised it above the head and dropped it uttering, 'bullshit!' What his people thought was world's best was nowhere near to the genius' expectations. His engineers got the right message and the rest is history—Apple's motherboard is world's best!

11. *Use a warrior's shield*: Shield is as important as the sword. A warrior must know how to shield himself, his people and his change plans. No one likes change except a baby who is wet. Resistance to change is as natural as resistance to death by a dying patient. So, be conscious of this fact and carry out the mission using a systematic plan for removing the doubts and apprehensions of the people.

Be aware:

- Change is inevitable—die, die, you must do!
- Change is resisted—do not force change instead make people aware.
- New ideas can be threatening—allay your people's apprehensions.
- People love status quo—burn their existing boats if need be.
- Kepler was ridiculed, Copernicus was imprisoned, Socrates was made to drink Hemlock, Christ had to bear the Cross—making change is not sleeping on a bed of roses. Your bed is made of thorns. If you are not prepared for sacrifice for a better cause, better withdraw before it is too late and collect alms at the temple from those who make change happen.

12. *Be a seller of your thoughts*: I love to hate those who say, 'My best ideas were not accepted.' Why do you blame others for your failure, blame yourself. Your ideas were not accepted because you did not know how to sell them? And if you could not sell your best ideas what else can you sell then? How can you make your

idea more attractive to other people? Answer the following three obvious queries:

- What does your idea promise?
- What benefits does it provide to me?
- If I throw it will my competitor pick it up?

13. *Set deadlines*: With all said and done, crisis management does work. Create crisis once in a while, if need be. Time frames play an important role in change management and especially in managing creative changes. It is like selling ice. A creative idea is highly perishable. If you do not execute it, your competitor will.

Where is your sense of urgency? What tight deadlines can you give to yourself and your people? Deadlines work.

- Crisis management does work, if not always, sometimes.
- 'Do or die' gives an option. 'Die, die must do' is a better phraseology.
- Creative tension is a good technique—it is better to keep your people in tension than to allow them to continue living in the comfort zones—the former is inconvenient, the latter is deadly.

14. *Be persistent*: Success depends on your persistence. Most of the time warriors fail because they do not give the same importance to the task at hand at the finish line, which they give in the initial stage. 'People usually fail when they are on the verge of success; so, give as much care to the end as to the beginning; then there will be no failure', the Old Master Lao Tzu gives this golden tip in his famous book, *Tao te Ching*. Not initiative, but 'finitiative' gets you the final success. Initiative opens the door of success but if one lacks 'initiative' he or she does not deserve to retain the company's identity card. Beginning is important but it does not give any guarantee of success. But lack of initiative surely stands as the testimony of failure. As I mentioned earlier, initiative opens the door. You must

walk in and continue walking until you reach the destination. Your job is to create excitement and sustain it throughout.

There is a story about two frogs who fell into a churn of milk. They swam around and tried to hop up. As there was no solid support under their feet, it was not possible for the frogs to hop out and escape. One conceded and died. The other persisted. So, he went on swimming and paddling. His movements churned the milk and turned it into butter. After some time, the frog climbed up on the pat of butter and hopped out of the churn. This only proves that persistence and perseverance are two techniques that directly take you to the finishing line.

15. *Self-appreciation*: Last but not the least; learn to pat your back. Remember, you are playing the role of a warrior. Your job is to inspire and motivate others. Once you reach the top, no one will motivate or inspire you, so you must learn to motivate yourself. Pat your own back. If you are a shy person and do not like patting your own back, stand secretly in front of a life-size mirror and pat the back of the guy you see in the image. Self-stroking is not bad it is just a technique.

Creative change is not a simple change management programme; it is a different cup of tea. For instance, when you benchmark, you do some cut and paste. That is good, not bad. At least you are trying to change. But that is not enough. You must learn to add value even to the mundane cut and paste change. When the corporate world is busy creating blue oceans is it not sinful that we are still content with matching and benchmarking. You have to raise the bar of change management.

Never forget this last tip. The entire creative process should be carried in two phases: (a) Imaginary Phase and (b) Practical Phase.

IMAGINARY PHASE

The first phase is the imaginary phase, which includes—soft, divergent, lateral and intuitive thinking! Ask questions using the technique of 'what if?' What if I do it like this? Think what rules can you break or override? What assumptions can you drop or discard? Can you borrow a metaphor from some other discipline? How about if I look at this backward? Such questions will get you variety of ideas. At this stage, lock out the judge and the sufi. They have no role to play at this imaginary phase. Allow Columbus and the artist to play around like a child. Allow them to say anything they want to say. You are not supposed to analyse or assess anything at this state.

The motto at this first phase is: Think something different!

PRACTICAL PHASE

The second phase is the practical phase—it involves hard, convergent, vertical and logical thinking! Now it is time to lock out Columbus and the artist, and allow the judge and sufi to examine the suggestions from practical and ethical angles. First allow the judge to examine asking certain questions—is this idea any good? Do we have resources to implement it? Is the timing right? What is the deadline? What are the consequences of not achieving the objectives or targets on time? Such searching questions will help you in identifying the ideas that are practical and suit your present requirements.

Now, the judge can lay back and allow the Sufi to examine the ethicality of the ideas. Is the idea value-based? What impact will it create? Will it help build the company's image as a value-based company? Is it the ethical way to earn profits? Such questions will help you in assessing the righteousness of the strategies and the chosen path. If your sufi wants to drop certain approved ideas, allow him to do so—overriding the views and judgement of your judge. You can compromise with business strategies but not with your value system.

The motto at this second phase is: Getting something done good!

In the imaginative phase your focus should be on quantity and not on quality, and in the practical phase the focus should be on quality and not on quantity. Following the technique 'first thing first' is absolutely necessary. You cannot reverse the process or carry them out concurrently.

Planning is an unnatural process; it is much more fun to do something. The nicest thing about not planning is that failure comes as a complete surprise, rather than being preceded by a period of worry and depression.

—Sir John Harvey-Jones

(Former chairman of Imperial Chemical Industries [ICI], he is best known for his BBC television show 'Troubleshooter')

Source: http://www.cybernation.com/quotationcenter/quoteshow.php?id=31850

7 Generating Creative Ideas—Tips and Techniques

Generating creative ideas is important for managing change, especially creative change. During the process of change some creative gaps always exist, which need to be filled first. What we really mean by creative gap is the gap between the 'desired level of creativity' and the 'existing level of creativity'. This gap hinders the creative change process.

There are two aspects in managing creative gaps—(a) assess, locate and fill the creative gaps or (b) create creative gaps on purpose by raising the bar of quality norms and innovation expectations. In the first case, you try to fill the existing creative gaps as you fill the existing competency gaps. It is a simple exercise.

In the second case, since you raise the bar and try to achieve much higher quality standards and innovative practices, products and services; a sudden vacuum is created. This vacuum is created on purpose. All of a sudden expectations are raised. This creates pressure or what is also called as creative tension. Building creative tension is a technique by which you can activate creative change at a fast pace. No vacuum remains unfilled. There is a general tendency to find the ways and means quickly to fill the vacuum, no matter how Herculean a task it may involve!

For filling the creative gaps—small or big—we must have many innovative ideas. 'How to get innovative ideas and unleash creativity of your people', is an important question. Many such techniques and processes already exist. I share some of these techniques by adding many tips from my own perception and experience.

The first and foremost issue in the entire process is to understand the problem or issue clearly. Unless the problem is properly understood, you cannot find the right solution. Likewise, unless the creative gap is properly assessed and understood you cannot find ways and means to bridge it. Thus, what is more important is 'articulation' of the problem or the creative gap.

ARTICULATION OF THE PROBLEM

In creative change management as well as in problem solving, understanding of the issue—or we may call it 'problem' to avoid complexity of words—is important. Unless you understand and define the problem, you cannot find the right solutions. 'A problem well understood and well stated is a problem half solved', is a famous saying!

What do we mean by a 'problem'? A problem is an undesirable deviation of what is happening from what should be happening! When we expect certain results and do not get them, we take it as a problem. Likewise, when we expect certain creative inputs, but do not get them then we consider it as 'creative gap'. Let me make it simple through an example. Suppose, you have bought a new car and it gives you a mileage of say, 10 kilometres per litre of petrol. You are quite satisfied with its performance. Later, you learn from your friend, who has also bought the same model of the car, that he is getting an average of 12 kilometres per litre. Now you have discovered that your car is less fuel-efficient. Will you still be satisfied with the fuel efficiency of your car? I know you will not tell a lie. So, now you have a problem! Nothing happened to your car; its fuel efficiency remained just the same, yet you have earned a problem by acquiring certain information, which was not there with you earlier. I will try to put this state through an equation:

> 10 km fuel efficiency (What is happening) – 12 km fuel efficiency (What should be happening) = (–) 2 km low fuel efficiency (Undesirable deviation)

So, before you start spending time on articulation of a problem and its possible solutions, ask yourself three questions:

1. Is there a deviation between what is happening and what should be happening?
2. Do I want to do something about it?
3. Is there anything that I can do about it?

On getting a positive response to all the three questions you start with the 'first thing first', that is, articulation of the problem. Edward Hodnett says, 'A good problem statement often includes (a) what is known, (b) what is unknown and (c) what is sought.' This means that the leader should undertake a tremendous amount of work before attempting to generate creative solutions for creative change.

'One technique for finding more answers is to change the wording in your questions', suggests Roger Von Oech in his book, *A Whack on the Side of the Head*. If an architect looks at an opening between two rooms and thinks, 'what type of door should I use to connect these rooms?' that is what he will design—a door. But if he thinks, 'What sort of passageway should I provide here?' he may design something different like a hallway, an air curtain, a tunnel or perhaps a courtyard. This shows how 'question framing' gives different perspectives to change leaders. Roger narrates an interesting story in this context:

Several centuries ago, a curious but deadly plague appeared in a small village in Lithuania. What was so curious about this disease was its grip on its victim; as soon as a person contracted it, he would go into a deep almost death-like coma. Most died within a day, but occasionally a hardy soul would make it back to the full bloom of health. The problem was that since 18th century medical technology was not very advanced, the unafflicted had quite a difficult time telling whether a victim was dead or alive. Then one day it was discovered that someone had been buried alive. This alarmed the townspeople, so they called a town meeting to decide what should be done to prevent such a situation from happening again.

After much discussion, most people agreed on the following solution. They decided to put food and water in every casket next to the body. They would even put an air hole from the casket up to the earth's surface. These procedures would be expensive, but they would be more than worthwhile if they would save people's lives.

Another group came up with a second, less expensive, right answer. They proposed implanting a 12-inch long stake in every coffin lid directly above where the victim's heart would be. Then whatever doubts there were about whether the person was dead or alive would be eliminated as soon the coffin lid was closed.

What differentiated the two solutions were the questions used to find them. The first group asked, 'What should we do if we bury somebody alive?' whereas the second group wondered, 'How can we make sure everyone we bury is dead?'

Do not go on the merit or the quality of suggestion. Try to understand how the articulation of the statement or question made the difference. If your question itself is framed incorrectly then do not curse the wise men who suggested implanting a big stake to the coffin lid.

A well-defined problem statement or a question can be extremely useful during the idea-generating phase. Ideally, it should be (a) stated in short and precise words, (b) clear and unambiguous and (c) defined in terms that will facilitate the ultimate measurement of results. For better clarity, I give below two examples of 'problem statements':

1. The sales of olive oil products are in trouble. We suspect that the cause can partly be attributed to bad packaging and partly to poor salesmanship. Brainstorming is conducted to discuss and recommend solutions for improving the packaging and design, and salesmanship.
2. The sales of olive oil products are disappointing. The preliminary analysis of the problem has shown that the root cause is unsatisfactory packaging (leakage, bad capping and poor packaging material). The team is invited to solve this problem. It is hoped that as a result of packaging improvements, sales of the product will increase by 12 per cent within one year.

One can say that the second statement is a better sample of 'problem statement'. It reflects that some preliminary exercises have already been conducted and the causes of problems have been identified. There are many techniques that can be used for finding the causes of a problem. This methodology is known as 'cause and effect analysis'. There are many tools and techniques for conducting such analysis; the following two techniques are commonly used and considered best and quite effective:

1. Ishikawa Analysis
2. Why–Why Analysis

Let me discuss these two techniques first, before I share with you many other techniques for creative idea generation.

Ishikawa Analysis

Professor Kaoru Ishikawa of the University of Tokyo, invented this technique for finding out causes for a particular effect by plotting them on a particular pattern. This diagram is recognised with his name and is known as 'Ishikawa diagram'. It is also popularly

Figure 7.1 Fishbone Technique

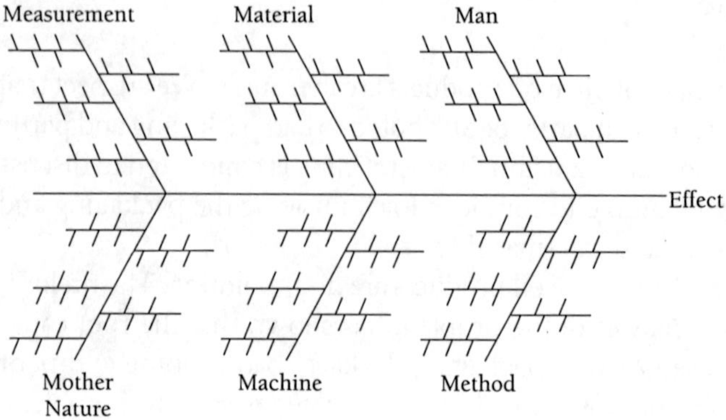

Source: Figure drawn by the author based on Professor Ishikawa's famous Cause and Effect diagram.

known as the 'Fishbone Diagram' because it looks like a fishbone (Figure 7.1).

As you can see, this diagram has a head, bones and a tail. The problem or end-effect is indicated at the head of the fish, and then ideas are generated and plotted on the various spikes of the fishbone. The great advantage of this fishbone diagram is that you see all the causes in a single diagram. Each cause can also have a few sub-causes. They can also be plotted on the horizontal and slanting–horizontal lines around the slanting–vertical bone.

For an ailment there must be some cause or causes. The ailment is seen with its symptoms. We cannot see the ailment—what we see are its symptoms (effect). So, if a doctor deals only with the symptoms without understanding the particular cause or causes, he or she can never cure the disease. Likewise for any problem (effect) there must be some particular cause or causes. So first we should find out that cause or causes then only tackle the issue. For instance, if the floor gets wet, you can wipe it dry with a cloth or foam brush. You can do this the second time. But if it once again becomes wet, it is foolhardy to wipe the floor for the third time. It is time to find out the real cause. So out of the many causes you find out, the real cause, which is causing the problem. Once you find out that the tap in the adjacent bathroom was left open, you have to close the tap first and then wipe the water off the floor. But in our day-to-day corporate life most of us are seen only wiping the floor again and again without closing the tap.

The following technique is simple but very effective. They say, boil the fish well till the bones appear. Do not take it literally it only suggests that what is needed is more patience and time. Do not try to finish the cause finding exercise in a single meeting. You may have to conduct such 'creativity unleashing' exercises many times. However, the frequency of the meetings depends on the gravity of the issue. Do not conduct many meetings only because someone has said that cook the fish well till bones appear. However, when you discuss a serious matter in a number of Ishikawa meetings, you get some additional benefits: (a) fresh ideas regarding possible causes that can flash in your mind during the intervals; (b) members will forget the originator of the idea and remember the idea alone which is a good tendency; (c) pressure will mount in the course of time unleashing many bright ideas and (d) seriousness of Ishikawa meetings will send very positive signals. The morale of the employees will be boosted when noticing management's concern for solving organisational issues as also for managing creative change.

Ishikawa diagram is a simple and logical process. It breaks the problem into some seeable components. This way you can eat the elephant (by cutting it into many pieces). There are many benefits. I discuss a few of them below, which are significant for managing creative change.

1. It studies the issue from many angles—you can see a holistic pattern.
2. It shows the reflection of a problem through many causes; against each cause you see the sub-causes in a single pattern.
3. It helps in unleashing the creativity of the people—this diagram is rated high as an exercise for leveraging the creativity of individuals and the group.
4. It stops 'squirrel caging'—it breaks the mental locks.

5. It brings a good degree of satisfaction to the team members as they have done their best.
6. It offers equal opportunity to each member to participate and share his or her views.
7. Every possible cause is discussed and plotted—this helps in finding the right solutions for corrective measures.

The 'Why–Why Analysis'

This technique is slightly different from the Ishikawa technique. It leads us to the root cause of a problem by repeatedly asking the same question, 'Why?'

This technique is a probing technique, which is very commonly used during the process of investigation. A questioning series of three or four 'Why?' links the effect with the probable cause or causes. Let me explain this through a 'Why–Why' example.

Unwittingly, children use this 'Why–Why' technique. Their inquisitive minds will not be satisfied with just one 'why'. Once you answer one 'why' the child will ask another 'why'. This process goes on until you get frustrated and somehow avoid answering.

Let us assume that while you were planning a creative change in the club, you discovered that the membership of the club is very low. So, the issue is, 'What is the cause of low membership?' Then you start a 'Why–Why' exercise (Figure 7.2). You ask, 'Why is the membership of my club so low?' You identify five possible causes: (a) fee is considered to be too high by the members, (b) inadequate promotions of your staff (so they might be frustrated and are not working properly), (c) ageing or old equipments, (d) bad club timings (it opens at wrong times) and (e) outdated activities. Let us assume that you find the last cause more meaningful. So, you ask, 'Why are the activities outdated?' You discover three causes: (a) do not know members' needs, (b) not using latest techniques and (c) no students (youth) are your members.

Now you are at a better position to analyse the cause. So, you come to the conclusion that the membership of the club is low because the club does not know the needs of its members. Once the root cause is identified, finding a solution is not difficult.

Figure 7.2 Why–Why Technique

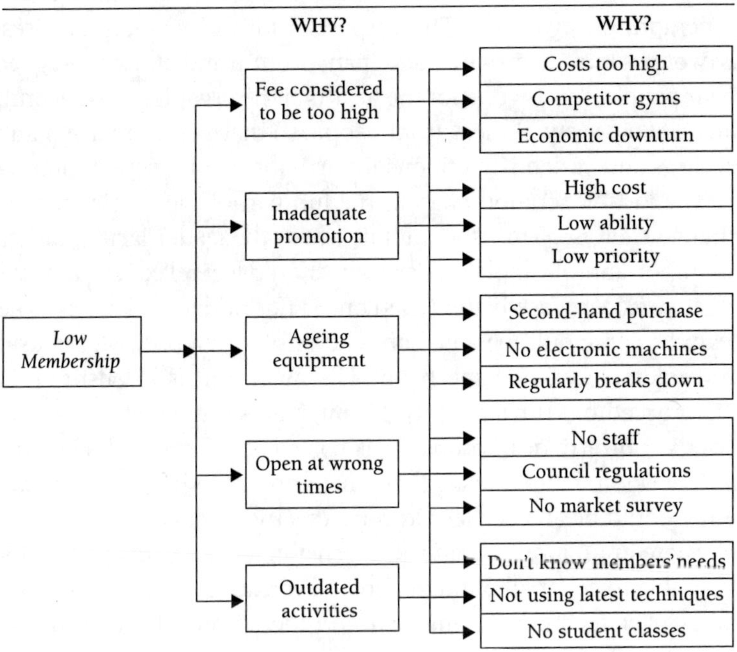

Source: http://www.tms.co.nz/in touch/issue8.htm

You may decide to conduct a 'club members' need survey'. Through this survey you may discover many needs of the members, which were not taken care by the governing body because it was unaware of them. So, you call for the governing body meeting and decide to take care of some of the important needs of the club members. Once you take care of these needs, the club members get satisfied. They do not withdraw the membership. They start talking well about the club activities, so their friends and office colleagues are attracted to it. The end result: club membership has increased. Wow!

CREATIVE IDEA GENERATION

Once you are able to identify various probable causes of problems and could articulate it with proper pattern of language, you are now in a position to find solutions. So, you must know the techniques of generating creative ideas. The purpose of 'idea-generation exercises' is twofold. First, to create a participative forum and utilise synergy of your people, this is good for the health of the organisation. Second, find out a variety of ideas from people so that you can have many options and varied perceptions for arriving at a better solution.

The idea-generation phase is the fun part of the whole creative change exercise. This is a point at which the leader/facilitator has an important role to play. The group should feel relaxed so that the creative juices work better when one is not ridden by anxiety. The team leader should be a person who possesses a positive mindset and tolerant 'attitude spectrum'. His main task is to ensure that the proceedings run smoothly. He must make sure that every idea, however bizarre or improbable, is voiced and discussed. He must have wisdom to appreciate that what appears to be 'stupid' sometimes could be an excellent idea for creative change.

There are many techniques to generate creative ideas. It is not desirable to cover all of them here. Nevertheless, there are certain time-tested techniques, which are considered very effective and are described in detail. They are:

1. The 'How–How' technique
2. Brainstorming
3. Brain stilling
4. Trigger sessions
5. Wild ideas sessions
6. Strengths, weaknesses, opportunities and threats (SWOT) analysis
7. Suggestion schemes
8. Quality circles

The first technique is a good blend of generating creative ideas as well as finding a solution to the issue that has been irking or creating the problem. It is more a 'problem-solving' exercise than an 'idea-generating' technique. For this reason, some change experts do not include this in the list of 'idea-generating' techniques.

The 'How–How' Technique

The 'How–How' technique is used for seeking a practical solution to a problem. By asking, 'how' a few times you can identify the right solution. It is a useful technique for managing creative change. Figure 7.3 shows us how.

Figure 7.3 How–How Technique

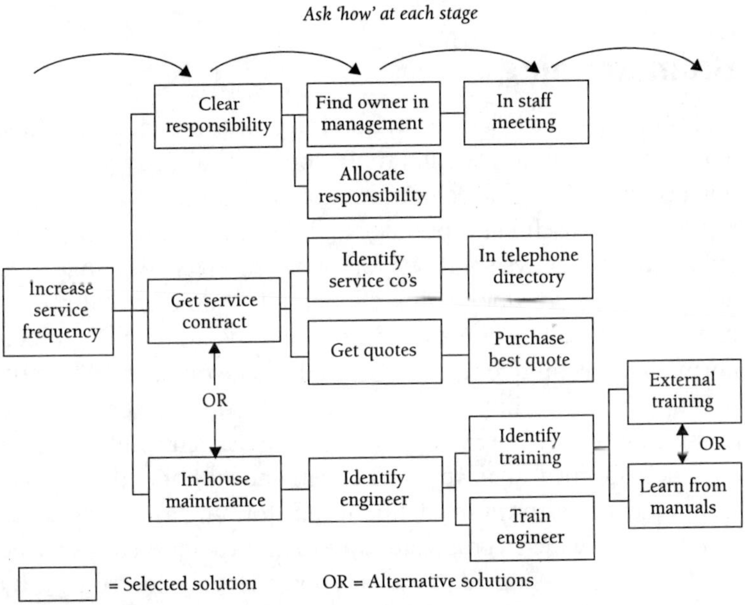

Source: syque.com/quality_tools/toolbook/Tree/vary.htm

Look at the 'How–How' diagram. 'How to improve housekeeping by increasing service frequency' is the issue. When you ask, 'how', for the first time, you get three possible solutions: (a) assign clear responsibility and accountability, (b) get service through a service contract agency and (c) provide captive (in-house) maintenance. Let us assume that the idea of 'outsourcing' appeals to you. So, you ask, 'How to get a "service contract"?' You discover that it involves two issues: (a) identify service contract agencies and (b) call for quotations. Let us assume, you know the procedure of calling for quotations, but you do not know the source of identifying the 'service companies'. So, you ask for the third time 'How?' to get the solution: 'In the telephone directory'. So, you refer to the telephone directory, see the yellow pages, locate various service companies, ask for quotations and assign a 'service contractor'. End result: your housekeeping is improved with the increased service frequency carried out by the service contract agency.

Brainstorming

Brainstorming is a good technique for generating creative ideas. Some authors call it a 'mental tool'. You may call it by any name, but it is a very powerful technique or tool—time-tested with proven results. It is a useful and popular tool that you can use for developing highly creative solutions for managing creative change. It is helpful, especially when you are looking for some breakthrough. It helps in breaking the established patterns and well-accepted norms. This technique can also be used when you need to develop new opportunities, improve the service that you offer, or when the existing approaches are not giving you the desired results.

Alex F. Osborn, an advertising expert and author of the creative technique 'Brainstorming', defines brainstorming as a 'conference technique' by which a group attempts to find a solution to a specific problem by amassing all the ideas spontaneously contributed by its members. The Indian name for this technique is *Parai-Prashna*. *Parai* means 'outside yourself' or 'foreign' and *prashna* means 'question'. Osborn believes that Hindu society used this technique for over 400 years in ancient India for finding spiritual solutions. But to my understanding, their way of brainstorming was different. It was rather brain stilling. I will explain this technique briefly.

The modern brainstorming sessions are creative conferences for the sole purpose of generating many ideas or developing a checklist that can serve as a lead to better ideas. The most important aspect that you must remember about brainstorming sessions is that your focus should be on quantity and not on quality. Once you gather many ideas, you can always choose the best and improve it further using other techniques.

Brainstorming and divergent thinking are indistinguishable and inseparable. The very purpose of brainstorming is to use the process of divergent thinking followed by lateral thinking. Through the process of divergent thinking you generate a variety of ideas and through lateral thinking you forcefully foster a relationship between two unidentical aspects thereby creating some sort of fusion. Today's remix music is the best example.

'Divergent thinking' is a way of thinking in which you try to look at the same issue from many angles and generate many possibilities. You try to find not just one 'right answer' but also many 'right answers'. You keep focus on generating many ideas. Thus, during brainstorming sessions you use both lateral thinking and divergent thinking. In this way, people come up with many ideas and suggestions. Since their inner urge is to generate many ideas looking from different angles, sometimes some of their ideas seem at first a bit crazy or senseless. But you can change these and improve them into creative ideas for managing creative change as well as for problem solving.

The process of brainstorming is very important. During these sessions there should be no criticism of ideas because here you are trying to open up possibilities and breakdown wrong assumptions about the limits of the problem. Judgements and analysis at this stage will only stunt idea generation. For this reason I say, 'Keep the judge away!' Ideas should only be evaluated at the end of the brainstorming sessions and not during the sessions. You must always remember this *mantra*.

How to use this 'mind tool'? Here are some tips:

1. The brainstorming sessions must be conducted by an expert who understands the purpose and the process well.
2. First clearly define the problem you want to solve and lay out any criteria to be met.
3. Keep focus on the problem; discourage one-upmanship and all attempts to outsmart others.

4. Ensure that no one criticises or tries to evaluate ideas during the session; let the judge be locked out.
5. Criticism introduces an element of risk for group members when putting forward an idea. This stifles creativity and cripples the free running nature of a good brainstorming process.
6. Encourage an enthusiastic, uncritical attitude among members of the group. Try to get everyone to contribute and develop ideas, including the quietest members of the group.
7. Let people have fun in brainstorming. Encourage them to come up with as many ideas as possible, from solidly practical to wildly impractical ones.
8. Ensure that no train of thought is followed for too long, discourage hair-splitting.
9. Encourage people to develop other people's ideas, or to use other ideas to create new ones.
10. Appoint one person to note down ideas that are generated during the session. A good way of doing this is to use a flip chart or a blackboard.
11. All the points should be studied and evaluated only after concluding the brainstorming exercise.

Four golden tips exclusively for the team leader of the brainstorming session:

1. *Lock the judge out*: Ensure you suspend your judgements during the session. Do not allow the participants to criticise each other because mud-slinging has no place in such creative sessions. Virtually you have to stop the 'judgemental thinking' at this stage. Anything and everything said must be accepted and recorded. Dustbins should be used after the session and not during the session.
2. *Allow 'freewheeling'*: 'The wilder the idea, the better', is the motto of brainstorming sessions. It is always easy to trim the sharp edges of the wild ideas later. Freewheeling means

that the flow of idea generation should be maintained. You should not allow any disruptions.

3. *Quantity must find focus*: The greater the number of ideas, the greater the probability of 'good ideas' being included in the list.
4. *Ask the judge to assist at conclusion*: Discovery means looking at the same thing as everyone else and thinking something different! Only after your Columbus and the artist play their creative roles, ask the judge to assist.

Brain Stilling

Brain stilling is the Indian version of brainstorming. As seen earlier, brainstorming is a collective method of seeking various alternatives to solve an issue. It is a Western approach—a vibrant and loud-thinking technique. But right and rational decisions cannot be taken in a state of turmoil when minds are overtaken by 'heat' generated by arguments and plus–minus exchange of thoughts and ideas. Brainstorming can be a better option, to discover alternatives. However, for rational and enduring solutions what is suggested is a situation of brain stilling when the mind is silent and can peacefully arrive at a lasting decision. Silence does not mean absence of speech; silence means perfect calm and tranquillity, joining the mind with the heart. Such a state of tranquillity opens the inner gateways. I will discuss this technique in detail in the Nagarjuna Group story in Chapter 8, where I introduced this healthy technique and found very fruitful results.

Trigger Sessions

Trigger sessions are different. Unlike brainstorming sessions, in trigger sessions you ask each member to write down his ideas or points on certain issues or problems. The process is as follows:

1. The problem owner defines the problem.

2. Each member of the group writes down his ideas in shorthand (5–10 minutes only).
3. One member reads out his list—others silently cross out ideas that are read out and write down 'hitch-hiked' ideas.
4. The next member reads out his list of ideas not already covered, followed in turn by other members.
5. The last member reads out his original list and his 'hitch-hiked' list.
6. The idea is that all repeated common ideas should become one well-worded idea. This way the final list is drawn listing out the ideas. For instance, 10 members have generated 50 ideas, out of which 35 ideas were repeated. So, the final list will contain 15 fresh ideas.

Wild Ideas' Sessions

The purpose of these sessions is to generate some outrageous ideas. From these wild ideas, 'down-to-earth' ideas are created. Dr Edward de Bono calls this process 'intermediate impossible'. A seemingly wild idea passing through the phase of 'intermediate impossible' is transformed into a sober and a practical idea. Edward de Bono had observed that it happens quite often that such impractical or even ridiculous ideas are the ones that trigger the imagination of the group and stimulate them towards developing remarkable and down-to-earth solutions.

For instance, the problem statement says: How can we reduce the cost of medical reimbursement? Obviously, genuine medical claims are not the cause of anxiety. The problem is owing to false medical claims. This is a very common problem in most public sector organisations and government departments. So, the members are asked to generate wild ideas. They might suggest:

1. Do not allow medical claims. Once the scheme is withdrawn, there cannot be any misuse.

2. Investigate a few suspected claims and initiate criminal legal action against them. Others will get a good lesson and may improve.
3. Each time you reimburse a medical claim, give money in a cover, boldly inscribed, 'For Thief'.
4. Display the names of 10 highest claimants on the Internet, with the caption: 'Company's Top Ten Sick Families'.

Likewise many wild ideas are gathered. Now from the above 'intermediate impossible' the members are asked to draw some workable solutions. So, someone may say, 'Do not display the list of top 10 sick families on the Internet because it will amount to washing dirty linen at the roadside. So, display the list on the office notice board.' Another person would say, 'draw the list and send it to those "10 people" in a cover so that only they know.' Now a person who is listening to these wild ideas may say:

> Let such a claimer know only his position; why should he know about others? Moreover, there could be some genuine cases as well. So, just write a simple letter mentioning that this month the medical claims for him and his family are the highest (or the second highest) in the company. Then say, we share the concern and pray for good health!

You may like this idea, which is practical and does not involve any humiliation. One can see a wild idea becoming sober and practical during the process!

SWOT Analysis

The acronym 'SWOT' stands for Strengths, Weaknesses, Opportunities and Threats. It is one of the best tools of audit to locate an organisation's strong and weak aspects both internally and externally. Through this single tool you can make both inward and outward scanning—strengths and weaknesses related to internal aspects, and threats and opportunities related to the external environment.

SWOT analysis is the first stage of planning, which helps organisations to focus on internal and external key issues. SWOT analysis helps business leaders to design their change programmes. On the one hand, it enables you to understand your positive and negative aspects and on the other, your internal and external position.

They say a picture is worth a thousand words. Figure 7.4 indicates all the four aspects: internal and external as well as positive and negative characteristics.

Figure 7.4 SWOT Analysis

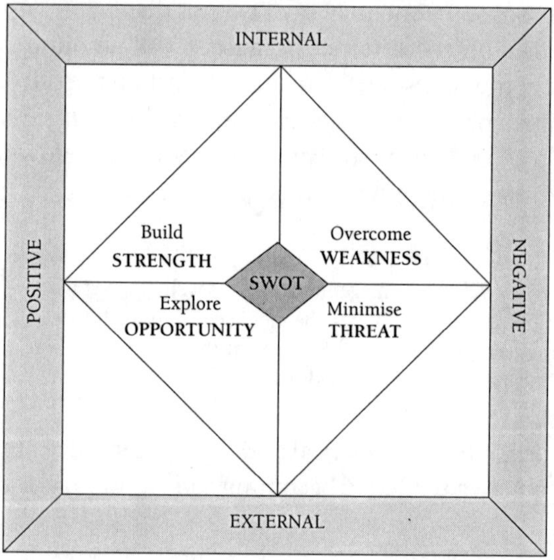

Source: A typical matrix of SWOT Technique propounded by Albert Humphrey.

The north-west quadrant shows internal strength and the south-west quadrant shows external opportunity—both are positive aspects with inward and outward focus. On the other hand, the north-east quadrant indicates internal weakness and the south-east depicts external threats—both are negative aspects with inward and outward focus.

Let us examine each parameter vis-à-vis examples of ABC Company. As mentioned earlier, strengths and weakness are internal factors, and opportunities and threats are external observable facts. I give below some examples of strengths and weaknesses of the company:

1. *Strengths*: Competent workforce; specialist marketing experts; good R&D; quality norms and SOP; and many such internal positive aspects.
2. *Weaknesses*: Lack of good designers; union rivalries; indiscipline; weak supply chain; outdated machinery; lack of skilled workers; and many such internal negative aspects.
3. *Opportunities*: A developing market; opportunities for joint ventures and strategic alliances; government support (subsidies, grants, allocation of funds, provision of supportive statuses, and so on); and many such external positive aspects.
4. *Threats*: Emerging new competitors; multinational companies (MNCs) entering the arena; changing unfavourable legal situations; politically infested locale; and many such external negative aspects.

A few tips to work for good SWOT:

1. Be realistic about the strengths and weaknesses of your organisation when conducting the SWOT analysis.
2. SWOT analysis must distinguish between where your organisation is today, and where you want it to be in the future.
3. SWOT must always be specific—avoid grey areas.
4. Always apply SWOT in relation to your competitors, that is, better than or worse than them in different aspects and on different parameters.
5. Keep SWOT short and simple. Avoid complexity and overtoning.
6. Plotting of points in the appropriate quadrant is extremely necessary—look carefully at the flip chart to check whether the point is placed properly in the right quadrant.
7. The doubtful aspects can be discussed threadbare. You write down the point only after consensus has emerged or broadly

accepted. Wrong observations and irrational plotting of points can lead to a skewed analysis.

8. First write down SWOT on a flip chart or on a blackboard, on a four-dimensional plotter. Analysis can be done later.

Once the key issues have been identified and rightly plotted, they fit into various business objectives. SWOT is a very popular tool especially among marketing students because of its simplicity and quickness for scanning the saleability of the market vis-à-vis market trends. Further, SWOT helps in developmental aspects and general improvements.

SWOT can also be used for visioning exercise—it is an 'outside in' technique. It covers many dimensions and has a multipurpose use.

Suggestion Scheme

Suggestion scheme is one of the best techniques but the worst practice—it is a wonderful tool, which is grossly misused in application. You find dirty 'suggestion boxes' gathered with dust, which makes it evident that no one is interested in your suggestions or suggestion box. This may be an Indian scenario. Japanese and most of the South-east Asian companies take the suggestion scheme seriously and attach a good deal of importance to it. What they call Kaizen is the progeny of the suggestion scheme. Let me briefly explain Kaizen.

Kaizen—Japanese term—means continuous improvement. The word Kaizen has two halves—'kai' means 'continuous' and 'zen' means 'improvement'. Some translate 'kai' to mean change and 'zen' to mean good, or rather better. So, 'Kaizen' is an effective tool for creative change. It brings about incremental improvements. Kaizen philosophy is in sharp contrast to the Western approach to innovation. Some people ask, 'Whether you need Kaizen or innovation?' To my understanding it is a wrong way of framing the question in terms of 'either/or'. We need both 'Kaizen' and 'innovation'. This approach is called 'Eastern Windows; Western doors'.

Incremental improvement is the spirit behind Kaizen. The Kaizen mind will tell you not to exert but to use your brain.

The key aspect of Kaizen is that it is an ongoing, never-ending improvement process. As mentioned earlier, it is a soft and a gradual method opposed to the usual Western habits to scrap everything and start something new.

Kaizen activities can be conducted in several ways. The first and foremost common objective of Kaizen is to simplify the operations of the worker, make his job more productive and efficient, less tiring and safer. To get his buy-in as well as significant improvement, a worker is invited to cooperate and re-engineer by himself, with the help of his teammates or with the support of the Kaizen group. The second purpose is to suggest improvement of equipment, like installing foolproof devices and/or changing the machine layout, and so on. The third objective is to improve systems, processes and procedures. All these goals can be combined in a broad improvement plan, which, in turn, helps in managing change.

Kaizen is controlled; it is not acceptable to let anybody change designs, layouts or standards for some so-called improvement. Improvement groups most often control Kaizen. Everyone, regardless of rank or position, is encouraged to make suggestions through suggestion schemes, what is known 'Teian' in Japanese. The authoritative committees discuss suggestions. Suggestions that are likely to be turned into applications are usually rewarded under the suggestion schemes.

Suggestion schemes do not merely consist of dust-clad suggestion boxes—it is much beyond, it is a better and beneficial system. It enables you to harness the power of your in-house creative ideas. The companies, which use suggestion schemes as change management tools for improvement, constitute 'suggestion committees', who consider the suggestions given by the workers and managers. Some provide specific easy-to-compile formats. All the suggestions received must be acknowledged for recognition, which send very positive signals not only to those who give suggestions but also to the entire workforce. People must feel happy that their views are being acknowledged and examined.

The 'top-down' approach is good for certain strategic decisions—it should not become the organisational attitude. Companies can no longer survive with people, who always look up for solutions, expecting that the management would provide 'all the right answers'. Today, companies require a steady flow of ideas and solutions from those who are closest to the processes and the customers, those with their 'ears to the ground'. To maintain an adaptable and responsive organisation, you must develop a culture that actively solicits inputs and suggestions from every level of hierarchy.

Suggestion schemes work well in organisations where empowerment is practised. The old Suggestion Boxes with rusted locks will not work in today's high-tech environment. It is time that we use information technology and modify the system.

Quality Circles

Dr Kaoru Ishikawa (1915–1989) who gave the corporate world the Ishikawa diagram—cause and effect tool—practised and promoted the quality circles (QC) movement as a part of his total quality control (TQC), which in Western terminology is called total quality management (TQM). Following are the central tenets of QC:

1. Solution of a problem lies at the grass-roots levels.
2. Respect human relations at the workplace.
3. Increase job satisfaction through total employees' involvement (TEI).
4. Draw out employee potential.
5. Small suggestions produce big results.

As can be seen in Figure 7.5, QCs have three-dimensional focus: TQM, risk assistance and industrial engineer (IE) related issues at the shop floor. These circles work with a profound product–process understanding.

The QC is a technique that has played an important role in the success of Japanese manufacturing companies. They are currently being adopted by many European and American enterprises.

Figure 7.5 Quality Circles

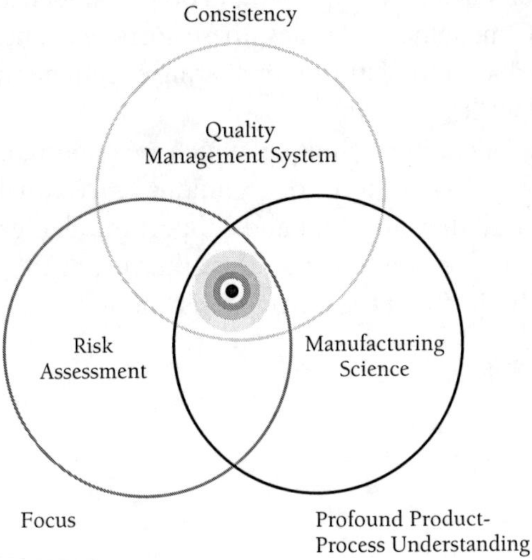

Source: Drawn by the author based on Dr Kaoru Ishikawa's technique of Quality Circles introduced by him first time in Japan.

The QC are normally composed of a small number of volunteers (typically between six and ten) from a particular work area or department who focus on improving quality, productivity, and risk and cost reduction. The circle meets under the guidance of a facilitator to identify problems and help generate possible solutions. After gathering the possible solutions the circle identifies which of these are likely to be most appropriate suiting the company's culture, structure, cost-effectiveness and time frames for effective implementation. In most of the QC programmes there are no direct financial rewards for coming up with good ideas or cost savings. However, people are indirectly paid for attendance in the sense that circle meetings occur during company time. Quality circles normally meet on a regular basis, often at two-weak intervals, for perhaps one or two hours.

Yearly meeting of these QC is conducted at the corporate level, where some important Kaizen are shared. The employees who give suggestions are publicly honoured and rewarded. Such high-level functions boost up the morale of the employee and build confidence of the people in the QC movement. Besides, these corporate conferences also serve as a common platform for sharing experiences; one can call it 'talk the walk'!

There are many idea-generating techniques which are important tools for managing change. These tools or techniques serve dual purpose. On the one hand, they augment and support the change programme by serving as positive tools; on the other hand, they help in controlling or diminishing the change resistance.

'Bury me on my face,' said Diogenes; and when he was asked why, he replied, 'Because in a little while everything will be turned upside down.'

—Diogenes
(Greek philosopher 412–323 BC)
Source: Lives and Opinions of Eminent Philosophers

There is nothing more difficult to take in hand, more perilous to conduct, or more uncertain in its success, than to take the lead in the introduction of a new order of things.

—Niccolo Machiavelli
(Italian Political Philosopher 1469–1527)
Source: The Prince

8 Walking the Tightrope—Change Stories

After floating my consulting company 'Intellects Biz' when I announced the first two-day workshop on 'Work Smart', Ranga Shahi, General Manager—Corporate Planning, Bharat Heavy Electricals Limited (BHEL), gave me a ring. He wanted to know more details about the workshop before sponsoring his managers. I shared all that I had in my mind.

'Mr Siddiqui, if you don't mind, can I suggest something?' he asked. On getting an affirmative he suggested something which I can never forget—like an etching on a stone his words are engraved on my mind.

> Sir, you have been an active player in managing change. You are also a witness to the rise and fall of some gigantic public sector and private sector companies. Why don't you share those rich experiences with corporate managers and conduct your next workshop on 'How to Walk the Tightrope?'

I liked his suggestion. I promised, but I never conducted a workshop on that theme. To be honest, I did not dare. Managing change is one thing, teaching the technique is a different cup of tea!

Whenever I feel threatened, I get back to the basics. That is the only way to stay alive in the corporate world. There is no other way. It is always better to set your pace with the change of time, rather than trying to chase it with dragging feet. Yes, today I feel confident that I can dare walk the tightrope—my future plans include workshops on 'change acrobatics'. Change is not a dance; change is a gymnast's acrobatics! I heard many gurus saying, 'Change or Perish!' I have seen companies who have 'changed and perished'. This does not mean that companies should not go for change, it simply means that companies must take the 'change process' seriously. I have seen many giant companies falling like withered trees because they did not know the art of managing change. Hindustan Machine Tools (HMT) is one such unfortunate public sector company—I have seen its glory and I have seen its downfall—it could not walk the tightrope!

HMT STORY

Pandit Jawaharlal Nehru considered HMT as the crown of all public sector undertakings (PSUs). He gave it the title 'Jewel in the Public Sector'—a title the company deserved most. Hindustan Machine Tools had survived and thrived amidst cut-throat competition in all its products like machine tools, tractors, printing machinery, bearings and watches. Today, a common man knows HMT by its product watches. But HMT did not begin with manufacturing watches; it began with machine tools. This giant public sector came into existence in 1953 under the name 'Hindustan Machine Tools'. S.S. Iyngar, a genius in the Ministry of Industry, Government of India, had prepared the project report and served the company as General Technical Manager until 1956. Aftab Rai was the first managing director of HMT. However, it was M.K. Mathulla, who had strengthened the foundation of the company during his eight years of tenure from 1956 to 1964. He added many units, almost one factory each year. Hindustan Machine Tools grew at a fast pace under his leadership. Dr S.M. Patil, who had joined HMT as superintending engineer in 1953, and worked shoulder-to-shoulder with Mathulla as in-charge of many projects, took over as Chairman and Managing Director (CMD) in the year 1964. Dr S.M. Patil is the legendary CEO who raised HMT to a pinnacle. Initially the multi-product, multi-unit, multi-location company grew following a decentralised structure. Dr Patil's book, *Twenty-five Years with HMT*, which was published by HMT under my guidance, reveals many stories of success and failures.

In 1972, HMT decided to go for major restructuring. At the instance of our ministry, we had assigned the task of studying the requirements of rapidly expanding HMT and suggesting a suitable structure for the company to Dr (Mrs) Kamala Chowdhary, Professor IIM (Ahmedabad). She conducted a study and visited all the units of HMT with her team causing a huge financial burden on the exchequer. Finally, she came out with the 'Restructuring Project Report', but to Dr Patil's dismay her report was good only for the academicians. She made some 'arm chair' suggestions, which did not make any sense to Dr Patil. Dr Patil observed,

> We didn't agree with most of her recommendations, one was to divide the company into various subsidiaries with independent marketing set-ups for each of the companies. This form of structure for HMT could perhaps be an ultimate solution when all product divisions would have reached a stage of financial self-sufficiency.

One must admire his business acumen and a sense of understanding the ground realities. He put his foot down despite heavy pressure from the ministry. Dr (Mrs) Chowdhary once again worked out the report with slight modifications, yet it was not acceptable to Dr Patil as he saw many flaws. The ministry decided to conduct a joint meeting to sort out the issue.

Finally, Dr Kamala Chowdhary's report was discussed at a joint meeting of all the top executives of HMT along with R.V. Subramaniam, Additional Secretary in our ministry. At this meeting we decided that the recommended restructure was too premature, and could perhaps be reviewed after some years when all the divisions would have grown to be more or less self-sufficient.

This way, the sleeping dog was allowed to sleep for quite some time and eventually this academic work met its own death. 'Since we did not hear from the ministry any further in this regard, it was presumed that the matter had been closed', writes Dr Patil in his memoir. So, a disaster was averted boldly.

Dr S.M. Patil decided to restructure the company using his mother wit with the support of his internal talents. He formed a cross-functional team, giving representation to each unit and discipline. It was the time when competition in machine tools industry was becoming stiff with major players like Kirloskar, Batilboi, Bharat Fritz Warner, Telco and Godrej already in the arena, competing directly with HMT. Yet HMT was an unchallenged leader amidst big killer sharks. The solitary reason for gaining the cutting edge was thinking ahead! 'HMT was the only company which thought ahead', writes Dr S.M. Patil.

The restructuring team—internal people—found 'decentralisation' as an obstacle rather than strength. Most amazingly the recommendations tilted in just the opposite direction to what the IIM professor had suggested.

Dr Patil writes in his memoirs:

> 'Decentralization had outlived its utility', discovered the restructuring team. Such a decentralized set-up threw up certain problems. The most important problems were in the co-ordination and overall controlling function, which was my responsibility as the Managing Director and Chief Executive. When we had only one unit, one product located in one place, it was comparatively easy for the Managing Director to exercise the supervisory control effectively. But with multiunits and multiproducts, at different locations this task was becoming more and more difficult and control had somewhat become diluted and ineffective. Hence we evolved and considerably strengthened the staff functionaries to guide and monitor the unit managements. Gradually, the so-called 'staff-and-line' structure of organization emerged strongly in HMT.

To understand Dr Patil's rationale of restructuring one has got to understand the Indian business scenario in the early 1970s. Let alone 'empowerment', even some staff functions were not recognised fully. Dr V. Krishnamurthy's 'corporate model' was new, and most of the public and private sector companies were not prepared to go for it unless they saw results. No doubt it was Dr V. Krishnamurthy who brought 'corporate culture' to corporate

India. He then knitted the scattered units of BHEL with a single thread by creating a strong 'corporate office'. A stand-alone unit of Bhopal, Heavy Electrical Ltd (HEL), was brought in the corporate fold of BHEL. Dr V. Krishnamurthy, a great visionary, simultaneously ensured that the corporate pharaohs, who were fond of 'back-seat driving', did not rob the unit's autonomy. However, Dr Patil did not borrow 'VK' model and independently evolved his own corporate model with the help of his internal talents. Although his model was not as powerful as Dr VK's, he deserved credit for daring to do something diagonally opposite to what the external consultant Dr (Mrs) Chowdhary had suggested. Besides restructuring, he created place for staff functions. Functional directors in the disciplines like 'personnel', 'finance', 'marketing' and 'corporate planning' were inducted to the board. Today it is not quite easy to visualise the 'wow factor' because these models have now become a routine. But during his time it was no doubt a daring step, which could be taken only by a man of steel like Dr Patil.

After battling the teething problems, HMT started gaining heights. Dr Patil shares the success story of restructuring as follows:

> Hitherto, we had been mainly a company of 'doers', now we had to learn to call on the staff and rely on their ability to think about answers to many of our corporate problems, therefore, cadre of specialists for each of the corporate functions. Now, we had the Chief of Finance, Chief of Personnel and Chief of Marketing, all reporting to me.

HMT grew at a very fast pace and became the pride of the nation. With its entry into watch production—a product, which never fell into the zone of its core competency—HMT proved its mettle and earned another nickname—The timekeepers to nation. The success story is long. There are many things and many events to share, but brevity is a compelling need that stops me from going on.

The second major restructuring was carried out during early 1980s. For the first time HMT adopted a 'business group' (BG) based structure under the leadership of T.V. Mansukhani. This structure was a good blend of centralised and decentralised models. The units of same or similar products were included in a single BG, where they were extremely centralised. On the other hand, each BG was autonomous and decentralised. So, the company was divided into four major BGs—Machine Tools BG; Watch BG; Tractors BG; General Engineering BG, that included all miscellaneous products like lamps, bearings, and so on. The unit chiefs within each BG had to report to the BG chief; each BG chief would then report to the CMD. Thus, there was only one board with a CMD and functional directors for major strategic decisions. HMT also constituted a non-statutory board at corporate level, calling it an executive committee. The board would meet four or five times in a year whereas the day-to-day business of the entire company was carried out by the executive committee, which comprised the chairman, functional directors and BGs' chiefs. At the BG level, again there used to be an executive committee, comprising the respective BG chief and unit chiefs. This structure took a 'gestation' period of over a year or so. During this initial phase there was utter confusion. People made fun of the new structure and passed sarcastic comments. One reason for elongating the transition was the non-judicious way of selecting the BG chiefs, where caste politics played a major role. As a result, some bright performers either withdrew or resigned in frustration. However, slowly the dust of confusion and frustration settled down, and the company once again picked momentum and showed good results. Once the morale of the senior team was rebuilt, the company started showing good profits.

However, the story of HMT is not full of success—it too has its share of failures. The first pitfall came with the creation of HMT Lamps, which caused an accumulated loss of more than ₹3,000 crore during the period of its existence. There is a saying, 'Nothing succeeds like success!' But, in case of HMT this saying went upside down. The successful entry into the new product category of watches created some sort of overconfidence—anything we touch will turn gold! Hungary wanted some special robotic chains for making lamps. HMT made those massive robotic chains for the first time, exported them and made huge profits. Some of them from HMT came up with a bright idea, 'When we can make the chains for manufacturing of lamps, why shouldn't we get into lamp-making business?' Some wise men advised, 'You cannot do it—that's not your core competency.' But the success of watches had made the top management arrogant. Having succeeded in watches—their non-core area—they thought they would get success in manufacturing lamps as well. What the top brass did not realise was that in making watches at least their 'machine-making' competency was involved at the micro level, but they knew nothing about 'vacuum technology' needed to manufacture lamps. 'Nothing fails like success' was the new maxim that dictated their fate. Hindustan Machine Tools hired expert managers from private sector; the worst stuff came forward. Each so-called expert came with a fleet of his people—his 'kith and kin'—branding them as 'experts'. HMT did not have any experience of selling goods. So, marketing had become another major bottleneck. Those who were managing institutional sales were asked to deal with petty retail shopkeepers, which brought down their morale and confidence. Those who were booking orders in millions of rupees were engaged in selling bulbs for ₹10 or so. This created hostile attitude towards the top management—'Top is so ignorant of marketing! Today the management is asking us to sell bulbs, tomorrow we will be selling vegetables in the market, holding a basket on our heads!' In a way they were right. A crocodile cannot swim in shallow waters, nor can sharks or whales! As they say, 'insult to injury', private lamp manufacturers made a cartel and bought some of the senior people of HMT lamps and union leaders. Then, everything was put in the reverse gear until the lamps unit eventfully closed.

Hindustan Machine Tools was one rare PSU that did not know the meaning of loss making. It never made huge profits. It consistently made moderate profits. When it started bleeding through its lamps unit, it faced the financial health problem. While such hiccups were on, the Chairman of HMT, T.V. Mansukhani, decided to start a watch factory in Uttar Pradesh (UP) under the political pressure of the then industrial minister. I need not mention his name; anyone can guess who was the most powerful political guy in UP from the then ruling government? Here the focus was not on business—the focus was on providing employment in the backward area of Ranibagh in the vicinity of Nainital. By that time, HMT had already started another 'political unit' of watches at Srinagar. The Ranibagh unit was the beginning of disaster in the watch business. Slowly the watch BG of HMT too started suffering. As if this shock was not enough, one of the genius and highly competent persons, I.K. Amita, Director Watches, was ill-treated by the rest of the top corporate team at the fag end of his career. So, he decided to teach a good lesson to HMT. After his retirement he joined TATA, and played the pivotal role in taking Titan Watches to greater heights within a short period of time. He picked up all the best talents from HMT Watches and offered them fat salary packages. In a single bout HMT became bankrupt of talented people—the cream had gone. The unexpected sudden vacuum was filled by eagles and vultures who were waiting to take their pound of flesh from the dying watch unit—corruption became the goddess of worship in the watch BG. When time is bad everything goes wrong. The sickness of a company sickens the mind of the top management too. A weak mind then easily compromises with values and morality. HMT watches lost their business character. They say, 'You can't hold the tea in the strainer!' Thus, HMT could not retain its profitability; everything started going into black holes.

When a part of the body gets maligned, cancer spreads to the other parts. At such a crucial time Dr M.R. Naidu came as a stalwart, but he could not do much except to prevent the company from going down further. Somehow, he could maintain the overall profitability of the company. He was a very cautious person—brooding was his decision making style. He used to delay decisions to the point of frustration, but once the decision was made he would ensure its efficacy. His entire attention was on reconsolidation of HMT. During his tenure, H.R. Alva joined the top team as a Director, Personnel. He was a genius. He rationalised the existing HR system and infused a fresh lease of life. The morale of the people started to lift. He became very popular in a short time. After M.R. Naidu's retirement, H.R. Alva was the best candidate to take the reins of the company in his hands. But the ministry was not willing to consider an HR professional for this post. So, P.C. Neogy was brought from

HECL. Alva, in frustration, left HMT and did not mind joining a sick company, Hindustan Photo Films Ltd, as the CMD.

P.C. Neogy was a genius. He spoke ahead of time. He was a very energetic person bubbling with enthusiasm—honest to the core. The HMT team which was tired now could not keep pace with his speed of thought and actions. When you do not understand lofty thoughts, you start making fun of genius people. So, Neogy was nicknamed as Mohammad Tughlaque. It was sheer bad luck that HMT for the first time made huge losses to the tune of ₹1,700 million or so, during his first 'full' financial year. So, Neogy had to bear the cross of past corporate sins.

During early 1990s—the time of turmoil—Government of India decided to go for total transformation of some major PSUs, and HMT also figured in the list. Japanese International Cooperation Agency (JICA) was assigned the task. The teams of experts worked with the key professionals of HMT. I was picked up to assist JICA in rationalisation of the HRD systems and matching them with the proposed restructuring plans. After a massive hectic task, JICA gave its reports in two phases. They were the best documents I have ever seen. Japanese International Cooperation Agency job was over and they had gone. We had plans but no money to implement them. So, the board and executive committee of HMT took a historical decision—implement all JICA proposals, which do not have financial implications; defer all those plans, which warrant fresh investments. It was the most stupid decision. 'It is like advising a patient: take all those medicines which he can afford to buy and do not take the medicines which he cannot manage to pay for', I opposed this decision. But my cry went unheard in wilderness.

The proposals of JICA were implemented immediately with a lot of fanfare. The structure of the company was drastically changed, as it did not involve any financial issues. A few new functional groups and BGs were created in the areas of information technology (IT), TQM and 'precise machinery and components'. The regional marketing, sales and services departments, which were hitherto established and were functioning on 'product-wise' pattern, were brought under a single roof with 'Matrix' controls. Seniority was taken as the criterion to decide who will head the common regional offices. So, if the Regional Manager, Lamps was the senior most guy, he headed the marketing functions of machine tools, watches, and so on. Great!

When the company was going through a phase of massive confusion, the ministry questioned Neogy about the downsizing plans suggested by JICA. Again, downsizing did not implicate any financial burden, as funds were extracted from the National Renewal Fund (NRF). Thus, massive campaigns were carried out under the lucrative—Voluntary Retirement Scheme (VRS). Negotiations were held with the unions, and within a short time the most dreaded word 'exit' became the dream of most HMT employees. Strict targets were allotted to BGs and SBUs. When targets are set in numbers, human beings too become numbers. Numbers became important and everything else took a backseat. Only those who still had saleability in the industry opted for VRS. When VRS money was considered as a reward, managers could not convince or prevent the highfliers from flying away. Even if they were denied the benefit, unions came forward to their rescue. Whenever a highflier was refused separation, he challenged the managers that he would turn a poor performer to avail VRS. Management was not ready for such situations. Under tremendous pressure from the government and corporate office, the company could meet the targets of downsizing—targets were fulfilled and the company's human assets went bankrupt. One should not jump to the conclusion that only talents separated—talents also separated. In the common bell curve, which is highly relevant to PSUs, highfliers hardly constitute 20 per cent of the total workforce. In total separations of say 1,000, if 400 highfliers separate, in effect, the talent pool loses 100 per cent! Who did not separate were mostly from the 37 per cent reserved-class segment, and other portions of workforce like 'physically handicapped', 'ex-servicemen', and so on. At that cut of time, HMT had a workforce of 29,700 and over two dozen units and factories were located in more than 10 states in India, with many regional marketing offices. During the first year itself a big chunk of 3,000 people was chopped off. Then, 'chop, chop ...' became the corporate habit. As the company started losing business, it started chopping off the workforce to match the downturn of turnover. Today the size of the company, by and large, is same in terms of the number of SBUs and regional offices but manpower has come down from around 30,000 to 9,500. Amazing!

Going back to the JICA days, after losing the balance 'perfectly', the ministry imposed, what they called, 'promotion holiday' and 'wage-freeze'. On the one hand, I was told that corporate HR should not promote anyone because the vacancies created by VRS cannot be refilled with promotions, and on the other, HMT employees were denied wage revision and salary revision. P.C. Neogy fought with the ministry, but shortly realised his limitations as the Chairman of a public sector company. He was bound step-by-step through the Memorandum of Understanding (MoU)—a one-sided document! With a lot of struggle and hue and cry pay revision came with many riders. Once the morale of the people was brought down and the cultural fabric was tarnished, nothing much could be done. The company went through a series of chairmen. Later N. Ramanujam (a man with a large heart and great wisdom), R.A. Sharma, M.S. Zahed (an IIM-MBA) came and went but the elephant who once sat down did not get up, let alone dance. Like the lost chastity of a virgin, HMT could not regain its glory.

The climax of the story of HMT is most amazing. As an outsider now, I heard that during the years 2002–2003 HMT again needed some massive funds for survival. So, the ministry asked them to come back with their plans for restructuring. As the story goes, HMT corporate planning department (some say that some guy in the Ministry of Industries) hurriedly made a search in the archives and to their good luck they hit the jackpot! They could locate the report of Dr (Mrs) Chowdhary, Professor of IIM (Ahmedabad), from the archives. They dusted, polished and updated it and submitted it to the ministry. The ministry gave its clearance. I do not know whether the story is true or false. But what I know is that today's restructured HMT has the same or similar pattern—one holding company with all other subsidiary companies. The BGs converted into subsidiary companies; each segmented company has its full-fledged board. The erstwhile BG heads became managing directors, head of departments and functional directors, of course after certain 'rituals'. But these subsidiary companies are not really autonomous. I have reasons to say so. Even for sponsoring a manager to the workshops I hear from the managing director, 'Mr Siddiqui, you know all about HMT—nothing moves here without the consent of big boss! The proposal is pending in the Chairman's office.' Great! When a managing director of the subsidiary company is not authorised to take a decision involving money in a 'single-digit K', how can he take a business decision implicating a risk worth a few millions? If the idea was to carry on with the same patriarchal control, why was such a huge structure with so many 'boards' created at the cost of the taxpayers' hard-earned money? Every taxpayer has the right to question such decisions.

In brief, what was resisted by Dr S.M. Patil tooth and nail in the early 1970s has ultimately become the fate of HMT with the dawn of the new century. I would not have believed this story, had today's HMT not been the 'mirror image' of Dr (Mrs) Chowdhary's rejected project report. The other possibility could be a remarkable coincidence! Yes, this possibility cannot be denied because such things do happen.

Let me show where HMT stands today on the normal curve of change management! This pictorial presentation will help the new leadership to take some preventing steps. It is not going to be an easy task. Whether HMT needs my advice or not but a person who gave the best part of his professional life to this company cannot sit in the gallery as a silent spectator.

Even if his opinion is unsolicited,
a minister should speak his mind at such times
and when his advice is specially sought
it should be for the good of the king.

(*Panchatantra*)

So, the first job that the new leadership is required to do is to rebuild the confidence of the people, which is at the lowest ebb. As you can see, HMT stands in the 'Valley of Death' (Figure 8.1).

Figure 8.1 Valley of Death

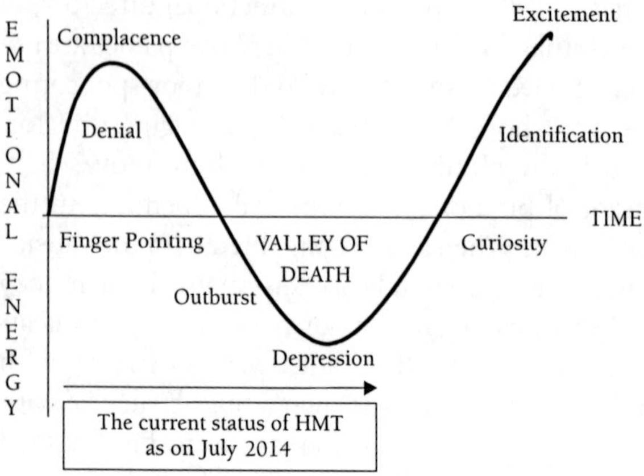

Source: Drawn adapting the popular 'Kubler–Ross Grief Cycle', comparing 'Depression' with 'Death Valley' of the United States, which is located in the lowest elevation in North America at 85.5 metres below the sea level.

Today HMT is facing the leadership crisis. After R.A. Sharma and M.S. Zahed, came A.V. Kamat. Though he got into the saddle could not make the horse move. He proved to be most ineffective Chairman of HMT. He was recognized as a leader who simply pondered upon without taking any decision. His entire focus was to somehow pass the tenure. Kamat was superseded by S.G. Sridhar as the Chairman of HMT. I know Sridhar when he was a deputy manager of printing press section of HMT corporate office. He was a young and dynamic guy. He climbed the ladder of hierarchy successfully and then left HMT and joined another public sector company. When Kamat superannuated, Sridhar was selected as Chairman and Managing Director of HMT as an outside candidate.

By the time Sridhar took HMT it was almost on the deathbed. People expected miracle from Sridhar, but he couldn't do much except financial fudging. In the month of June 2013, he was booked for fudging the financial figures. As per the news published in the *Hindu*, June 18, 2013,

> The Department of Heavy Industries has suspended Chairman and Managing Director of HMT Ltd S.G. Sridhar with effect from June 14. The

action was based on the findings of an internal inquiry into the running of the Tractor Division of the books having been dressed up, resulting in substantial losses to the company. The notice said, *Mr Sridhar indulged in fudging of accounts and providing incorrect reports to the stock exchanges and other authorities.*

When I am writing the text for the revised edition, Mr Harbhajan Singh, Joint Secretary, Ministry of Heavy Industries, has been assigned the additional charge of CMD of HMT. I wish him all success.

The prime task of a leader in such a situation is to first push the organisation out of the valley of death. It is possible only when leadership would succeed in creating some excitement. The first thing first ... At this stage, the first job of the leader is to convert anxiety into excitement—some enthusiasm! The excitement must be genuine not fake. How one creates this is the challenge to the leadership.

Managing change is walking the tightrope without any safety net, which is not quite easy. Even Wallenda, world's best tightrope walker, had fallen and met death. But the tightrope walkers do not fear death, after the death of Wallenda, his son Nik Wallenda took the baton and crossed the Niagara Falls walking the tightrope. The real change makers are daredevils—death is not threat to them.

Today HMT needs a Nik Wallenda—a reckless risk-taker who can demonstrate courage to walk the tightrope without any safety net. HMT is certainly not a hopeless case. It needs a fearless, bold, courageous, and above all, a most honest CEO who should be capable of performing major surgeries with minimum blood loss. When A.P.V.N. Sarma and R.H. Khwaja can get SCCL from the jaws of death—BIFR—not once but twice, no wonder if the new leadership plays a similar miracle in HMT.

BEML STORY

The story of Bharat Earth Movers Limited (BEML) is quite different. Sometimes you mistake a face with thick layers of make-up as beautiful. During her youth, BEML was really slim and beautiful.

Today, she looks prettier than ever—I must admire the make-up masters. Only people of wisdom can see its real face. Not the ageing process but the bleeding heart is the cause of its sorrows. She is growing with an empty soul!

After being selected as a Director of HR, Public Enterprise Selection Board (PESB), I left HMT and joined BEML. It was a moderate medium-sized company with all its manufacturing units in Karnataka. I had many dreams to fulfil. One thing that I had observed was that the company was moving without any specific goals or objectives. Since the company was making money no extra efforts were made for planning the future.

It was when the Indian economy had already opened up and many multinational players had made their entry. I was aware of their dirty tricks. These MNCs play a foul game. Their first objective is to kill the existing Indian companies, which stand in their way as their competitors. So, initially they sell their products at rates lower than the cost price and as a part of their strategy incur the 'planned losses'. Incurring a loss of a few million dollars is peanuts for them. This way they beat the competition. Obviously, the Indian companies cannot afford to bring down their prices because their ability to compete on price is limited. They cannot reduce the price without cutting costs. They can cut costs to the bones, not beyond that. You can cut your margins just so far without jeopardising your operations.

So, gradually the Indian companies start losing market, as they cannot cut their costs beyond the bones. The mathematical equation of these MNCs is simple: Once the costs are high, you cannot reduce the prices. So, after sometime the Indian companies lose market and start bleeding. Unlike their MNC competitors, they cannot afford to stay longer. So, either they are sold out to the MNCs, or they close down their business, providing a monopolistic situation in favour of the competing multinational company.

Once these MNCs get the monopolistic position, they enhance the prices and within no time recover their planned losses. In BEML, we had already started getting clear signals from the ministry that if we were not competitive in prices, the Government of India would not hesitate to purchase the defence equipments from Caterpillar or any other multinational players.

So, the need of the day was to plan a clear-cut vision for survival and growth based on solid bedrock. After scanning the organisational culture and understanding the organisational need, I tabled my proposal for 'BEML Vision 2002', which was approved in the second board meeting (Figure 8.2).

Figure 8.2 BEML's Vision 2002

Source: Scanned copy of the original.

The focus of the mission was on a balanced growth. For this I had chosen four aspects: (a) *internal focus*: processes, systems, practices, development of competencies, capabilities and cultural aspects; (b) *external focus*: Customer delight and market-related issues, including the changing business scenario; (c) *focus on present*: current affairs; and (d) *focus on future*: R&D, training and all such activities, which will make the future bright and help the company to float smoothly with time.

Vision gives you direction, but it does not have any measures of righteousness. For this purpose, one has got to follow a set of values. After many brainstorming sessions, we identified the supportive set of values:

1. Customer satisfaction is of cardinal value to BEML.
2. Human assets are an invaluable resource; develop their competencies.
3. Transparency in all our operations.
4. Mutual trust and mutual prosperity determine healthy vendor-relationship.
5. High concern for quality, safety and work environment in managing operations.
6. Passion for stakeholders' interest.
7. Emotional and intellectual integrity.
8. Humility is akin to dignity in business.

The mission statement and the set of corporate values were printed on a pocket-sized card and each executive was given this card through a well-organised process. Once the process was successfully completed, I decided to conduct a focused training programme. The training calendar was designed covering all the four important dimensions. A plotter was designed which can work as some sort of a dashboard. Each training workshop was plotted on the matrix. So, just in one glance one would see whether the desired balanced focus was maintained.

We also identified 'change agents' from the cross-section of departments and SBUs. Hierarchies were neglected while making selections. So, in all a team of 25 change agents was developed who belonged to different units and different disciplines. This cross-functional hierarchy-less team was called 'warriors'. Their main task was to fight against status quo and the change-barriers.

A consulting agency was identified that was assigned the task to train the warriors (we called them 'mentors') about the art of managing change with focus on values and BEML's Vision 2002. It was a well-thought out plan and great deal of care was taken for its execution. Within a short span of less than one year, BEML's Vision 2002 became very popular with an overwhelming support from the SBU chiefs and the officers' federation. If I were asked to rate the success on a 10-point scale, without any hesitation I would have rated it 7. With clear focus, each of our activities was aligned to one of the four dimensions of the balanced growth mission.

The only regret that I have in my mind today is that I could not continue in BEML for long, as I had decided to join the Nagarjuna Group. It was my strategic mistake. Once I left BEML, things started changing. My 'warriors' were in touch with me for some time, but later they lost interest. The 'spoils system'—a very common political practice in America—is followed in Indian public sector companies too. The new guy meticulously ensures to undo what was done by his predecessor. Sometimes some good people become victims of such a system. Vision 2002 was not an exception to such vengeance—it was hammered out.

Apple-polishing doesn't work in change management. Makeup and facials can hide some deficiency but it cannot hide ugliness permanently. You can fool some people sometime but cannot fool all people all the time. The entire focus of the Chairman and Managing Director (who retired in 2012 ungracefully) remained on apple-polishing and painting a rosy picture of BEML. He never allowed people to express their views—dissent or disagreement was taken as disobedience. He sacked many people and transfer was used as one of the way of punishment. He sacked even a board level director. The focus was not on performance—the focus was to create terror so no one dares oppose him or his policies.

Keeping the entire focus only on financial results is like flying a plane, which has only one meter—fuel meter—on the dashboard. Would you choose to flying on such a craft? The lopsided growth is not growth; it is swelling! BEML swelled but did not grow. A blacksmith only knows hammering—it hardly matters much whether it is the head of a nail or the head of a human. There is a Zen saying, 'When you accumulate virtue with continued practices, you do not see the good of it, but in time it will function; if you abandon right and go against truth, you do not see the evil of it, but in time you will perish.' BEML is no exception to the universal law of energy response—*Nemeses do work!*

NAGARJUNA GROUP STORY

There was a time when Nagarjuna Group was considered as one of the largest groups in South India. It had ambitious plans to be one amongst the 10 largest companies in India, but some setbacks impeded the progress. Nagarjuna Group went through many ups and downs. People say, the group had passed through good and bad phases. But my approach and understanding is different. An experience should not be taken in terms of good or bad—every experience is rich. You become richer with each new experience. You learn something new! Life is nothing but a series of experiences.

K.V.K. Raju was the founder of the group and Nagarjuna Fertilizers and Chemicals Limited (NFCL) was its first child. It grew healthy both physically and spiritually under the special care of K.V.K. Even today, it is the flagship company of the group. K.V.K. was a visionary leader. He was a dreamer who turned his dreams into reality. He was a noble soul and gave the company a strong foundation of ethical and human values. So are his son and grandson, K.S. Raju, the present CMD of the group, and Rahul Raju, one of the Directors on board, respectively. In 1999, I had joined this group as Executive Vice-president, Human Potential Development (HPD). I studied the systems and policies that existed during the time of K.V.K. Each policy of the company was based on logic with focus on human values. The salary management during his time was nothing but a reflection of his great wisdom. Some senior people, especially the Director, Finance, did not understand head or tail of the deeper aspects of his policies and tried to convert the wage philosophy into a mathematical cost to company (CTC). KVK's philosophy was to give a lifestyle to his people, not mere salary. Cost to company cannot give you a lifestyle. If people lack such simple wisdom, they do not deserve to rise, let alone occupy the board level positions.

I have many stories to tell and many experiences to share. However, I choose to tell one of those, which is of contextual importance to this chapter—managing transition. In 1999, the company decided to implement the Enterprise Resource Plan (ERP). KPMG, one of the best global consultants, was hired for assistance. Their job was to provide technical support, which I call the 'hard track'. The other track is the 'soft track', which is more important in change management. An outsider can never take care of the human aspects and culture-related issues, that is, the soft track can only be taken care of by the insiders. So, as the corporate HPD chief, I kept my entire focus on the soft track.

We took a lot of proactive steps to ensure that the proposed change should not create anxiety or shock, as it normally happens in a change process. As a first step, we carried out the news about the proposed change plans in the monthly house journal. Once people became aware, we decided to give a name to the mission. Many ideas were suggested, but K.S. Raju's idea was the noblest. His idea was to get the suggestions for the name of the mission from the workforce. Let people decide the name for the change campaign. So, a competition was organised inviting names for this campaign from the employees. This process created the desired 'stir', what is called 'percolation'.

Stirring plays a very important part in change management. It is easy to stir sugar in a teacup. But when it comes to an organisation, you have got to find the ways and means—the right processes. Once you decide the 'nature of change'—the 'what' part—you must then think seriously about the processes for managing change—the 'how part'. The best idea can get killed if the 'how' aspect of the process is not properly taken care of. Here communication plays an important role. But, a perfect 'stirring' goes beyond communication. For instance, a CEO might say, 'I want my company should follow the principle, "Honesty is the best policy".' A nice idea, then what? Would people become honest if we cover all the walls, floors and ceilings with big posters of this slogan? No, never. Posters are but posters. They can at best be considered as 'important means', but can never be taken as the be-all and the end-all. The change process needs a much wider range of communication than mere posting of posters.

So, the idea of giving a name to the campaign had helped us in two ways. On the one hand, it percolated the idea of change across the organisation effectively by sending positive signals, and on the other, converted anxiety into excitement. In addition, this 'naming campaign' also provided a new platform for participation or what the Japanese call TEI—total employees involvement. Thus, the campaign jelled well with central tenet of change—'People whose lives are affected by a decision relating to change must be part of the process of arriving at that decision.' I could see the excitement all around. Simple things give you bigger results. As Collin Powell says, 'To achieve excellence in big things you must develop the habit in little matters.' Excellence is not an exception—excellence is a prevailing attitude.

This process created more excitement than we expected! A lot of names were received in English, Hindi and Telugu. We constituted a committee and the committee selected the best name. Thus, the ERP campaign was given the name 'Parivartanam'. The Hindi word 'parivartan' or Telugu word 'parivatanam' can be translated in English as change or transformation but these words carry a much deeper meaning. The employee who suggested this name got a handsome cash award and our newsletter carried the photos of the award distribution ceremony. This boosted the morale of the people—it is our programme for our company and we shall carry it forward.

Enthused with the enthusiasm of the employees, we decided to start a new bilingual series of the newsletter, giving it the name

'Parivartanam'. Monthly progress on ERP and the related news was reported through this special news bulletin. In this bulletin we printed some good articles on change management, so that the employees understand the need for change and also learn various ways by which other world-class companies had espoused ERP and standard operating procedure (SAP). We also introduced a 'suggestion scheme' exclusively on 'Parivartanam'. Good suggestions were rewarded and used in making the process simple and workable.

To get many good ideas we used the technique of brain stilling. Brainstorming is a wrong phrase; in Nagarjuna, we did not subscribe to this Western terminology. You cannot get the best from your brain by storming it. Contrarily, when you storm the brain it stops functioning, it does not work well. It may even work negatively, what is known as 'negative motivation'. If you want to get the best from your brain, you must first learn how to calm it down. What you can achieve from your brain when it is in peace and tranquillity you can never get it from the so called storming. When your mind becomes the mountain's lake, you start seeing the reflection. You can see the moon, the stars and even the Milky Way, in the reflection, on the calm surface of a lake. One cannot see a reflection in disturbed water. So, make your mind a 'mountain's lake' first.

Before every such meeting, we used to meditate for one or two minutes to calm our brains. The idea behind such two-minute silence was simple. Everyone would come carrying many problems in one's mind relating to his or her department. If the brain was not brought to a tranquilizing state, it would not be productive; it would remain busy thinking about many other issues. Thus, meditation helps. Brain stilling follows the following pattern:

1. In the mind's silence the transcendent acts.
2. The hushed heart hears the unuttered words.
3. Hidden in silent depths the words are formed.
4. From hidden silences the acts are born.

It would be advisable for business organisations to provide for a 'room of silence' which must have a different ambience.

The ambience of a conference room is not ideal. For this reason, sometimes I used to avail Brahama Kumari's meditation rooms, which were in the adjacent complex.

The brain stilling sessions did not recognise ranks. After meditation, anyone would decide to lead the group; it could be the junior most member of the team. We had our own credo—it is reproduced as shown in Figure 8.3.

The leader ensured that every meeting of brain stilling must conclude with 'closing the loop'. We did not believe in encouraging people to indulge in verbal acrobatics without results. If anyone hurt other's feelings by passing sarcastic remarks, which created discord, the leader would declare a one minute time off.

Figure 8.3 Brain Stilling

TOWARDS ENHANCING EFFECTIVENESS OF MEETINGS

- *There is no rank in this room; let one lead*
- *Observe a minute's silence; calm the mind*
- *Be open; speak your mind*
- *One speaker at a time*
- *Stay focused*
- *Be smart; don't outsmart*
- *Let everyone participate; every view is precious*
- *Shrink differences; shed the ego*
- *Don't end up with intellectual acrobatics; close the loop*
- *Look for solutions; not the issues*
  &
- *Be an active listener*
- *Humour, in the right place, is a bonus*

NAGARJUNA GROUP

Evolved by : Human Potential Development & Corporate Communications, Nagarjuna Group.

Source: Scanned copy of the original.

Once again we used to observe one minute's silence to calm our minds. Brain stilling became very popular. I got the brain stilling credo printed and distributed it amongst all the employees of the Nagarjuna group. We got many good results from this healthy practice of brain stilling.

At one point of time, when the management was thinking in terms of constituting a cross-functional team exclusive for this change mission, an employee floated an idea on an almost similar pattern. We decided to give credit to the employee and announced that based on someone's suggestion a 'Parivartanam Team' has been constituted. We inducted the best brains from different disciplines—not the ones who were 'spareable' but the ones who were 'difficult to be spared'! Thus, this empowered team became the nodal agency between KPMG and the Nagarjuna Group. This team was also responsible to remove the bottlenecks, by discussing with the concerned 'discipline head'. For instance, when I resisted that HRD must be excluded from the ERP process, the team members came to me with a clear mind, 'either convince or get convinced'. I argued on two issues.

First, the 'lotus notes', which were introduced recently did not get fully accepted by people and our 'paperless office' plan was passing through a crucial phase. So, it was not an opportune time to introduce another big dose of change. Second, I was not quite satisfied with the then HRD SAP package, as it did not go well with the 'Indian HR' pattern—HR with a human face! I was not ready to accept a mechanical system for dealing with people, which was 'spiritually empty' and not sensitive to feelings and emotions. I had no objection in putting the routine HR processes such as benefits administration, time management, corporate communication and other administrative areas like guest houses, transport, and so on, on ERP, but not the total HR processes per se.

The same team of KPMG had carried out the ERP project in my earlier organisation, BEML, where I was the HR director on board. I had faced a similar problem there. I had internal information that within a couple of years the 'India-friendly' HR model of SAP was likely to be introduced.

'So, it is better to defer', I argued. My arguments were taken well by the Parivartanam Team. Once the team was convinced, I did not bother much about the top brass.

Percolation of change through newsletter was not an adequate communication channel. So, I decided to take this major aspect as a part of our training programme. Many training workshops were conducted, associating all those who were affected directly or indirectly. The desired change took place smoothly. As expected, business process re-engineering (BPR) exercises created redundancy, which warranted cutting the fat. Downsizing was not a new exercise for me—I had carried it out in HMT. But this time, being the commander-in-chief, I wanted to deal with it on a different footing. Instead of saying goodbye to the guys whose positions were rendered surplus, I decided to go for 'mix and match' principle. I was not convinced that I should blindly say goodbye to all those people whose positions (due to some reason) were rendered surplus.

A highflier is always a highflier. Retention of talents and highfliers was a part of my duty. I was not convinced that just because the position was rendered surplus we should mechanically go for a golden handshake with the so-called surplus people. On the other hand, some deadwoods would continue to be safe because the positions they occupied were not rendered surplus. Right from the time I was in HMT, I was not satisfied with such mechanical exercises, which are normally carried out in the 'downsizing' organisations. So, instead of going with the well-accepted formula of 'good-fit', I went with my own formula 'talents and highfliers will remain; the deadwoods will separate'. There was a good deal of resistance, but ultimately I could prevail. The BG chiefs of new businesses were upset as it restricted their freedom for recruiting people from the open market. As per my formula, first they were supposed to interview the internal lot and see whether 'good-fit' can be created by an additional dose of training. This clicked well—more than 70 per cent of good people from the category termed 'surplus' were adjusted and relocated. I know, business wise it was not the best option, but from the ethical and human values point of view it appeared to be the best solution to me. Having completed the first exercise successfully, I was in a position to say goodbye to the deadwoods without any feeling of professional guilt. A golden handshake with 'low performers' and 'deadwoods' was not an uncomfortable exercise.

Politics and change management are twins, which cannot be separated. The reason is obvious—with every change process some people, disciplines or departments get adversely affected and no one likes to die by one's own sweet choice. So this happens when the sword of change cuts the fat and foul flesh—some people get affected. But sometimes certain change programmes also hit the best talents. For the change maker it may be a mere process, but for the affected people it is a question of life and death. So, they use all possible methods to protect their interests. Such politics is well understandable. But, sometimes change is also taken as the opportunity to settle old scores. For settling such scores, taking the consulting agency into confidence is not a difficult task instead it is quite a common practice. Certain 'authorities' are always 'important' for the consulting agency—the nodal authority or those who settle the payments. They have a better say. They can always influence the consulting agency to get what they want through the 'change programme'. It is done very articulately by using professional jargons and giving them 'extra' inputs as the buttress to manage what such vested authorities ultimately want from the consultants.

This is an important aspect, about which most of the CEOs or top people are not aware. The purpose of sharing some secrets is to educate them and caution them so that sufficient safeguards are taken to protect the victims.

Some top guys, especially the ones who enjoyed good positions and built their own 'power centres', took my entry into the Nagarjuna Group as a threat. K.S. Raju had not involved anyone in my selection process—it was an informal chat over a cup of tea in his office and he invited me to join his group. This created a great deal of suspicion in the minds of those who were at the helm of affairs. Another aspect was that my predecessor was a 'too submissive' type of a person—he would never oppose or clash with these 'power centre' pharaohs. They expected the same 'brownnosing' from me but soon they realised that I was not the guy who would feed to their inflated egos. So, some feelers were sent to me to 'cooperate' with them. Their stooges also shared with me that whosoever had opposed them they were fated with a bad exit. Somehow, I did not pay any heed to those words and there were some occasions when I had to go against them. Again, feelers were sent to me that I must learn how to swim with sharks and live in peace with their support and blessings. I just neglected all such whispering campaigns. One of the directors talked to me directly and threatened me, 'When you have decided to drink poison, you shall have it.' I did not bother much. I didn't even feel carrying all this to KS. I always believe in bearing one's own Cross. KS was unaware of all that was happening to me.

Now, I will reveal to you a very interesting technique used by the corporate pharaohs to get me out of this organisation. There were two guys—one was the chief of one of the BGs and the second one, who had threatened me that I would have to drink poison, was the finance chief. They were always together—the bondage of some common interests is always strong. During Parivartanam, the HBR came out with an article on a ground-breaking theme, 'The Centreless Organization', it was a new theme with focus on extreme degree of 'decentralisation'. This model well-suited the sector (BG) chiefs for further strengthening their autonomy. All through my career I preached and practised 'empowerment'. I was not against functional autonomy. But when it comes to overall business strategies with focus on larger interests, such autonomy needs to be mended sometimes. The maxim 'power corrupts—absolute power corrupts absolutely' is not all that senseless. To cut the story short, the idea to demolish 'corporate HR' was sold by these two corporate pharaohs through the consulting agency with the help of the HBR article. It was not their first attempt; earlier also they tried but could not succeed. When you throw many types of spaghetti, one may stick; this last spaghetti stuck well. It was decided to go for a 'centre-less organisational structure'. Since it was an equal threat to some other corporate disciplines, including corporate finance, the consulting agency was used to suggest that the implementation process must be carried out in a 'phased manner'—corporate HPD (HR) became the first casualty. K.S. Raju never wanted me to leave. He had many alternative plans. But, in principle, respecting the new 'centre-less structure' I chose to part from the group.

By virtues raised to lofty heights; by those same virtues the noble fall. I left the organisation with my head held high. The second phase, as I could foresee, never materialised. The so-called centre-less organisation, which was planned with a skewed objective, never became the reality. Even today the corporate 'HPD' exists in the Nagarjuna Group.

But it was a great lesson for me—a change maker must know that sometimes he may have to bear his own Cross. Socrates drank Hemlock; Jesus Christ bore the Cross; Prophet Mohammad had to migrate from Mecca.

'Trickery succeeds sometimes, but it always commits suicide!' How true was Kahlil Gibran, in saying so! Having committed many sins, both those top guys eventually got exposed and they were asked to leave the Nagarjuna group. They left with their heads held low in shame. This reminded me of Visnu Sarma's famous verse from *Panchatantra*:

All of a sudden
a nobleman may fall;
but his fall,
like that of a ball,
is upspringing.
But the crooked who falls stays
fallen—
call it the 'flattened-out' fall of a
lump of clay!

I continue to be a proud member of the loving Raju family. Whenever I feel hungry, I go to K.S. Raju or Rahul and collect the honey drops of wisdom.

9 Injelititis—The Kiss of Death

'Change or Perish' is a catchphrase. But, if management does not know the art of managing change the organisation perishes. I have narrated the classical example of HMT in Chapter 8—*how this company mismanaged the change and suffered*! Not HMT alone, many organisations have perished owing to mismanaging the Change. Even healthy organisations can perish if the change is not managed properly. This is one extreme. But on the other hand, those who are afraid of managing change also suffer. If change process is delayed the organisation shows some symptoms of disease, called *Injelititis*.

What is *Injelititis*? *Injelititis* is a deadly organisational disease. It is so deadly that this disease is recognized as the 'Kiss of Death'. Many organisations suffer from *injelititis* and if preventive measures are not taken they succumb to this deadly disease.

Change management is the most delicate and sensitive process, which should be managed by experts with utmost care. Organisations suffer if change is not managed properly. Organisations also suffer if change is delayed or denied. Like human beings, organisations are also living beings. Health and diseases are relevant to organisations as relevant to human beings. Like human beings many organisations also suffer from diseases, some are curable; some are deadly.

Injelititis is a deadly disease—It was Northcote C. Parkinson, who first discovered this organisational disease and gave it the name 'Injelititis'. He claims that this disease has no cure, so the top management must always be watchful, observing the symptoms and taking precautionary measures to ensure that the disease does not incubate.

Parkinson describes *Injelititis* in terms of an equation: *I3+J5 = Injelititis*. Seems to be some sort of quiz or riddle? Let me explain. In this equation *I* stands for 'Incompetence' and *J* stands for 'Jealousy' (against the Intelligence or Intelligent people). The figures '3' and '5' are the measures in terms of ratio. In simple words when 'Incompetence' grows 3 times against *competence* and 'Jealousy' 5 times against the Intelligent and competent managers, the deadly disease, Ingelititis develops.

Believe it or not, 'Jealousy' is disastrous! It is one of the strongest negative forces. Almost all scriptures of various faiths caution mankind against the evil effect of jealousy. Let me quote one of the verses from the Old Testament, which describes that one can withstand cruelty and brutality, but not jealousy:

> *Wrath is cruel and anger a torrent,*
> *But who is able to stand before jealousy!*

'Jealousy' plays havoc in business organisations. Parkinson's Injelititis is no fiction; it is based on his lifetime study and meticulous analysis. One must be careful with those who have a jealous mind and an envious soul for no one can withstand their jealousy and ill-will. Jealousy and greed are the signs of death that undermine corporate prosperity. The CEOs keep focus on competence, capabilities, and attitudes of people but quite of them forget the softer aspects—positive and negative. Jealousy is one such negative softer aspect, which goes unnoticed.

When *incompetence* and *jealousy* reign and competence and competent people are marginalised through conspiracies and negative strategies, there remains no healthy competition among employees to perform better. As fish do not survive in polluted water, intelligent professionals and the real contributors feel suffocated under such a depressing, cursing and melancholy atmosphere. Suspicion of one's own abilities as also those of others rules the roast. One-upmanship to prosper at the expense of other becomes a normal practice. Nobody does any useful work that adds value to the products or services as is often seen in some of the defunct government departments. Work expands so as to fill the time available. Everyone is busy to justify his or her position or workload. In such situation the expenditure rises to meet the income. Many a time expenditure tends to surpass the income. People are seen busy filling the void created by the human failures. Everyone is seen sweating in cleaning the soiled floor without much value addition to the customer.

Fighting 'injelititis' is not an easy task. It needs a lot of patience to change the mindset of people suffering from it and enough commitment to streamline the organisation by retraining highfliers, setting standards of work, monitoring their daily performance, constantly motivating them, ensuring that there is little time to waste and finally rewarding the deserved and also punishing those who are responsible for polluting the culture of excellence.

When the organisation keeps focus on internal issues giving precedence to rules, regulation and procedures, the external factors, especially the customers, go out of focus, the company suffers from this deadly 'corporate disease'. A few symptoms are quoted below:

- Work expands so as to fill the time available—everyone is busy to justify his or her position and workload.
- Action expands to fill the void created by human failure—everyone sweats in cleaning the soiled floor without much value addition for the customer.
- Expenditure rises to meet income and tends to surpass it.
- Delay in throughput and output by the employees as also in rewarding the people by the management incubates the disease fast. Delay is the deadliest form of denial—incompetent CEOs with a *jealous heart* fail to understand this.
- The time spent on any item of the agenda will be in inverse proportion to 'customer focus'—more time than required is given to non-issues in terms of 'customer orientation'.

All this brings the company to a stage, what we may call Coma. At this stage some peculiar tendencies can be witnessed. For instance:

- People on the helm of affairs are seen plodding and walking heavily.
- *Jealous* and *incompetent managers* remain active in intriguing and scheming against the highfliers, technocrats, marketing guys, etc., to put them down with the power of rules and procedures.
- The hangmen gain strength by virtue of code of conduct and discipline and appeal rules of the company. They grow powerful. Holding the noose, they search for competent and risk-taking managers who have guts to defy the rules and override the procedures in the interest of business and customer. When such competent managers with risk-taking muscles are punished, the highflyers and bold managers start sulking. This way, the game Escapism begins.
- Committed people begin to withdraw their emotional investment and flex not their risk-taking muscles.
- Dissent is not tolerated and considered as insubordination or disobedience.
- If the *boss* is second rate, he will see to it that his immediate subordinates are all third rate and, in turn, they see to it that their juniors are fourth rate.
- Smugness is the cardinal symptoms. Everyone is seen hitting the target—either the bull's eye is too big or the sitting duck is at too short distance.
- The specialist when observe the jealous incompetent managers who manage or mismanage keeping internal focus, without understanding the need of customers and market, start withdrawing.
- Sycophancy from top to bottom broods in. People learn the art of buttering the royal toast and speaking what creates melody to the ears of their bosses.
- The risk-taking competent and brave managers having diagnosed the disease—Corporate Injelititis—coolly find the fox

holes, for no one would listen to them even when they voiced their dissent from the top of their roofs.

- No spark of intelligence is left in the whole organisation—the corporate Pharaohs talk about HR and creativity without even understanding the basics of such softer side of human assets.

The final stage may linger for years while company slowly dies with kiss of *incompetence blended with jealousy*, leaving the corporate Pharaohs wondering— 'I controlled "costs" at all costs; I followed the systems, rules and procedures so scrupulously and unerringly, yet the organization has collapsed!' Strange! We defend our wrongs with more vigour than we do our rights!

The worst is not that some of us behave like pen pushers; the worst is that they take pride to be pen pushers. 'The man whose life is devoted to paperwork has lost the initiative. He is dealing with things that are brought to his notice, having ceased to notice anything for himself,' believes Parkinson.

Death pops up no red flags on CEO's table.

Change is hard because people overestimate the value of what they have—and underestimate the value of what they may gain by giving that up.

—James Belasco and Ralph C. Stayer
(Authors of *Flight of the Buffalo: Soaring to Excellence, Learning to Let Employees Lead*)

10 Managing Transition—Hard Track and Soft Track

You must have observed from the three case studies discussed in Chapter 8 that there are two important aspects of managing transition. On the one hand, we introduce new systems and processes using technology, and on the other, we have to focus on the humane aspects as well—the emotional aspects. Most unfortunately, we take the physical aspects seriously and give no heed to the emotional aspects. To me the latter is an obverse phase in change management. I call the physical and technology-related aspects 'hard track' and the emotional and cultural aspects 'soft track'. I have yet to find a consulting agency that gives its clients a comprehensive package for soft track and their total involvement in bringing about the cultural change and change in the mindset of the people. Let me explain what I mean by hard track and soft track.

HARD TRACK

The hard track approach to change includes all those activities that are related to physical aspects such as structure-related changes like de-layering, business process re-engineering (BPR), downsizing, rightsizing or smart-sizing, enterprise resource plan (ERP) and Global Positioning System (GPS). If you care to see, you will realise that each of them is related to the physical aspects. Another important aspect is that these activities or exercises are not stand-alone exercises. They have a great degree of connectivity. Since we are not in the habit of seeing business management as a big picture, we see these activities in snapshots and carry out these activities in segments.

Let me explain what I mean. Restructuring is normally designed based on a new objective or a set of objectives. We may call it 'vision'—where we want to go from here? So keeping the vision in mind we rework the structure, to suit our mission. Thus, when an organisation decides to re-transform, the first thing that warrants change is its structure. So restructuring is planned on paper. Once the new structure is finalised we then think of systems and subsystems, processes and other SOPs.

One of the accepted patterns for organisational restructuring is de-layering. But once you de-layer, you cannot exercise controls because the de-layered structure and the concept of 'span of control' do not go together. Span of control can work only in tall pyramid type of organisations where many hierarchies are created keeping in mind the limitations of span of control. Our stone-age gurus had told us that you can at best control 10–20 people and not beyond. So, when you plan a structure on the basis of span of control you have got to create more layers to make control workable. As you have more number of employees, you create more layers. This way we worked and created the organisation structure in the form of tall pyramids with many layers. But when you flatten the structure through the process of de-layering, controls do not work.

Why do we need to de-layer? We de-layer, keeping two major objectives in our mind. First, to speed up the decision-making process, and second to cut costs by eliminating the superficial layers. In a de-layered organisation, span of control fails. Even if you want to control, you cannot control when people are many and layers are only two or three. One can control 20 but not 200 people. So if you want to control, then you need to create 10 levels of hierarchy. The mathematics is simple; I need not explain the obvious! So, once you de-layer, by default, you have to empower your people. Even if you do not like it, you have no choice. When controls go, empowerment gets in to fill the void.

De-layering warrants revisiting your processes. So, you go for BPR. Once the business processes are re-engineered, a lot of obsolete practices are rejected and discarded. Hence, those who were engaged in such non-productive activities are no more required. So, whether you like it or not, downsizing becomes a necessity. Since it befits the redesigned business processes, it is called 'smartsizing' or 'rightsizing'. Downsizing, in turn, necessitates golden handshake. Once you have completed all these exercises, you are now fit to go for ERP. If you do not polish the processes and perfect the structural design first, ERP cannot get you success. One of the major limitations of ERP is that it is like being 'etched' on a stone, you cannot change the processes easily. So, it is always advisable to rationalise the processes first, and then go for ERP. Technology has no limits. Global positioning system can be used in making ERP more hi-tech.

Enterprise resource plan integrates the process through technology. It first captures the details and then gives support to supply chain management and many other disciplines at micro levels. At the macro level it integrates various strategic business units (SBUs) across the country or globe, at various locations. It also provides the best platform for financial integration. ERP streamlines the processes, and discards all those that do not add value to the customer, product or people. Enterprise resource plan works through process groups as against the conventional pattern of unifunctionalism.

In a nutshell, ERP improves operational efficiency. It cannot by itself produce cheaper, better and more profitable goods and services. Only people can do that. If you agree with this, you must also agree that people must also be transformed simultaneously. This calls for soft track.

Once you understand the inbuilt sequence of a hard track, even a child will be able to say that all these exercises will help you acquire physical fitness. Now your organisation with the cutting of fat has become slim and smart. But the question is, whether such physical fitness is the end or just the means? Obviously, physical fitness is not the end; it is the means to achieve bigger objectives and higher goals. The eventual goal is longevity—a happy, satisfied long life, longing for attaining greater heights! These aspects are taken care through soft track.

SOFT TRACK

Working on soft track means working on the softer aspects of change management. For example, the hard track process may demand downsizing. To achieve this objective, soft track process will help you to ponder upon: How good is the exercise of 'downsizing' not only for human aspects but also for business results?' Thomas H. Davenport was a staunch supporter of downsizing. He was a pioneer of re-engineering who worked with Michael Hammer, the guru who coined the word BPR, and re-engineered business processes through the process of downsizing. After seeing the bloodshed caused by downsizing the same Thomas comes to a conclusion in *Liberating the Corporate Soul-Building a Visionary Organization* (authored by Richard Barrett) saying, 'Companies that embraced re-engineering as the Silver Bullet are now looking for ways to rebuild the organisation's torn social fabric.'

Those who do not know much about Michael Hammer's BPR must know that he simply adapted the age-old mechanics of F.W. Taylor's 'IE'—industrial engineer. Richard Barrett, the author of the famous book *Liberating Corporate Soul*, comes down heavily on hard track strategies saying that the survey conducted in 1999 revealed that two-thirds of the initiatives undertaken for re-engineering in 1994 were judged as producing mediocre, marginal or failed results.

Let me now explain through a figure both the processes—hard track and soft track. In Figure 10.1, you find hard track processes—mechanical processes—on the left side and soft track processes—organic processes— on the right side.

The mechanical process—hard track—starts with a defensive process—how to cope with resistance? Then the existing processes are scanned, mapped and measured in terms of the desired outputs.

Figure 10.1 Hard Track and Soft Track Processes

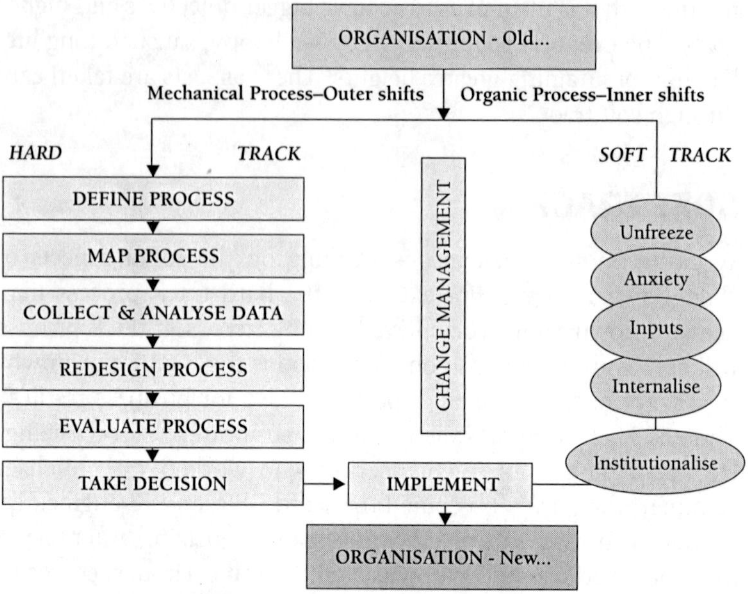

Source: Computed by the author.

At the third step, a lot of data is collected and analysed before suggesting new processes. Based on the outcome new processes are designed and introduced. These processes are carried out as some sort of 'dry-run' for the purpose of observation and recording the results. At this stage the legacy system is carried out concurrently. After examining the results thoroughly, once the ERP agency is satisfied, the final decision is taken with the consent of the CEO of the client company. And the new processes overtake or override the legacy system.

The organic process—soft track—begins with the 'unfreezing' exercise. Various techniques are used to allay various suspicions and apprehensions from the minds of people. Hectic efforts are made to clarify various doubts and well-planned massive exercises are undertaken. Once the anxiety is removed, people are ready to take new inputs willingly. So, at the third stage new inputs are poured in. Now the real challenge facing the leadership is how to percolate new information speedily, without giving rise to a fresh round of anxiety or suspicion? This stage of transformation is known as 'internalisation'. Once people accept the change and changed concepts, efforts are made to ensure that the change seeps into the organisation's bloodstream. This stage of transformation is known as 'institutionalisation'. Each stage is important. Success in making change depends in tackling each stage cautiously and thoughtfully. Mostly the consulting agencies take care of the hard track. They neither have the expertise nor do they have the sensitivity to manage the soft track related issues. So, I strongly recommend that the softer aspects—organic processes—must be taken care by the internal team of well-trained change experts. If you cannot do this, better not to go for change.

General Electric's (GE) single-menu model would give us a better understanding and clarity for managing transition. To simplify systems and processes, GE carried out BPR. To make GE slim, it was massively rightsized. To shed the controls, GE flattened the pyramid and opted for de-layering. The de-layered SBUs were empowered and, in turn, the SBU chiefs were asked to empower managers at each layer. So, the managers were converted into business leaders, what we call as 'entrepreneurs'. When the flow of decision making became fast and an entreprencurial organisational culture was created, GE progressed well. That is the reason why Jack Welch used to say, 'We are not managing better; we are managing less, which is better!'

To make restructuring perfect, you must know how to downsize by using the technique of rightsizing. Downsizing must always be balanced with upsizing through your expansion and developmental plans. When you follow the golden handshake to say goodbye, you must also follow the technique of 'golden handcuff' to retain talented people. After cutting the fat, you must then work to re-strengthen the muscles. De-layering and empowerment must ensure loosening the control systems and demolishing the power centres. And if you want to move forward and push your organisation towards future, once in a while you must look into the rear-view mirror. Lastly, maintain focus on both internal and external factors, and issues. While loosening the grip over controls with the intention to provide autonomy to the SBUs' heads, simultaneously tighten the grip over value system and other central tenets of your organisation. This unique technique is known as 'Loose-tight game'. Tom Peters coined this phraseology in his book *In Search of Excellence*, which he has co-authored with others.

'We are at the end of one period of "building modern organizations", and at the beginning of a "New Period" ,' said Peter Drucker at the fag end of his life. Transformation is inevitable, there is no choice with you! What is needed is transformation with a human face. For this you must know how to manage through your heart keeping your conscience alive all the time!

Transformation begins from 'Self'. So, in corporate sense it should begin with the CEO or the team leader. 'You change; others change' is the universal law of energy response. Never forget the fact that 'corporations do not transform, people do!' You can walk the talk only when you talk what you do. You can bring transformation only when you remove the difference between 'your thinking' and 'your doing'. For real success of transformation, it is necessary that you must hold the ethical and human values steadfast so that the 'belief system' becomes persuasive throughout the organisation. Let the espoused values seep into the bloodstream of the organisation.

Painting the 'big picture' is very important in change process. You cannot think of transforming the organisation and people through your 'snapshots-outlook'! If not all the top team members, at least the CEO must know what he wants. He must see the big picture clearly and vividly. Kenichi Ohmae, the author of *The Borderless World*, makes a powerful observation:

> Many of most globally successful Japanese companies—Honda, Nissan, Canon—have been led by a strong leader for at least a decade. These leaders can override bureaucratic inertia; they can tear down institutional barriers. Someone has to have a sense of overall programme—the Mental Map of the segments. Visualising the big picture is an important aspect of change management. Like an architect who visualises the finished building, the change agent must clearly see the big picture—How would the organisation finally look?

Managing change is managing transition, both hard track and soft track.

It takes a lot of courage to release the familiar and seemingly secure, to embrace the new. But there is no real security in what is no longer meaningful. There is more security in the adventurous and exciting, for in movement there is life, and in change there is power.

—Alan Cohen

(The author is a contributing writer for the best-selling Chicken Soup for the Soul series)

Source: http://www.brainyquote.com/quotes/authors/a/alan_cohen.html

11 Change without Pain—Techniques and Processes

Change is always painful. So what? So is surgery. Surgery always causes blood loss. A good surgeon does not look for a bloodless surgery—he looks for how best blood loss can be controlled! When I say, 'Change without Pain', I mean change with least pain, with least loss of blood. They are liars who say that change can be managed without pain. They are as bad as those liars who say that a major surgery can be conducted with no loss of blood. Similarly, if you do anything some people are sure to get affected—either favourably or adversely. Stewart Brand, an American author puts it nicely, 'You are either part of the steam roller or part of the road!'

Managing change is managing transition—I will say this until my tongue bleeds or the crows turn white—but in the same breath, I would also like to caution that we must clearly understand the meaning of transition first. By transition I mean a comprehensive seamless process. It is not a stand-alone phenomenon—it is preceded by unfreezing and succeeded by refreezing phases. Since change is a continuous process, it works like a cycle. The end point, after some time, becomes the beginning point and the change goes on. Those who choose to stay in their comfort zones in complacence eventually stand to be losers. As Anais Nin puts it, 'Life is a process of becoming, a combination of states we have to go through. Where people fail is that they wish to elect a state and remain in it. This is a kind of death.'

In this chapter, I will briefly explain the entire change cycle and share with you some important techniques and tips for making the change process smooth—what I call 'change without pain'. In the process, you can recap some of the concepts which I have already shared with you in the preceding chapters and in addition learn some new techniques.

We live in a competitive world, which is dynamic. What the biologists call 'Red Queen Effect' is *ipso facto* applicable to the business world. This term is meant to describe the evolutionary necessity to evolve faster than one's competitors. In fingerboard, or carom board, winning the 'red queen' is almost akin to winning the game, so everyone tries to win the red queen in the first opportunity. Lewis Carroll, the author of *Alice in the Wonderland*, makes an intelligent use of the 'Red Queen Effect' through the famous sentence, 'It takes all the running you can do to stay in the same place. If you want to get somewhere else, you must run at least twice as fast as that.' Those who follow the Red Queen gallop and avoid the hazards of comfort zones while motivating and energizing their people; they only will have a massive advantage; they will lead their people and organisation into the future through the path, most likely paved with the skulls and bones of their competitors. Change ability means survival—living to fight another day. One should plan out a clear mental map.

'Good leaders create vision, articulate vision, passionately own it and drive it to completion', believes Jack Welch, the former CEO of General Electric (GE). Change follows the following pattern:

1. Perceive (the need for change)
2. Conceive (the idea)
3. Sell it (convincingly)

4. Own it (passionately)
5. Commit for it (emotionally)
6. Complete it (untiringly)

As mentioned earlier, unlearning is crucial to the process of change management. Only when you stop doing what does not work, can things get better. Nevertheless, for a small period the legacy system can go parallel (Figure 11.1).

Figure 11.1 Change Process

- **Unfreeze**
- **Pour fresh inputs**
- **Internalise**

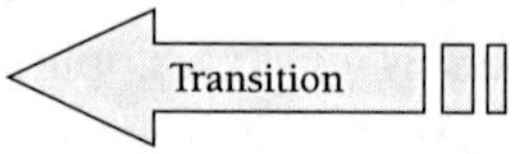

- **Institutionalise**
- **Refreeze (Cap it)**

Source: Computed by the author.

Alvin Toffler, the author of *Future Shock*, made this observation almost two decades ago, which is coming true in the 21st century: 'The illiterate of the 21st century will not be those who cannot read and write but those who cannot learn, unlearn and relearn.' The new age is the age of constant learning, unlearning and new learning. With the pace of change in today's world, if you are not making conscious efforts to make your tomorrow better than yesterday, you are not just standing still—you are getting farther and farther behind. You are becoming less and less relevant because those around you are moving rapidly ahead. You are not living in a static world but you are living in a world that is changing every nanosecond.

One should learn the art of transformation, rather 'corporate reincarnation' from Nokia, which is recognised today for its cellphones. You will be amazed to know that this company started with paper manufacturing, then went into rubber products, rubber boots, raincoats, hunting rifles, consumer electronics and finally secured the position of one of the major global players in cellphones.

Risk, failures and change go together; success is, of course, an important feature of change. But we learn more from failures than from success. 'You learn nothing from your successes except to think too much of yourself. It is from failure that all growth comes, provided you can recognise it, admit it, learn from it, rise about it and then try again,' believes Dee Hock, founder CEO, Visa International. You may call failures as failures, or you can as well call failures as new avenues to success. Thomas Edison used to say that he didn't fail 10,000 times; he successfully eliminated several thousand materials and combinations that didn't work. It is this type of learning that caused Thomas J. Watson to say that if you want to increase your success rate, you have to double your failure rate. It may appear very threatening. So, let me offer a modest suggestion, 'If you want to get success, do not be afraid of failures.'

Unlearning or unfreezing, transition and refreezing are three crucial phases of transformation. Let me describe each phase of change.

UNFREEZING

In organisations we constantly hear seniors talking about the need for change. Is their anxiety real or manipulative? Sadly, it is true. We live in change as we stay on a conveyer. Whether you stay or walk, you are moving. To save time, it is better to walk, and precisely this is what all of us do. It is better to understand the reality as it is. There is more excitement in movement, for in movement is life.

Change whether through innovations or wars creates disturbance. Change does not stop when people stop fighting on the streets—the battle just shifts to the negotiation table or boardrooms. The bottom line is that whether we like or dislike, we have to face change. On one hand, technology and science continue to revolutionise our workplace and on the other, the harsh winds of global trends go on biting deep into the foundation of our organisations. We have little choice. So, move, move fast. If you cannot move fast then at least move slowly, but move. 'Be not afraid of going slow; be afraid of standing still!' How true is this Chinese saying!

When you announce change, it creates anxiety. If the initial concern of people is not taken seriously and remedial techniques are not employed, then the change programme can get into trouble. 'Kubler–Ross Grief Cycle' graphically explains the initial concern—the gap between stability and acceptance of the new initiative for change (Figure 11.2).

Figure 11.2 Kubler–Ross Grief Cycle

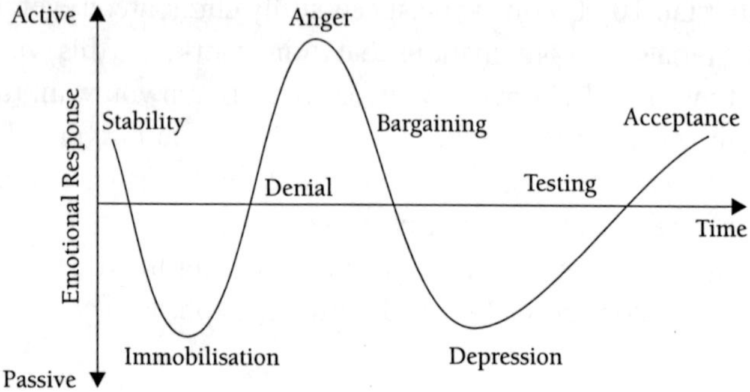

Source: Computed by the author based on Kubler–Ross Grief Cycle.

The Kubler–Ross Grief Cycle explains the emotional response to change. Look at the curve each time you go through the explanation: stability and immobilisation—positive and negative—are the two phases of the same coin. The denial or disturbance of this, what we call as the comfort zone, creates anger and unrest. Owing to this, some implicit bargaining takes place which not only reduces the anger but also causes depression. Only when they are convinced by using their 'touchstone'—testing process—the new idea or initiative is accepted.

The process of unfreezing is very important. Just as foreplay makes lovemaking a wonderful experience, unfreezing announces the success of a change programme.

TRANSITION

Transition is the soul of change management. As mentioned many times earlier, it covers a larger meaning. On the one hand, it denotes 'unfreezing'—the reason why all this is happening? On the other end, it needs a 'loop' closing, so that the new change inputs deliver the desired results for the expected duration. A change leader, or call him a change agent, must know the art of managing transition. If he does, fine; if he fails, he fails the change process. The reason is simple. During transition both morale and productivity come down. The single cause for this is uncertainty. If transition process allows uncertainty to prevail for a longer time, it generates a feeling of instability in the minds of people, which in turn, can cause a disaster in the organisation. For this reason I say, 'Managing transition is managing change.'

If the phase of unfreezing is not properly handled, it affects the transition phase. Heraclitus had once said that dogs bark at what they do not understand. How true! The dog goes on barking until he is convinced that there is no threat. For this reason, the unfreezing exercise should be handled with utmost care so that transition can be managed smoothly.

Involvement and participation of people make the process of change smooth. I have already shared various techniques and methods in the Nagarjuna Group story. Make every effort to involve people in the process, especially during the transition phase. Get your people involved in each change initiative. Invite them to participate in discussions, empower them and assign responsibilities of certain tasks related to the change process.

Involvement leads to bonding. When people are a part of something, they bond with it, making it a part of their identity. Bonding is a very powerful technique. One thing that stood out in the turnaround of SCCL (as you will read in the second part of this book) was corporate bonding—'One for All; All for One'. This slogan became the central tenet of the turnaround. The other statement of the chairman—'One Family; One Vision; One Mission'—was miraculous. These statements and slogans created a tremendous bonding effect and put life into the mission.

Physical bonds can be easily created by providing incentives and monetary gains, but 'intellectual bonds' can be strengthened by creating a learning organisation (Figure 11.3). Through emotional bonds you can inspire and motivate people, and a spiritual bond is most powerful in uniting people. When the feeling of oneness is created the entire workforce considers itself as one soul in many bodies.

Figure 11.3 Bonding Process

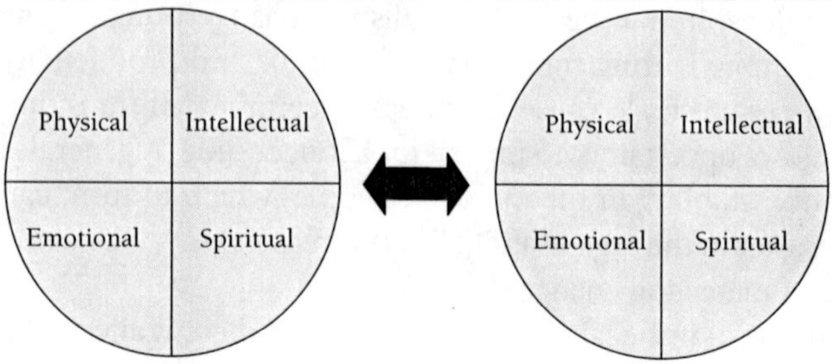

1. Physical–Monetary gains (Individualistic)
2. Intellectual–Creating a Learning Organisation (Collective)
3. Emotional–Inspiring and Motivating (Involving families)
4. Spiritual–Creating Oneness (Holistic)

Source: Computed by the author.

Before I move to the refreezing technique, let me put all that we have discussed so far through a pictorial graph, what I call the 'Transformation Path' (Figure 11.4).

Figure 11.4 Transformation Path

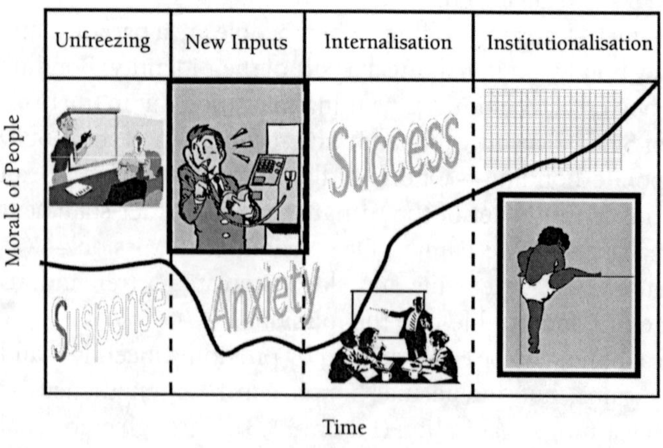

Source: Computed by the author.

In Figure 11.4, you will notice the importance of the process of unfreezing. When you announce the change it creates suspense; people suspect your intentions and try to find out the hidden agenda. If this part of transformation is not carried out with care, suspense and suspicion will create anxiety—people will start consulting their friends and well-wishers to find out solutions. They will be worried—wondering what will happen to them, their job, their career and their family? During the first two stages the morale of the people along with the productivity will come down. So, it is in the organisation's interest to hasten up the process of 'clarification' through well-planned and organised campaigns. Training can play a vital role during this crucial phase. You can start seeing success only when people fully understand the reasons and heave a sigh of relief.

At this stage, let me caution you about an important aspect which the change leaders mostly neglect and then commit mistake in ignorance. If some small segment is going to be adversely affected by your game plan, it is always better to announce it without mincing the words so that, at least, others—the major part—know that they are safe. One blunder, which most of the organisations commit is following the path of secrecy. 'How can we share the bad news; it will affect production and morale?' It is a silly apprehension. On the contrary, if you do not come out openly and maintain secrecy the void will be filled by some 'grapevine'. Once this happens—good or bad—you cannot do much. You might, as well, spend double the time and efforts to undo all that has erupted due to your approach of secrecy. On the other hand, if you announce boldly that 'these 20 people will have to quit' under the change plans, you protect rest of the 80 people from 'anxiety'. Which is better? The obvious is not explained.

Now look at the production curve in Figure 11.4. During the first two stages, it came down lower than the original point when change was initiated. If you speed up your 'internalisation' process articulately and meticulously, the production curve gradually moves up and goes above the original point. The curve scales its peak when the changed processes seep into the organisational bloodstream—what we call the stage of 'institutionalisation'. Eventually you reach at a much higher stage (see Figure 11.4). Now it is time for refreezing!

REFREEZING

Refreezing is the third of Lewins' change transition stages, in which people are taken from a state of being in transition, and moved to a stable and productive state.

Once the purpose is achieved and the objectives are fulfilled, it is time for refreezing so that the change programme remains frozen for some time. This creates a new place for stability. As mentioned earlier, you cannot divide time into cuts or slices. These phases, unfreezing, transition, refreezing, and so on, are not clearly finished stages; they are blurred and hazy at their finish points. You cannot take them into slices as shown in Figure 11.4. The transition process continues even during the process of refreezing. Therefore, in practice, refreezing may be a slow process as transition seldom stops—there are no visible finish points in change management.

Not only 'Walking the Talk' but also 'Talking the Walk' yields better results during Refreezing. It seems to be a bit odd, but that is the only way I can give words to this technique. It is just opposite to the technique of 'walk the talk'. Once you are able to walk the talk and create some impact, you must collect some good stories, incidences and unique experiences that occurred during the change making exercise and carry them to other parts of the organisation. 'Larry Chair' is one such metaphor commonly used to explain this technique. The Olive Garden Restaurant chain went for a massive campaign on 'customer delight'. The results were excellent. When the president of the restaurant was receiving all complimentary letters, he received a strange letter—it was a letter from one Mr Larry. He wrote in the letter that the other day he visited one of the Olive Garden Restaurants and found the food, ambience and service excellent, except that the chair was not comfortable. The president was shocked, as he knew that the best chairs were provided in all the restaurants. So, he decided to probe the matter. He got the feedback which was amazing. It seemed that Mr Larry was a fat rich guy. He was very fat and therefore the chairs of Olive Garden Restaurant could not provide him the desired comfort. The president immediately instructed all the restaurants to keep at least two extra 'Larry chairs', which should be replaced before such 'Mr Larrys' enter the restaurant. Thus, every hotel provided 'extra large chairs' and they were called 'Mr Larry's chairs'. This story was shared with many people in the organisation and they were asked to be more observant and look for doing different things lest we receive such letters in future. This technique is called as 'Evidence Stream'. The idea is whatsoever good things are happening in the company should be shared and spread across the lengths and breadths of the organisation.

These are some important tips that can be used at this phase of refreezing. Success depends how fast and how best you manage these three important phases of change management—(1) Unfreezing, (2) Transition and (3) Refreezing. Delay can cause many problems and mishandling or mismanaging transition can cause a total collapse. In the latter case the phrase 'change or perish' turns to 'changed and perished'. Never allow this to happen.

Managing change is the toughest of all operations of business management. It is unfortunate that the desired seriousness is not attached to such a significant process. Change alone is eternal, perpetual and immortal—you cannot vilify it, you cannot dodge it! 'We cannot adopt the way of living that was satisfactory a hundred years ago. The world in which we live has changed, and we must change with it', said Felix Adler, author of *Ethical Culture* and founder of New York Society for Ethical Culture. None will disagree to what he said. The heresy of one age becomes the orthodoxy of the next. It is better to be recognised as a heretic than orthodox in business.

Here is the last tip, which indeed becomes first on the circle of change where the ending becomes the beginning. Ask the following three simple questions:

1. What is one thing we are now doing that you think we should continue doing?

2. What is one thing we are now doing that you think we should stop doing?
3. What is one thing we are not doing now that you think we should start doing?

These three simple questions are of vital importance in change management. With this last tip, I end this part of the book.

In the second part of this book, you will read the exciting turnaround story of a company, which was brought back to life from mortuary. R.H. Khwaja—a bureaucrat-turned-business-leader—shares the ups and downs and various strides SCCL had passed through.

I have dealt with the easier part of this book—like the role of a consultant who gives some tips and disappears—and have highlighted various concepts and techniques of change management. His job is difficult— managing change is a Herculean task and giving it a pattern of language is not everyone's cup of tea. Only a genius like Khwaja can do it.

PART II

The Singareni Love Story

Turnaround from the Heart (Leadership, Strategies and Execution)

Men make history and not the other way around. In periods where there is no leadership, society stands still. Progress occurs when courageous, skilful leaders seize the opportunity to change things for the better.

—Harry S. Truman

(He was the 33rd President of the United States of America)

Source: http://www.brainyquote.com/quotes/authors/h/harry_s_truman.html

12 My Romance with Singareni—A Brief Historical Perspective

Singareni Collieries Company Limited (SCCL) traces its origins to a quaint historical event in 1870. A group of pilgrims on their way to the famous temple of Lord Ram at Bhadrachalam was camping near a village called Singareni. While lighting fire for cooking they were petrified when some stones caught fire. This strange occurrence was reported to the local authorities. Dr William King, an eminent geologist, was asked to conduct investigations. His detailed studies revealed the presence of coal in the Godavari–Pranahitha valley.

The discovery of black gold led to the formation of a company called The Hyderabad Deccan Company Private Limited in 1886. In 1889, the company commenced its mining operations in Yellandu area of Khammam district. It was on 23 December 1920 that the name of The Hyderabad Deccan Company Private Limited was changed to the Singareni Collieries Company Limited or SCCL. Interestingly, SCCL was registered in the London Stock Exchange in the same year.

In 1945, Mir Osman Ali Khan, the Nizam of Hyderabad, purchased majority of the shares and SCCL, thus, became the first state-owned mining company in the country. After India attained independence, the Government of India took over 49 per cent of shares while the Government of Andhra Pradesh continued with majority holding of 51 per cent of shares. The distinction of being the only joint venture government coal company in the country belongs to SCCL.

SCCL continued to mine coal and expanded its activities. Being a PSU, the functioning of the company was characterised by huge manpower and low levels of productivity. After 1965, the company fell into losses and was unable to pay dividend to its shareholders. In the 1980s communist-inspired extremist, locally known as 'Naxalites', infiltrated the company with extremely damaging consequences. In 1988, a front organisation called Singareni Karmika Samakya (SIKASA) was formed. Between 1988 and 1992, SIKASA engineered a large number of strikes crippling the organisation completely. In 1991–1992, a record number of 475 strikes took place in SCCL. The company became a sick unit in 1992 and was referred to the Board for Industrial and Financial Reconstruction (BIFR) for its closure.

The Government of Andhra Pradesh and the Union Government could not afford the only coal-producing company in South India to be shut down. Apart from catering to the energy requirements of four southern states, SCCL was located in the four districts of Adilabad, Karimnagar, Khammam and Warangal providing employment to over 114,000 employees. There have been movements in recent times demanding a separate state of Telangana. To add to the sensitivity was the influence of the Naxalites who were wreaking havoc in the company. Given this background, the state and the union governments were compelled to act forcefully in working out a bailout package to save the company.

In 1992, in order to stabilise SCCL, a series of measures were taken. Equity holding was increased, debts were waived off and generous loans were extended to the company to revive its financial health. Some half-hearted administrative measures were also taken to improve discipline in the workforce and to enhance productivity. But the all-pervasive influence of the Naxalites did not allow the company to regain its financial health. In 1996, the company was again on the verge of collapse and was referred to the BIFR for the second time within a period of four years.

To provide a balanced perspective for the reasons contributing to the sickness of SCCL, I must briefly mention some key issues. It is a well-known fact that coal mining is an inherently risky and hazardous activity. The geological conditions of the Godavari valley coalfields are adverse. There are a large number of fault lines in the area. The quality of the coal is of low grade. Till 1974–1975, only underground mining was being done. Underground mining using traditional board and pillar methodology is risk-prone, labour-intensive and has low productivity. Being a PSU, the company was looked upon as an 'employment provider' in the backward Telangana districts of the state. The governments in power did not have the political will to take on over 103 trade unions, some of whom were backed by the militant SIKASA. Weak and confused political policies created a fertile breeding ground for SIKASA, which indulged in a virtual reign of terror in the coal-belt area. There was political interference in the management and very few Chief Executive Officers (CEOs) (the company is headed by a Chairman and Managing Director [CMD] belonging to the Indian Administrative Service [IAS], Andhra Pradesh cadre) were given a stable tenure.

In the beginning of 1997, the then Chief Minister (CM) of Andhra Pradesh, N. Chandra Babu Naidu, decided that the company should be reformed and restructured to make it vibrant once again. A series of bold and innovative measures were taken between 1997 and 2001, which brought about spectacular improvements in the company. 'Political will' is the most vital component in a democratic society. Unless the political executive is clear about its 'mission statement' it cannot provide leadership. To Naidu belongs the credit of providing bold and visionary leadership for the stunning turnaround of SCCL, from a company on the verge of collapse to emerging as a premier coal mining company in the country within six years.

Naidu selected A.P.V.N. Sarma as the CEO of SCCL. 'APVN', as he was popularly known, served as the CMD, SCCL, with great distinction and tremendous success from 1 January 1997 to 27 October 2001. He formulated policies with complete support of the state government. Extremely tough management decisions were taken for bringing out bold reforms. In 1998, elections for trade unions were held by the secret ballot method. This drastically reduced the number of trade unions and dramatically lowered the strike rates. Indiscipline in the workforce was firmly curbed but with a human touch. Generous incentives were given to reward productivity and result-oriented performance. Communications channels at different levels were activated leading to some rapport between the management and the workforce. Two individuals contributed immensely in streamlining the administration of the company. The first was Heeralal Samariya, a sincere and dynamic IAS Officer, who worked as the Director (Personnel and Administration) with A.P.V.N. Sarma. He was succeeded by an equally competent and hard-working officer, Dr G. Srinivas Ayyangar. Both Samariya and Ayyangar were full of sincerity, dedication and zeal. They provided invaluable support to the CEO in their sustained and systematic efforts to revive the company.

It was against this background that I succeeded APVN on 27 October 2001. I consider APVN as the architect of the turnaround of SCCL. I was lucky to inherit a well-managed system—thanks to the great work done by my predecessor, APVN, during his tenure.

The story that I am going to share—my experience of 60 months in SCCL—is a passionate story of romance with the Singareni people and their families. The fundamental objective of this experience sharing is to reinforce belief in certain higher principles, which govern our day-to-day life. What apparently seems to be insignificant plays miracles when embarked upon with a human touch. Despite all pervasive scepticism that engulfs us today, it is my firm belief that we can still strive with utter honesty and dedication in dispelling cynicism and help in transforming the society for the better. They say, 'God favours the prepared mind and bends the heavens to pave way towards success!' I have seen this happening. There are many experiences that I am unable to explain. As Lao Tzu says that there are certain occurrences on earth and in heavens that even a sage cannot explain.

What people call turnaround is a passionate story of my romance with Singareni and Singarenians! I call it 'Singareni Love Story—Management from the Heart!'

There are seven things that will destroy us: Wealth without work; Pleasure without conscience; Knowledge without character; Religion without sacrifice; Politics without principle; Science without humanity; Business without ethics.

—Mahatma Gandhi

(He was a politician, philosopher, freedom fighter and spiritual leader of India)

Source: Quoted in *Principle Centered Leadership* by Steven R. Covey

13 Reforms with a Human Touch—Management from the Heart

Within a couple of months after taking charge, the extremely challenging demands of working as the CEO of SCCL became palpably clear to me: I was heading an organisation with over 100,000 workforce; dealing with trade unions who were generally unyielding and hostile in their relationship with the management; the company had not yet come out of the red having accumulated losses in excess of ₹570 crore; the danger of Naxalites was ever present in threatening our workforce and in engineering strikes; and trying to come to terms with the grave technical uncertainties that characterise underground (coal mines).

Our senior management team comprising company directors decided that we should continue the process of institution building and reforms, which had commenced in 1997. We decided to evolve our 'vision–mission' framework for aligning company policies. Our first task was to analyse the most critical problems we had to tackle. We then undertook inter se prioritisation of issues.

In a highly complex and mammoth organisation of the size and scale of SCCL, problems are always aplenty. But we decided to go ahead with single-minded sense of purpose.

Here I want to share a unique technique commonly known as 'Eating Elephant'. You can always make use of this technique when you are bogged down with many problems. When you are confronted with many massive problems it is better to sit down and think calmly on how can you break them into issues and put them in some logical sequence, so that you can tackle them one by one. This technique worked out well. After having broken the massive problems into issues, we regrouped them giving them some identity. What seemed to be messy and unmanageable at first was no longer fuzzy. This exercise boosted our morale and gave us clarity.

We could give clarity to a blurred picture. Now we were in a position to see the problems at micro- and macro levels.

After conducting many exercises of brainstorming, or call them brain stilling (though we did not use these terminologies), our senior team came to a conclusion and we decided to look at the problem from three angles—(a) modernisation, (b) upgradation of mining technology and (c) focus on underground mining.

Having decided upon the critical areas for improvement, we thought of evolving certain strategies to deal with them. The first thing that came forward was the need to further improve the communication channels for better industrial relations. Communication was also a felt need to reach people and their families. One thought that is deeply engraved in my mind is Victor Frankl's remark, 'Love is the only way to grasp another human being in the immense core of his personality!' Management from the heart demands reaching the heart of the people. Again the needle came back to the need for communication channels. The introduction and consolidation of environmentally sustainable coal mining practices was another major issue that attracted our attention. And the third strategic area that we identified was 'restructuring'. It was highly desirable to formulate strategies not for one-time restructuring but as an ongoing activity. Continued restructuring and introducing reforms in collaboration with officers and workforce became our major strategy.

I organised a series of creative, transparent and honest brainstorming sessions involving senior executives of the company. Officers from all levels were involved in this exercise, starting from mine managers to personnel in the higher levels of the hierarchy. In my first meeting with senior level executives, I introduced the concept of 'scriptwriting'. I told the executives that each one of them should imagine that he has been appointed as the CEO of the company and asked them to draw out a strategic plan based on his long years of experience suggesting, 'how to turnaround the company!' This was something very novel for the company executives. After some initial hesitation, many of them came out with pragmatic and good suggestions for improving the company. During this meeting, I emphasised that my personal mission statement was to continue with the wonderful work done by my predecessor. I made it clear that I would acknowledge, appreciate and reward sincerity, integrity and dedicated service. I would always be open to good suggestions from all quarters. I would not follow the rigid hierarchy in my interface with my colleagues, and they should be free to help me with their good ideas at all times.

My initial interaction with the executives generated its customary sense of doubt and mild cynicism. Many executives thought that every new CMD starts with the same platitudes and comes with Another Fine Programme (AFP)! This initial syndrome, 'we have seen it before also' did not deter me from pursuing my colleagues in their scriptwriting. After sometime, I started receiving extremely good ideas cutting across different disciplines in the company.

I then sat down with my directors and we formulated our vision–mission statement as follows:

> We would strive to become the best coal company in the country. We would adopt best global practices in coal mining. We would overcome all challenges and odds confronting us by team work and team spirit. We would try to restore to Mother Earth what we were remorselessly and relentlessly extracting from Her. We would make our workers as partners in progress by giving them *stakeholdership* in the Company's working and growth.

Vision statements are meant as motivators for inspiring organisations who have to then define their mission in more specific terms.

The mission is subsequently broken into achievable milestones within a specified timeframe. The vision statement must always aim for the stars. It should be idealistic and lofty and brighten up the team whenever it is surrounded by despair and gloom. At the same time, a vision statement should not be mere jugglery of words and a vague cocktail of ideas. It has to be grounded in reality and it has to be implemented pragmatically.

These were some of the guiding principles that helped us in formulating our mission statement. Our mission statement is based on the following key foundations:

> Adopt the best global benchmark practices in respect of mining and allied activities. To break the strike-oriented work culture and replace it with a culture based on self-belief of all workers.

To promote self-belief not merely by giving attractive slogans, but by pursuing hardheaded and logical annual action plans which would promote our overall objectives for growth.

It is relatively easy to frame ambitious objectives. But it is extremely challenging to execute what appear to be perfectly logical and practical programmes. Our senior management team wholeheartedly plunged itself into giving a practical framework to our vision–mission statement. From the very beginning, I was clear that a gigantic organisation like SCCL had to work in a transparent and equity-promoting mode. I encouraged all senior executives to shed their inhibitions and involve middle and junior level company officers in the decision-making process. The idea was to unleash the creative potential, which all individuals possess but are often afraid to utilise. The fear of ridicule in case of failure acts as a great deterrent to human beings attempting innovative solutions to nagging problems.

Coal mining industry in India is unique in many ways. It has a distinctive culture and like any other culture it has its positive and negative points. Amongst the positives is a strong spirit of fraternalism. Coal miners generally bond well with one another. This is due to the difficult situations in which they work. On the negative side, there is a strong sense of conservatism and a rigid hierarchical approach. Junior level managers rarely share their free and frank thoughts with senior level managers. This is one of the factors that contribute to lack of major improvements in mining practices in our country.

Our attempt was to gradually whittle down the hierarchical rigidity and promote junior level executives to give their ideas based on their experiences to the senior level management. For achieving this objective, I encouraged the practice of scriptwriting amongst the middle and junior management also. Understandably this took time. However, slowly but steadily we witnessed a substantial improvement in the quality of communications and good ideas started flowing in from all directions.

It is of paramount importance that the process of change management is slow and steady. High-speed changes often generate adverse responses, as majority of the people involved do not get adequate time to appreciate the change process. I encouraged our senior management team not to act with undue haste in the process of change making. We decided that reasonable time would be given so that people could adapt to the new realities. In hindsight, I feel that this was the correct approach as it yielded positive results.

I would not like to spell in greater detail a vast number of reforms that we undertook for transforming our company into a more efficient organisation. Instead, I would like to essentially dwell upon the human aspects of transformation—which my co-author, Moid, calls 'soft track'. Our emphasis was to avoid, to the maximum extent possible, human suffering while undertaking reforms. Our slogan was 'Reforms with a Human Touch—Management from the Heart'.

'Downsizing', 'rightsizing' and 'optimising workforce' are modern-day management *mantra*s. The challenge confronting us was rightsizing the organisation while simultaneously minimising human suffering. At the peak of its loss-making regime the workforce in SCCL was nearly 117,000 employees. This was in 1991–1992 when coal production was 20.51 million tonne.

The average earning of a worker per shift was meagre ₹151. When the company was referred to Board for Industrial and Financial Reconstruction (BIFR) in 1992 and again in 1996, reducing the workforce was one of the obvious and painful requirements. It took many years for the workers and the trade union representatives to realise that it was possible to reduce manpower in a humane manner. Vast efforts went into communication campaigns, which commenced in 1998, to convince the workers that unless redundancy is reduced the company would ultimately collapse.

I must acknowledge my intense admiration for the wonderful work done in this very effective communication exercise by A.P.V.N. Sarma, Heeralal Samariya, G.S.G. Ayyangar and others. In 2000, a Voluntary Retirement Scheme (VRS) was launched. After 2002, it was extended annually to the workforce. The 'Golden Handshake' package was an extremely generous offer. The minimum compensation package for a worker accepting VRS was ₹1,000,000 along with other benefits as well. The company management counselled the workers and their families for proper utilisation of the compensation received. Special attention was given to the spouses of the workers who were encouraged to avoid wasteful expenditure. Singareni Collieries Company Limited has extremely robust and efficient running voluntary organisations in its fold. These include Singareni Seva Samithi (SSS) and Singareni Employees Wives Association (SEWA). Both SSS and SEWA played an active role in providing a social safety net to employees availing VRS. Some studies conducted in the recent past have shown that workers who availed VRS are quite satisfied and happy. I consider this as a great success story because nearly 15,000 company employees availed VRS between 2000 and 2006.

After the commencement of the VRS scheme in 2000, we made constant efforts to refine the planning and execution of the scheme. We kept learning from our mistakes and shortcomings, and tried our best to constructively utilise the feedback that we got from our workforce. One key element of our strategy was to fully involve the trade unions in this exercise. After 1998, a system of company-level recognised union was adopted. At the area level if a trade union got majority votes, but it did not get overall majority at the company level, then it was given the status of representative union in that particular area. Thus, we had a two-tier union representative system.

We find this system working quiet smoothly, as it has withstood the test of time successfully.

We follow a structured system for periodic interface between the management and the unions at different hierarchical levels. At the bottom of the pyramid there are monthly meetings at the mine level with the local trade unions. At the second level, there are area-level meetings with the General Manager of the respective area. At the third tier, there are bi-monthly meetings with the Director (Personnel and Administration) and the company-level recognised unions. At the highest level, there are quarterly meetings with the CMD, the directors representing the management and the recognised trade union. The CMD also conducts quarterly meetings with representatives of all recognised and representative trade unions. These meetings are called Joint Consultative Committees.

After the path-breaking decision to hold elections to the trade union in 1998, the company management adopted the 'Code of Discipline'. This is a morally binding document also having certain legal implications. It provided an opportunity to institutionalise the relationship between the trade unions and the management. Initially elections were held for a term of two years. Later in 2003, the term of elected unions was extended to four years. The regional labour commissioner (Government of India) supervises the conduct of these elections. After the declaration of results, formal orders are issued by the company management according recognised status to the union which commands the majority. Whenever formal negotiations are held a Memorandum of Settlement (MoS) is signed. It is the responsibility of the regional labour commissioner to supervise the negotiations and get the agreements signed.

The decision to hold elections based on secret ballot is unparalleled in the history of Indian coal mining industry. The credit of adopting this novel and highly successful method goes to SCCL. Whenever the management wants to undertake sensitive changes, this institutional framework provides an effective mechanism for conflict resolution. From 1997 onwards, when the company embarked on massive reforms and restructuring, the management invariably took the trade unions into confidence. I must clarify that by 'confidence' I do not mean concurrence of the unions. It also does not mean that the unions extended their support to all key management decisions. On many occasions, the unions organised major company level strikes which lead to stalling or delaying of vital reforms.

Despite the drawbacks, which are inherent in management–union relationships in large organisations, I must record with great satisfaction that the code of discipline has been a great success in SCCL. We utilised the trade union platform while advocating the VRS scheme in the company. After initial resistance by the trade unions, to our pleasant surprise, they turned supporters of the scheme. During 2004 and 2005 the trade unions were pressing us to increase the coverage of the scheme. I recall having some interesting conversations with the representatives of the recognised trade unions on this subject. They said that the workers were very happy with the scheme and they were supporting the scheme because of its outstanding success. Management gurus can deduce interesting results if a detailed study is made of the VRS schemes implemented by us. In fact, the smooth implementation of our scheme became a source not only of inspiration but also of envy to other public sector undertakings (PSUs) in the state.

A striking feature during implementation of the scheme was the absence of political interference from Members of Parliament (MPs) and Members of Legislative Assembly (MLAs). This is of great significance given the way our democratic polity functions. But another unpleasant truth is that in the majority of cases trade unions get underhand payment from workers for including their names in schemes which give them individual benefits. The absence of political interference in the formulation and implementation of our VRS scheme is a splendid success story in SCCL.

I entirely agree with the old adage, 'Man does not live on bread alone.' I would like to add that giant organisations like SCCL do not live on wages and material comforts alone. The human touch is the most vital ingredient for promoting a sense of wholesomeness and contentment. The PSUs in our country are considered as avenues that provide employment. The motive of the workforce is on furthering their own interests. They usually demand higher wages and more infrastructural facilities—without committing themselves to higher levels of productivity. This invariably leads to conflicts between the management and the workforce. After nationalisation of the coal mining industry in India in 1973–1974, Coal India Limited (CIL) was formed in 1974–1975. The workforce of CIL was the largest in the Indian public sector, next only to Indian Railways. The management–workers relationships were difficult to handle and strikes were common.

During the late 1980s and early 1990s, SCCL attained the dubious distinction of having a large number of strikes for four years successively. Between 1989 and 1992, the average number of strikes in the company was in excess of 400 per annum. A record was created in 1991–1992 when 475 strikes took place. It was only after the reform process was initiated in 1997 that the situation started improving steadily. I have provided data in Annexures I–III about the profile, performance and welfare measures of SCCL before and after the reforms.

In my initial days in the company, I was very keen to understand why SCCL was such a strike-prone organisation. I spent long hours consulting colleagues at different levels. I interacted extensively with representatives of different trade unions. I had long conversations with my illustrious predecessor, A.P.V.N. Sarma. I picked upon the brains of G. Srinivas Ayyangar, who was then serving as Director (Personnel and Administration). I spoke to a wide cross-section of people who were familiar with SCCL. Slowly but surely, the realisation dawned on me that one of the primary reasons for trade unions instigating strikes was that the management was portrayed in negative light. In Chapter 15—'The Magic of Communication'—I have dwelt upon in detail on our communication strategy for promoting the philosophy of Singarenism, which contributed vastly in improving the relationship between the management and the workers. Here I would like to mention a few examples which dispelled the notion that management was hostile to the workers and was interested only in increasing the company's profits.

The total workforce of Singareni exceeded 100,000 when I assumed charge in October 2001. During my initial orientation exercises, I realised that nearly 90 per cent of the active workforce engaged in coal mining operations was working in underground mines. I asked our senior management to give some good ideas for positively influencing the underground workers. I must mention here that our underground workers endure great hardships. Their working conditions are exceedingly demanding and danger is always lurking round the corner in many forms. At the end of an eight-hour shift the worker is drained both physically and emotionally. Due to the relatively lower productivity of underground mining, the wage packet of these workers is substantially less as compared to their brethren working in opencast operations in far more congenial work environment. Hence, it can be understandable why underground workers are victims of depression, alcoholism and often disruptive family life. Their health suffers because of the tedious working conditions and they develop backache and other ailments.

Despite this, I was deeply touched to see the inherent optimism, sincerity and dedication of our underground workers when I inspected the mines. I promised myself that I would try my best to improve their working conditions. After all our underground workers constitute the backbone of coal mining operations in SCCL.

After extensive consultation with my colleagues we decided to undertake various measures to improve the working conditions in the underground mines. We invested substantial amounts in improving the condition of man-ways and haul-ways. We also improved the ventilation in the mines. Strict instructions were given to maintain the prescribed moisture levels. The drinking water and toilet amenities in the mines were improved as well. The resting areas were given a facelift. The felt needs of our workers determined enhancement of infrastructural facilities. The workers responded with enthusiasm to the improvements in their working environment, and their morale went up by several notches.

One of the most difficult aspects of working in underground mines is the long distances to be walked for reaching the workplace.

A majority of our underground mines have steep gradients involving walks ranging from a minimum of 2 kilometres up to 7 kilometres. Imagine a worker in an underground mine having to walk for 14 kilometre simply to reach his workplace! What would be the motivation level of an individual in such circumstances? It is not surprising that all underground mines were running in losses. We were frequently receiving requests from workers to get transferred to surface jobs. Many applications were genuine as there were medical reasons. The sheer drudgery and tediousness of working in underground conditions is counterproductive to leading a contended and pleasant life.

We decided that we have to reduce the strain and stress of working in underground mines by installing man-riding systems. There are two types of systems in use in our mines. They are called chairlift type and rail type. We launched a massive drive to identify mines where the workers' fatigue was maximum. Other factors taken into consideration included the life of the mine, quality of coal and safety-related parameters. A systematic campaign was then launched calling for tenders for installation of man-riding systems.

In October 2001 when I joined SCCL, there were only eight mines having man-riding systems. In September 2006 when I left SCCL, there were 35 mines with man-riding facilities. I call this a 'mini revolution' in underground mining in India. The numbers assume greater significance when they are contrasted with CIL mines. In SCCL out of 47 underground mines, 35 mines have man-riding systems whereas in CIL out of nearly 315 mines not more than 15 have this facility. The provision of man-riding systems within a short span of five years proved inspirational for our underground miners. It would not be an exaggeration to say that this single welfare-oriented initiative has generated tremendous goodwill for the top-level management. It had effectively countered negative and often baseless propaganda of trade unions, who loved to project themselves as workers' saviours pitted against a dehumanised and money-centric management. The spirit of Singarenism has its deep roots in man-riding facilities for underground workers.

I recount an anecdote regarding this initiative. Sometime in 2005, one of the chairpersons of a Coal India subsidiary, V.K. Singh of Northern Coal Fields Company Limited, visited SCCL. He went around and saw different facilities. On his return from the coalfields, we had a discussion in my corporate office in Singareni Bhavan, Hyderabad. While narrating his impressions and experiences Mr Singh commented:

> Khwaja Saheb, I must tell you that I am thoroughly impressed by the enthusiasm, commitment and morale of your underground workers in the field. What particularly impressed me is the high awareness level of the underground workers. In one voice they all expressed their happiness and gratitude to the management in reducing their work drudgery by installing man-riding facilities. I am determined to impress upon my colleagues in CIL to emulate the example of Singareni.

The genuineness and the passion with which Singh made this observation further reinforced my commitment to pursuing more welfare-centric policies for the workers in the company. Genuine compliments like these are worth living for. They not only make your day but also inspire you to work even harder for attaining your personal objectives in life. Anne Frank observes:

> Then, without realizing it, you try to improve yourself at the start of each new day; of course, you achieve quite a lot in the course of time. Anyone can do this, it costs nothing and is certainly very helpful. Whoever doesn't know it must learn and find by experience that a quiet conscience makes one strong. (As quoted in *Manners do Matter*)

It appears as if she had written these beautiful lines to draw this chapter to conclusion.

Yes, my 'quiet conscience' was making me stronger. I could feel that. My enthusiasm was getting renewed with each cockcrow. I felt a strange soothing effect in my heart and a new happiness which was until now unknown to me.

Though negotiations are a rough game, you should never allow them to become a dirty game. Once you've agreed to a deal, don't back out of it unless the other party fails to deliver as promised. Your handshake is your bond. As far as I'm concerned, a handshake is worth more than a signed contract. As an entrepreneur, a reputation for integrity is your most valuable commodity. If you try to put something over on someone, it will come back to haunt you.

—Victor K. Kiam

(He was a renowned American entrepreneur,
who was known for his ethical values)

Source: Live to Win: Achieving Success in Life and Business

14 The Power of 'Bonding'—Singarenism

I always believe that the key to human happiness is to unlock the intrinsic quality of humanism, which we all possess. As I have journeyed in life experiencing the good, the bad and the ugly, my belief in upholding the principles of honesty, transparency and sincerity is being renewed constantly. I am irrevocably committed to the concept of every individual being fully responsible for his/her actions. Most of us are tiny specs on the sands of time. Where and when the wind will blow us away, no one knows. I sincerely and passionately believe in 'Indianness'. My definition of Indianness is respecting pluralism in all its multi-hued colours. I do not subscribe to a way of thinking that promotes 'exclusivism' in any form. With all our civilisational weaknesses and problems, I consider Indian society to be one of the most cosmopolitan and tolerant ones in the world. Narrow-mindedness, bigotry and a clannish mentality are anathema to me. My intellectual development has been deeply influenced by my cultural background where we were taught to respect people for their actions, and not to like or dislike people because of their religion, caste, language or other such chauvinistic considerations. The name, Rajen Habib Khwaja, given to me by my parents epitomises this philosophical background.

I have very briefly stated my fundamental value system as it is indelibly linked to the philosophy of Singarenism, which I have tried my best to conceive and promote. I have sublime satisfaction that in a relatively short period of five years, Singarenism has become a mighty force in the organisation. In this chapter, I will share how Singarenism was developed.

It struck me as very odd that even though Singareni Collieries Company Limited (SCCL) was in existence since 1886 and the name 'Singareni Collieries Company' was adopted on 23 December 1920, nobody in the organisation had thought of calling members of the Singareni family as 'Singarenians'. Upon making enquiries, I was offered very interesting explanations for the absence of the term 'Singarenian'. The most common (and truthful) explanation was that any recognition or identity with a 'loss-making company', which lacks team spirit and feeling of belongingness, would not inspire people. They prefer not to be recognised with that identity. For this reason, most employees used to avoid telling others that they worked in SCCL, as the outsiders use to recognise SCCL as 'Strike Collieries Company Limited'. The morale of the employees was at the lowest ebb when the company was referred twice to Board for Industrial and Financial Reconstruction (BIFR) in the early 1990s. I was also told that there was an undercurrent of caste feelings and regional feelings which prevented genuine bonding amongst the employees.

I was now determined more than ever before to experiment promoting my personal value system based on honesty, transparency and justice on the Singareni family. I thought this was a unique opportunity given to me to demonstrate that the need of the hour is to promote 'Indianness' in our society. Traditionally, SCCL has been a 'CMD-centric' organisation. I had nothing to lose by boldly injecting liberal doses of a value-based system.

The first thought which came to my mind was that we should promote the concept of 'One Family, One Vision, One Mission'. I consulted my senior colleagues and asked them to suggest ideas which would contribute to building a feeling of belongingness to the company. One of the first decisions that we took was to coin the term 'Singarenian'. My colleagues enthusiastically supported this idea. I started referring to our employees as Singarenians sometime from mid-2002 onwards. I was delighted when this term started becoming popular with great rapidity. Today, all members of the Singareni family take great pride in calling themselves Singarenians.

With the passage of time and by constant observation of the working ethos of the company, I decided to expand the term 'Singarenian' and to evolve a way of thinking and living which we decided to call 'Singarenism'. The underlying philosophy of Singarenism is promoting the concept that unless all of us bond together we will not be contributing our full potential to the organisation. Historically, SCCL has attracted people from all parts of the country. In addition to people from the state of Andhra Pradesh, we have officers at junior level, middle level and even senior levels from places as far away as Bihar, Punjab, Jammu and Kashmir, and West Bengal. I was keen to combine my concept of 'Indianness' with Singarenism.

In order to effectively communicate with all members of the Singareni family, we adopted different modalities. These included bringing out a newsletter called 'Singareni Samacharam'; letters from the CMD addressed to all workers in the company; telefilms produced in the company and widely exhibited in all coal mining areas; and bringing out monthly coloured posters depicting important events and activities. The theme of 'One Family, One Vision, One Mission—the Spirit of Singareni' was directly as well as subtly conveyed through our creative and extremely effective media campaign. I was privileged to have extremely brilliant and dedicated colleagues helping me in realising my dream. I must specially mention Dr T.R.K. Rao, S. Chandrasekhar and Ghana Sankar Pujari. All these persons were the fountainheads of creativity producing high-quality telefilms, composition and recording of Singareni Geetham (Singareni song), and in promoting local folk arts like *Burrakatha* and *Oggu katha*.

As an Indian, I have always taken great pride in the multicultural and pluralistic civilisational values that we practise. It is no coincidence that our country is the birthplace of great religious traditions and inspirational thought systems. Religious tolerance has been the hallmark of Indian culture. It causes me unbounded anguish when I find narrow-minded elements promoting bigotry and intolerance in our country. Despite our history of respect for different cultures, in recent times we have not exhibited the requisite degree of discernment in responding to parochial and self-serving viewpoints aggressively promoted by some vested interests. I am alluding to the unfortunate outbreak of discriminatory behaviour our society is witnessing owing to religion and caste fanaticism.

My basic objective in promoting the concept of 'One Family, One Vision, One Mission' is to negate this line of thinking. I wanted to emphasise the great diversity of the Singareni family. I wanted my colleagues to consider Singareni as a microcosm of Indian society, where we had a workforce of over hundred thousand. We had people from all castes, communities, regions and religions. I wanted 'emotional bonding' to take place. I wanted all of us to think and act as members of a single family.

The principles of Singarenism are embedded in high moral values. I was keen that we are honest and transparent in our interaction with one another. I wanted the dark clouds of negative thoughts to be taken away by the strong winds of fair play and equity. As Indians, we are habituated to look up to our seniors as role models. I urged all senior executives to first practise what we were attempting to preach. I pointed out our national weakness of rarely acknowledging our faults and weaknesses but promptly pointing out the mistakes of others. As the old saying goes, 'Physician, heal thyself', I motivated our senior colleagues to lead by example following this inspirational message. I was very clear that pious appeals without being supported by correct actions would not yield the desired results.

Human behaviour is highly complex, multi-dimensional and often unpredictable. Motivational theories often flounder when impacted by harsh ground realities. I have always believed in the directness of approach complimented by 'practising' and not 'preaching'. In Singareni, I had the rare opportunity of experimenting with some ideas I have very sincerely believed in. I was convinced that if the top management led by personal example then the vast majority of Singarenians would not be found wanting in imbibing a value system grounded in the philosophy of Singarenism.

As I look back, I am enveloped by a warm glow of contentment as Singarenism is a vibrant and constantly evolving way of life. Readers may consider the statement to be an exaggeration. They may snidely remark that 'Khwaja, like a narcissist, suffers from "I syndrome". He is indulging in pompous self-praise.' I would like to say with utter humility that mercifully I am not yet a victim of self-delusion. Knowledgeable visitors to Singareni never cease in expressing their astonishment in the change of mindset of the Singarenian in less than half a decade. Let me narrate some specific instances to buttress this statement.

In July 2006, a team of very senior managers of TATA Coffee visited our coal belt areas. The team members were specialists in evaluating corporate social responsibility. After extensive visits and detailed interaction at different levels, the team leader, K.N. Changappa, expressed his amazement about the very high morale and feeling of well-being in the Singareni employees. He was particularly impressed by the fact that all the persons with whom the team interacted always referred to themselves as 'Singarenians'. They were all aware of the path-breaking and zealously implemented principles like 'One for All—All for One' and 'One Family, One Vision, One Mission—the Spirit of Singareni'. All of them liked Singareni song and many of them remembered its lyrics too. When enquired about the relationship between management and workers, most employees spoke highly of the wide range of welfare measures being implemented in the company. Mrs Ganga Changappa, an expert in dealing with differently enabled persons, was equally generous in her appreciation of the work being done by spouses of Singareni workers. She mentioned about her visit to Manochaitanya in Ramagundam area where Krishna Kumar and his dedicated team are doing wonderful work in serving handicapped children.

My distinguished co-author, Moid Siddiqui, has been lavish in his appreciation of what he calls 'the Pygmalion effect in Singareni'.

I cannot match Moid in his fluency of expression, but the phrase coined by him is a great source of strength and satisfaction to me in my occasional moments of despair. Moid speaks and writes about 'The lovebird in the green pastures of Singareni'. He used this terminology while addressing the top-level management team in a one-day retreat organised at the enticing Alankrita Resort on 26 August 2006. He mentioned that earlier he used to dread visiting the barren sand traps of Singareni. He now loves the green pastures of Singareni.

A team of Germans from WIRTH Company sent us an e-mail in December 2004. They wrote about the enchanting environment, gardens and parks of Kothagudem, and the emphasis on the quality of living which they experienced during their stay. They simultaneously appreciated the professionalism of our colleagues while discussing the subject of rescue drill rig.

My main objective in recounting the three incidents is to highlight the fact that they come from independent sources who are highly knowledgeable in their respective domain areas. We received equally encouraging and supporting appreciation from the coal mining fraternity. Distinguished persons like P.C. Parakh, former Union Coal Secretary; Mr Abhiram Sharma, CMD of Mahanadi Coal Fields Limited and Mr B. Bhattacharjee, Director General of Mine Safety (who passed away in a tragic accident in December 2006) visited SCCL, and were generous in their appreciation.

From 2003 onwards, the concept of Singarenism started taking firm roots. Full credit goes to my senior management team. I must specially mention Mr P. Vasudeva Rao who retired as Director, Operations in September 2006. Rao is one of the most competent and distinguished mining engineers in the country and an exceptionally good human being. These are rare qualities. Rao, ably assisted by other equally efficient and talented colleagues, played a key role in 'walking the talk'. With his impeccable ethical conduct coupled with his technical brilliance, Rao motivated and inspired his team to bond together and since he was highly respected he got excellent support.

We got great ideas from T.R.K. Rao, G. Srinivas Ayyangar, D.L.R. Prasad and S. Chandrasekhar. But having great ideas is not enough. It is vital to implement them effectively. I would like to share some important initiatives, which promoted bonding in the organisation.

We decided that there should be a 'company anthem'. All Singarenians should learn the company anthem, which we called 'Singareni Geetham'. This song melodiously rendered by the famous singer, S.P. Balasubrahmanyam, was recorded in 2003. Unless one hears this song one cannot realise its hypnotic power. The song has become an integral part of the make-up of Singareni. It is played in all offices and in mines on a regular basis. Many workers know the song by the heart. The song is a personal favourite of mine. It never fails to lift my drooping spirits. I consider the introduction of Singareni song as a great success story in promoting team spirit, bonding and Singarenism.

On 5 March 2004, I dedicated the Singareni arch at the entrance of the bungalow area in Kothagudem. It has now become a symbol of Singareni's stunning turnaround in 2002–2003 and reflects the sacrifices made, determination shown and stupendous hard work put in by Singarenians in the company. I thought that a fitting symbol to the spirit of Singareni characterised by its indomitable spirit should mark the momentous occasion of the company paying dividend after 37 years. The Singareni arch reflects local Kakatiya period architectural style. Today, it stands as a dignified yet imposing symbol of Singarenism. The arch has come to symbolise the company's indefatigable spirit.

In December 2003, the company paid dividend to Government of Andhra Pradesh and the Government of India after a long gap of 37 years. We thought that we must have a symbol that reflects our credo of 'One Family, One Vision, One Mission'. Throughout history, humankind has constructed imposing gateways, forts, palaces and arches as symbols of civilisational values and achievements. Our objective in constructing the Singareni arch was far simpler. We do not believe in grandeur and show. But we certainly believe in modesty and humility. Both these virtues do not preclude us from construction of a simple but attractive arch. The plaque on the arch has a powerful invocation, which is reproduced below:

> Dedicated to all 'Singarenians' who have served the company with utmost zeal, total devotion and sustained hard work enabling the company to achieve a stunning turnaround and enter net profit regime after 27 years in 2003—Inaugurated by Shri R.H. Khwaja, IAS, on 5 March 2004.

Later we decided to construct a similar arch at the entrance of the bungalow area in Ramagundam, which was dedicated to Singarenians in March 2006. The plaque on this arch is equally inspirational which reads as follows:

> The spirit of Singareni: 'One Family—One Vision—One Mission'. No institutional journey is ever complete and no success is forever. This is the basic *mantra* which motivates and inspires SCCL as it marches forward in its journey to emerge as the premier coal producing company in the country. Destiny beckons all Singarenians to once again rededicate themselves to work with exemplary zeal and complete sincerity in contributing to the growth and prosperity of the company. The strength of the Singareni—our people, our environment and our indomitable spirit.

Moid Siddiqui, who served corporate India on senior and board level positions, is widely respected as a management guru. He has written about 'hard track' and 'soft track' of management in the first part of this book. The evolution of the concept of being a Singarenian and a practitioner of Singarenism falls in the category of soft track management practices. It never ceases to disappoint me as to how many people adopt contradictory and confused approaches in the management of change. It is extremely popular to hire professional consultants who study the organisation and submit bulky reports. Such consultants very rarely utilise the great storehouse of information, experience and knowledge that insiders working in the organisation possess. The organisation that commissions such studies is overawed by the reputation of their external consultants. It is common knowledge that many organisations have come to grief while thoughtlessly implementing the advice of experts.

One of our abiding strengths in SCCL was our ability to effectively tap the expertise available within our organisation. The constant encouragement given at all levels for making constructive suggestions, the transparency in our management policies, the system of liberal awards for meritorious work and the constant dialogue with all employees at different levels immensely contributed to our reforms process. Thanks to the constant and effective communication policies, there was a significant reduction in communication gaps between the management and the workers. We were vigilant in immediately combating any disinformation campaign engineered by vested interests. Within two to three years, the belief gained wide currency that the top management of the company was extremely tough, but transparently fair in settling problems and grievances of executives and workers. After all, trust is the cornerstone of the edifice of human relations. You cannot win trust by being hypocritical and contradictory. One has to take the difficult and less travelled road of implementing high moral values and ethical principles.

With a workforce of over 100,000, it was vital that genuine grievances of workers and executives are speedily redressed. How can employees regard themselves as members of one family unless their problems are resolved and difficulties understood? We made constant efforts to streamline our personnel management system. The major credit goes to the trio of Heeralal Samariya, G. Srinivasa Ayyangar and Sriram Taranikanti who worked in that order as Directors (Personnel and Administration) in SCCL during the crucial turnaround years. These three gentlemen selflessly and sincerely developed systems which became institutionalised with the passage of time and greatly contributed to good man-management practices in the organisation.

Emotional and psychological feelings are basic foundations of bonding. We cannot force people to 'feel good'. Ground realities have to create an environment where people start 'feeling good'. All human situations are inherently dynamic. What works at a given point in time, may not work at another time even though the group is the same. Our emphasis was always on keeping our eyes and ears in constant touch with ground realities. Whenever we perceived that certain issues were creating resentment in the workforce, we speedily acted to resolve them. In many cases, we did not agree with the viewpoint of our executives or workers, as the case may be. However, even in complex and difficult situations we were generally able to convince our colleagues to see reason. The relationship of trust, which evolved over a period of time, constitutes a vital backbone of the bonding process and the acceptance of Singarenism as a way of life.

Many moves, initiatives and strategies were carried out, but if I am required to identify the cardinal one, I would say, it was 'corporate bonding', which made things happen. Having said about bonding let me share with you the process of 'bonding'.

Corporate bonding can be created at four levels—physical, intellectual, emotional and spiritual. All these levels are significant in our life. As they say, 'A hungry man listens to the music through his stomach!' Unless the physical needs of people are taken care of, they cannot, or rather will not, respond to any moves that serve to their intellectual needs. You cannot create a learning organisation when people's basic needs are not fully satisfied. Corporate bonding at emotional and spiritual levels cannot be created unless and until the physical and intellectual needs of people are adequately satisfied. This wisdom led to success. It took time, but we could create corporate bonding which led to many other successes.

When you conduct management using the heart, no specific strategies are needed. Just listen to the whispers of your conscience and move ahead. The 'man in the mirror' never tells a lie. Trust him. I trusted him and got results. The purpose of telling you this love story is to give you confidence in the softer aspects. It is the 'intangible' that gets you 'tangible' results. Take care of the softer aspects, things will move better. Allow your heart to lead, if not always, mostly!

It takes time to grow in trust—trust gets you the goodwill. Goodwill of your people is the greatest intangible asset. Admiral

James B. Stockdale, one of the most highly decorated officers in the history of the United States Navy, said:

> Leadership must be based on goodwill. Goodwill does not mean posturing and, least of all, pandering to the mob. It means obvious and wholehearted commitment to helping followers. We are tired of leaders we fear, tired of leaders we love and tired of leaders who let us take liberties with them. What we need for leaders are men of the heart who are so helpful that they, in effect, do away with the need of their jobs. But leaders like that are never out of a job, never out of followers. Strange as it sounds, great leaders gain authority by giving it away.
>
> (*Quotes of Leadership*)

Without credible communication, and a lot of it, the hearts and minds of others are never captured.

—John P. Kotter

(Former Professor of Harvard Business School)

Source: Leading Change authored by him

The Magic of Communication 15

My predecessor, A.P.V.N. Sarma, was a bold and visionary leader. Early in his tenure, he realised the huge importance of using innovative strategies for improving communications between management and workforce. In January 1997, when he assumed charge as chairman and managing director (CMD), the total employees in the company was over 114,000. Imagine the magnitude of the challenge: mines stretching for over 400 kilometres from north to south covering four districts and 512 categories of employees working in 34 departments. It is impossible for the chief executive officer (CEO) to visit each and every establishment of the company and to personally communicate with his workforce. Such a void was haunting! The lack of effective communication gives rise to grapevine. Once it is scotched, it is not easier to control or counter.

Sarma decided to introduce new methods of communications. He started writing letters addressed separately to the executives and to the workers at periodic intervals. The contents of the letters were simple. He not only shared the serious problems and issues the company was facing but also shared the efforts of the management to resolve them. This was a masterstroke by him. Combined with a concerted drive to increase the literacy level of the workers the CMD's thoughts started directly impacting the workers. The false and baseless propaganda commonly indulged in by some trade unions stood exposed. From time to time pamphlets were published, countering disinformation or rumours, which certain trade unions were floating in the company for grinding their own axes.

The dormant system of organising mine-level grievance resolutions meetings, called 'MINE SADASSU', was activated. Srinivasa Ayyangar (director, Personnel and Administration) played an important part in improving the quality and content of communications at cutting-edge levels with the workers. Many pressing problems of the workmen were resolved in the mine-level discussions. Relatively simple issues like poor quality of food in the company canteen, lack of hygienic toilets, delays in disbursement of special incentives, lack of proper ventilation in underground mines and personal problems of some workers were resolved in these meetings. Gradually the morale of the workforce improved and the credibility of the management soared.

I have always believed that good-quality communication is the key to success in life. Most problems arise either due to lack of communication, poor quality of communication, miscommunication, or wrong communication. I quickly realised that in a mammoth organisation like Singareni Collieries Company Limited (SCCL), communication will be vitally important. We then undertook a series of steps, which further reinforced the excellent initiatives, which commenced during Sarma's time. I encouraged all colleagues to come up with ideas, which could be practically implemented in field conditions for presenting the correct facts to the workforce.

One of our primary concerns was the palpably false propaganda of Singareni Karmika Samakya (SIKASA) and other extreme left-oriented trade unions. Without going into the polemics of any ideology, I have no hesitation in stating that the Naxalites and their front organisations caused the greatest damage to SCCL for many decades. One can understand exaggerations and half-truths, but blatant falsehoods cannot be accepted. The crux of extreme ideology which SIKASA propagated in the company was that the management was always harming the interests of the workers. The extremists took advantage of the simplicity of the workers and their lack of awareness. Till mid-1990s, the literacy levels amongst workers were poor. Partly out of fear and ignorance, the workers were forced into a strike culture with devastating consequences for the company and for themselves. At the peak of Naxalism in SCCL, strikes were organised at mine level without any advance notice but merely by oral commands of SIKASA activists. Violence was common. Two senior level officers were kidnapped, tortured and killed. Six workers, including some trade union leaders, were also brutally exterminated. This occurred between 1988 and 1994.

Our think-tank was sensitive to ground realities of countering the grave challenges posed by extremists in the company. We came out with some novel and innovative ideas which, in retrospect, have proved to be very successful in weaning away workers from extremist influence. I would like to mention some of our most successful initiatives.

Keeping in mind the trend of the times, we gave much emphasis to audio–visual media. We were lucky to have an exceptionally talented and creative artist in our company—Gana Sankar Pujari. He is a great actor and scriptwriter. He combined these qualities with undiluted sincerity and inspirational energy levels. We made T.R.K. Rao (Executive Director, Marketing and Movement) in-charge of our Public Relations Department in addition to his normal duties. TRK is a multi-faceted genius. Within a short span of time, he displayed amazing creativity, skill and energy in galvanising our Public Relations Department to new heights of creative activities. In 2002, a bimonthly news round-up of important and interesting events in the company was launched. G.S. Pujari worked as the anchor for 'Singareni Tarangalu', the name given to the news round-up. It was T.R.K. Rao who persuaded the famous singer S.P. Balasubramanyam to render the Singareni song. In January 2002, we revived our bimonthly newsletter called *Singareni Samachar*. New columns were introduced encouraging the workers to share their views. Slowly but surely the newsletter became a powerful tool of communication between the management and the workforce.

We realised that we must reach all our far-flung areas for effectively communicating the spirit of Singarenism, which was evolving. T.R.K. Rao came up with a brilliant idea in 2003 of fabricating a high-tech mobile publicity vehicle fitted with modern communication systems. This van was named 'Karmika Mithra' and was launched in June 2004. The van toured all areas of the company as per a specified calendar. We showed our telefilms and other programmes. The deployment of the van was indeed a great success story in improving our communication with the workers.

Not contented with producing short-length telefilms on some specific themes, we decided to produce a full-length 90-minute telefilm in 2004. It was named *Shramika Bandham* and was released in December 2004. This powerful film proved to be extremely successful in promoting the philosophy of Singarenism. It has powerful characterisation coupled with heart-moving dialogues. The film depicts the successful turnaround of our company and the united team efforts of all sections of the company employees which made this turnaround possible. Some characters of the movie like Raghavaiah, Singanna and Ramkoti are now part of the Singareni folklore. We had entered this movie as an official entry for the prestigious Nandi Awards instituted by the Government of Andhra Pradesh for 2004. Although we did not get an award, we got an honourable mention. Encouraged by the success of this venture, SCCL has produced a large number of telefilms. Most of them are of high quality and have evoked appreciative response from the audience. The themes of these short films are centred on safety; promoting saving habits by avoiding wasteful expenditure; tips for good health by avoiding bad habits like alcoholism and smoking; increasing awareness on dreadful diseases like AIDS; emphasising good practices which contribute to environmentally sustainable mining; reducing waste by promoting use of recyclable products and promoting greenery and water conservation.

Chandrakantha Sarma (chief general manager, Human Resources Department) is a committed Singarenian. To him goes the credit of implementing some very useful innovative ideas. I would especially like to mention the suggestion he gave me in November 2005—to print a 30-page booklet which would be enclosed with my New Year and Sankranthi greetings to the workers for 2006.

Chandrakantha Sarma suggested that we mention our concerns and strategies for further progress of the company. We included useful information for promoting good health by giving tips on treating ailments like diabetes, hypertension and general hygiene. We published this booklet in Telugu entitled *Pragathi Pathamlo Singareni Payanam—Oka Mata*, meaning 'Singareni's Journey and Path to Progress'. The response to this booklet has been heart warming for us. We had circulated feedback forms. More than 90 per cent of the employees had expressed their appreciation and suggested that this initiative should be continued in future years.

As we journeyed along in infusing creativity, professionalism and efficiency in our company, we realised the importance of adopting a flexible and accommodative approach in our management systems. Noticing the growing success of our communication policies where we were making liberal use of good ideas from all quarters, we decided to reward novel and practical suggestions. K. Karunasree, the daughter of a Singarenian, suggested that the highly popular Singareni song should be used as ringtone for cellphones. Our Public Relations Department worked on this idea enthusiastically. On 15 August 2006, during the Independence Day celebration function, I launched the Singareni song as a ringtone in collaboration with Airtel. This proved to be a hugely popular measure. Since then thousands of Singarenians adopted this ringtone in their cellphones. We received envious compliments from certain corporate houses, who wanted to emulate our scheme. It was a great pleasure for me to give a gift to Karunasree for her innovative idea in the presence of thousands of persons in the function held on 15 August 2006. It is my firm belief that this single act of encouragement to Karunasree conveyed a very powerful message to the Singareni family and enormously promoted goodwill for the management.

One of our most effective and ever-growing popular decisions has been to launch an exclusive Singareni channel on 1 May 2006 (May Day) on MANA TV. This programme was anchored by our popular Singareni telestar Ghana Sankar Pujari. Within a short span of few months, our MANA TV programme emerged as the most powerful medium of communication between the management and the workers. The programme included interviews of Singareni achievers; question and answer sessions between workers and departmental heads; informative talks on subjects such as health care, education of children and other important social issues. The informative Singareni news round-up 'Singareni Tarangalu' was also telecasted. This initiative was unique in many ways. It opened the windows of opportunity for creative employees and their children to appear on TV and enhance their confidence and levels of skills. The feeling of closeness and belongingness to Mother Singareni was constantly intensifying as beautifully crafted programmes were beamed on the televisions in the house-holds of the workers. We live in an electronic age of cellphones, Internet and cable TV, which are an integral part of the current civilisational milieu. It would be truism to say the TV has emerged as the most powerful and successful communication medium for SCCL.

One day during my discussions with the senior management team I realised that Singareni did not have a tradition of celebrating its foundation day. I found this extremely strange. My enquiries did not bring forth any convincing explanations for this unusual situation. We decided that we would celebrate 'Singareni Day' on 23 December beginning with 2003. This date was chosen as the name of the company changed from Hyderabad Deccan Company to SCCL in the year 1920 on this day.

Keeping in view the vast geographical spread of our organisation, instructions were given to celebrate 23 December as Singareni Day every year in all 11 areas. The nature of the programmes varied from exhibitions depicting the different activities of the company; cultural programmes and organisation of competitions in company schools and colleges. In December 2004, we started organising 'Singareni Day Run' in all areas. We provided free T-shirts and caps to all runners. The T-shirts carried the powerful messages: 'One for All. All for One', and 'One Family—One Vision—One Mission'. A Singareni torch based on the pattern of the Olympic torch was carried by the runners. On the final day of the celebrations, which culminated in the corporate headquarters at Kothagudem, the Singareni flame was symbolically handed over to the Chairman and the

Managing Director (CMD). I recall the incredible atmosphere generated when I received the Singareni torch from one of the relay runners on 23 December 2005 in Prakasam Stadium, Kothagudem. There was a sea of Singarenians of all age groups. Despite heavy rain, nothing could dampen the indomitable Singareni spirit. Everybody burst into spontaneous and prolonged applause, when I lighted the Singareni flame. I was overwhelmed by emotion as I saw officers, trade union leaders and workers all jostling one another in the true spirit of friendship and a passionate attachment to their beloved Mother Singareni. I knew this was my last Singareni Day function as my tenure would end in October 2006. This lent special poignancy to the occasion, and even today I cherish warm memories of that evening with the same intensity, which I felt that day. I silently said in my heart 'Long Live Singareni'. The pouring rain only dampened our bodies, but it ignited our spirits even further. We all felt supremely proud to belong to our company which has rewritten a 'believe-it-or-not script' of success by rising from the ashes of despair to astounding heights of achievements.

T.R.K. Rao and his dedicated band produced an attractive dance-drama entitled *Singareni Spoorthi* in December 2005. Later this programme was beamed on cable TV and was shown a number of times on MANA TV channel. I am making special mention of this effort because this play proved to be a powerful and emotional communication success story. The play narrates the history of SCCL. It starts by explaining the process of coal formation in nature and briefly traces the different phases of growth of SCCL. The most powerful section of the play is dwelling upon the failures of the company, the main reasons contributing to these failures and then how by dint of sustained and dedicated teamwork the spirit of Singareni has been evolved. The play extols the virtues of continuing to work for the future glory of the company in the true spirit of the Singarenism. Shot on actual locales with lilting music and sensitive poetry, *Singareni Spoorthi* never fails to touch the hearts of viewers and is a great source of inspiration.

Now I briefly mention some other important initiatives taken by us for building the self-image of our employees and their belief that with teamwork and team spirit it was possible to take the company to great heights of achievement and glory.

In October 2005, the official logo of the company was modified. The motto, 'One Family, One Vision, One Mission' was incorporated in the logo. The colour was changed from just black to a band of black and gold. The idea was to look upon coal as 'Black Gold'.

From 2003 onwards, we started giving attractive colour calendars featuring different activities of the company, free of cost, to all employees. All the executives received high-quality diaries in addition to calendars.

The practice of *padayatras*, which was introduced in 1998, was constantly refined for increasing its effectiveness. Multi-departmental teams started going to the doorsteps of the workers for solving their immediate pressing problems. Spouses of workers were encouraged to interact actively during the *padayatras*.

Encouraged by the thrilling response to the launch of the Singareni song, we organised song composition competitions in all areas among workers for displaying their creative talents. We announced that a special CD and audio cassette will be brought out by the company containing the best composed songs. The winners would be provided services of a professional studio to record their songs. In December 2005, as part of the Singareni Day celebrations, we released the CD and audio cassette entitled 'Singareni Swaralu'. This cassette has become immensely popular, and all Singarenians have hailed this novel idea.

For promoting the spirit of Singarenism, attractively designed T-shirts, caps and badges were distributed in the past few years. This gave a sense of identity to the employees. They felt proud to call themselves Singarenians. We also designed a Singareni flag. This was unfurled for the first time on 30 June 2006 in an impressive parade in Prakasam Stadium, Kothagudem, by the specially trained Singareni Protection Core (SPC). On the same day, a flag depicting the motto of SPC was unfurled. I must mention the wonderful work done by Col. Zafar Naseem in training the 'jawans' of SPC. He organised a passing out parade of the newly trained personnel in a very impressive manner. The Singareni flag now proudly flies in the corporate office and in area offices. It has become a symbol of identity for all Singarenians. It never ceases to inspire them. In a way we had brought a process to its logical culmination—the process of effectively using symbols by amending our logo, coining the term Singarenian, designing a company flag, constructing Singareni archs, bringing out Singareni badges, and Singareni calendars and diaries.

Communication is what people understand—what I mean is not important, but what people understand is important. 'You can have brilliant ideas, but if you can't get them across, your ideas won't get you anywhere', said Lee Iacocca (*Iacocca: An Autobiography*), a famous business leader known for turning around Chrysler Corporation in 1980s. Communication plays an important role in cultivating culture and establishing corporate bonding. The art of communication is not 'language leadership', it is 'heart leadership'. When you speak from your heart, people listen through their souls.

The basic building block of effective communication is the feeling that every human being is unique and important. Language plays a very important role. Studies reveal that people are more sensitive in the matter of language than religion. I have always followed the local language to make our communication effective.

When we communicate, we communicate the four F's—facts, feelings, folklores and fantasies. Experts say, hearsay (folklores) and self-assumptions (fantasies) can be neglected, but facts and feelings cannot be overlooked or ignored. Such negligence becomes costly. In 'management by the heart', feelings assume highest significance. Whatsoever success we could achieve it was owing to our sensitivity and respect for others' feelings for their religious beliefs, language, community and customary practices. It may not mean much to you and me, but for them it is their purpose of being.

'Without credible communication, and a lot of it, the hearts and minds of others are never captured', says John P. Kotter. How true! We could directly reach to the hearts of our people and for that reason we take a genuine pride for our efforts for 'credible communication'.

There is a tide in the affairs of men, which taken at the flood, leads on to fortune. Omitted, all the voyage of their life is bound in shallows and in miseries. On such a full sea are we now afloat. And we must take the current when it serves, or lose our ventures.

—William Shakespeare

(Famous, poet, writer and playwright)

Source: The Tragedy of Julius Caesar

16 Learning from Adversities—The Test of True Leadership

When I joined the organisation I was repeatedly told that Singareni Collieries Company Limited (SCCL) is a 'Chairman and Managing Director (CMD)-centric company'. Knowledgeable persons mentioned that the company employees do not fail to respond positively to good leadership at the top levels. I noted that even after a lapse of three decades, B.N. Raman was fondly remembered for the path-breaking work he did in establishing educational institutions, formulating welfare measures for the employees and substantially upgrading medical infrastructure. In more recent times, my immediate predecessor, A.P.V.N. Sarma, was affectionately remembered for his human and caring approach towards the company. It was he who provided bold, decisive and inspired leadership enabling reforms, restructuring the company and rescuing it from the brink of utter disaster.

Leadership in an organisation is always a key factor in determining its destiny. In the Indian context, leadership acquires more pronounced importance. Indians in general have a somewhat feudal tinge in their thought process. They look up to their leaders and expect them to be their role models and exemplars. They like to be led rather than lead others. Leadership acquires acute relevance in huge and complex organisations like SCCL. Wrong moves by the top echelons of the company can be a good recipe for failure and disaster.

It dawned on me that I had to be exceedingly careful in evolving my personal leadership style. Here I was, a postgraduate in history, heading one of the largest public sector undertakings (PSUs) in the country without any previous experience of coal mining. The service to which I belong, Indian Administrative Service (IAS), has been frequently at the receiving end of trenchant criticism of being out of depth when dealing with specialised assignments in areas of financial management, industrial management and other fields which require solid domain experience. I could sense a distinct undercurrent of negative energy when dealing with some of the senior-most mining engineers of the company. They had an air conveying the message that it is unfortunate for the country to have a system where technocrats have to be subservient to generalists, who do not have an inkling of professional and technical knowledge required in dealing with highly specialised operations like coal mining.

My friends and colleagues regard me as a cautious person by nature and temperament. According to me, this is an accurate assessment. I have rarely attempted to catch the attention of my seniors by trying to indulge in sensational actions. I am acutely aware of my limitations as a generalist administrator and as a human being. I normally try to learn from my peer group as much as possible in the initial stages after taking charge of a new assignment. I avoid taking dramatic policy decisions merely to create an impact and to announce my arrival. These instincts held me in very good stead in SCCL. I spent the initial months in trying to learn as much as I could about the complexities of coal mining in the Godavari–Pranahitha valley coalfields. I believe in all humility that I am a good and quick learner. After a few months in the chair, I could notice a favourable trend, as I was eliciting better response from the top technocrats in the company. They realised that the new CMD will not unnecessarily tread on their domain and that he is always receptive to the advice they give.

I have always believed that communication channels should be kept open with different hierarchical levels in any organisation. In the case of SCCL, it would have been suicidal not do so. From my first days in office, I encouraged receiving ideas and inputs from anybody who was interested in giving them to me. This proved to be extremely invaluable in my process of self-education of coal mining operations.

One characteristic of the trade unions in SCCL has been to test new CMDs by organising strikes as soon as they join. Handling a strike in an organisation with over 100,000 employees is obviously a forbidding challenge, but at the same time it is an opportunity for the CMD to seize the initiative and to stamp his authority. It is also an acid test of leadership. I had to face a general strike in August 2002 within 10 months of my joining. Readers may think that 10 months is a long time. Only those who are familiar in managing gigantic organisations like SCCL will understand that 10 months is like 10 days. There are so many issues and problems which the CEO has to deal with on a daily basis. Sometimes when my people felt bogged down with incessant problems of people, to motivate them I used to quote the famous sentence of General Colin Powell: 'The day soldiers stop bringing you their problems is the day you have stopped leading them'. I am fully aware of their challenging roles. The workload is extremely demanding. Human relationships are constantly tested on the anvil of bitter truths and harsh realities.

The 'build up' to the August 2002 strike in fact had started almost immediately after my joining in late October 2001. The issue raised was our move to pay wages through the bank. The union threatened that they would oppose payment of wages through banks to company employees, and would organise a general strike if the management persisted with their declared policy of abolishing cash payments to workers. The union had its well-entrenched selfish motives for opposing payment of wages through banks. Workers used to pay their monthly subscriptions to unions in cash. Moneylenders, chit fund operators and some union leaders used to exploit the simple and illiterate workforce. Societal pressures and conspicuous consumption left large number of workers in debt to private moneylenders. Historically speaking, this was one of the main reasons for the low morale of the workforce. Being in constant debt they resorted to negative personal habits like drinking and gambling. Exploitative elements were keenly interested in the indebtedness of the workforce so that they became easy pickings from them.

I must briefly mention why the management decided to discontinue with the cash payment system to workers. We were disbursing over ₹80 crore in cash. These amounts had to be dispatched to 165 different establishments. Due to the ever present threats of Naxalites, we were always on tenterhooks until the payment was done. The district police was under immense pressure as there was danger of cash being looted by the Naxalites. Moreover, we wanted to improve the quality of life of workers and their families. We wanted to break the hold of exploitive elements who were pushing workers into indebtedness with multifarious adverse consequences. The bank management in the coal belt was equally keen to improve their business. They were aware of the saving potential of the workers.

I have forgotten to share a unique fact about the multiplicity of trade unions in SCCL. Until 1998, there were more than 103 trade unions and trade associations in SCCL vying with one another for keeping the workers in their fold. This was one of the main reasons that contributed to the plethora of strikes in the company. The emergence of a large number of bogus chit funds led to the harassment of workers by moneylenders. Some workers even committed suicide causing untold misery to their families. On numerous occasions the management tried to force the policy of disbursing wages through banks. It had to retreat when faced with strikes jointly inspired by chit fund operators, private moneylenders and trade union leaders. This battle was going on since 2000.

When it became apparent to me that a general strike on this issue was a certainty we held our 'War Council' meetings. With extreme care, we chalked out exigency plans on how to counter the strike.

We assessed that if we worked on our opencast mines we would not suffer any losses as all underground mines put together contributed only 35 per cent of the total production. We decided to be open and transparent, so we shared the facts with the workers. They were explained the benefits of getting wages through banks, and slowly, we won their confidence. However, the strike threat still remained.

I may share some of the efforts that we made for creating awareness about the evils of strikes and their negative impact on their lives. The company had started a campaign focusing on workers and their families for improving the literacy level; emphasising the need for education of their children with particular attention to girls and discouraging wasteful and conspicuous consumption. We launched our information campaign to expose our workers to the correct facts of the case in the face of bogus propaganda carried by the trade unions. Intensive *padayatras* were conducted. Pamphlets were published explaining the truth. Special attention was given to the spouses of the workers so that they motivate their husbands and persuade them not to join the strike. It was encouraging for us to realise that there was silent opposition to the strike. But due to the threat of Naxalites and the powerful hold of trade unions, they were afraid to speak their mind. We focused our strategy on channelising the silent resentment amongst the workers who were not very keen to go on strike. Apart from the financial losses that workers would suffer we explained that this would be a setback to the ongoing reforms in the company.

Special efforts were made to persuade trade union representatives not to precipitate a strike, but the trade unions were adamant. I met senior officers in the government and informed them about the emerging situation. They were apprehensive about the adverse consequences of a strike and advised me to give some more time to the trade unions. I pointed out that sufficient time had already been given to the trade unions and this issue was in the process of negotiations since two years. I informed that we were confident of operating our opencast mines despite the strike. I pointed out that the company would not suffer any financial losses if we worked on our opencast mines. Despite their reservations, I informed the government that once we had taken a decision, we would not back out on principles.

I have always believed in adopting the *Lakshman Rekha* principle of administration. This principle implies maintaining complete transparency and effective communications with all stakeholders. We have to convince those adopting confronting postures that the decision of the management on a particular set of issues is based on logic, administrative requirements, legal position and commonsense. Whatever concessions are required they should be done through the process of negotiations in a spirit of mutual accommodation. However, once the management has announced its final decision we would under no circumstances compromise on our fundamental principles to appease trade union and workers. This is the essence of what I call the *Lakshman Rekha* principle, which we adopted in SCCL during my time.

I am very clear that nothing damages the interest of an organisation more than surrendering to unreasonable demands as a direct consequence of threats or coercion. If we want to concede a bargaining point to the trade unions, then it should be done across the negotiating table. Our stand should be based on reasonableness, hard ground realities, ethical principles, and within the constitutional and legal framework of the system within which we operate. There is adequate historical data on management–labour relationship to support my views. I have always believed that when the trade unions make a reasonable request, then why should the management disagree with them? On the contrary, if the management has taken a correct decision, then why should it succumb to threats and strikes? In huge organisations like SCCL, with a history of strike culture, taking a principled stand assumes even greater importance. We decided to face the consequences firmly.

In April 2002, we started payment of wages through banks. Immediately the recognised and representative trade unions of the company launched an indefinite general strike. It came as a great shock to the trade unions that the strike did not disrupt our opencast mining operations.

As mentioned above, we had planned meticulously. The district administration headed by the collector and superintendent of police was taken into confidence. Law and order arrangements were worked out with the district magistrate (DM) and superintendent of police (SP). We got full support in all four districts from the local machinery. This was one of the fundamental reasons why the strike failed and was called off within five days.

With the active cooperation of our dedicated officers and loyal workmen, we managed to achieve 80 per cent of our daily targeted production of coal from the very first day of the strike. After five days the trade unions panicked. They made vain attempts for face-saving formula.

However, we refused to budge. On the fifth day, the strike was called off by the trade unions.

The failure of the strike is a landmark in the management–trade union relationships in SCCL. This was perhaps for the first time that despite a general strike the company actually earned a profit. This was possible because we operated only 11 opencast mines. These mines are mechanised and give handsome profits in contrast to the 47 underground mines which were all loss making. Our wage bill came down drastically due to large-scale absenteeism in underground mines. As we maintained very high level of production from opencast mines with minimal manpower, we could make a tidy profit of ₹7 crore during the strike period. The trade unions like wounded tigers were left licking their wounds. They were dismayed at the lack of enthusiastic support shown by the majority of workers to the strike. It started dawning on them that the management's effective communicative policy and the ongoing reform process had started exposing the hollowness of their claims.

I have always emphasised the importance of teamwork and team spirit in administering complex organisations like SCCL. We succeeded in neutralising the trade unions because there was complete clarity in our communications with our field machinery. We received excellent support from the district administration in the maintenance of law and order. Due to protection of sensitive and vital installations even the Naxalites could not engage in violence.

The 'feel-good factor' was very much evident in 'Team Singareni' when the strike failed. We made detailed analysis of the strike and prepared a case study in which we objectively looked at our strengths and weaknesses. We were fully aware that the trade unions would organise another strike as elections to the trade unions were scheduled for May 2003. We started our contingency planning for the next anticipated strike instead of resting on our laurels.

In January–February 2003, there was a 17-day long general strike in the company. I will not go into details of the strike because I have already dwelt upon the approach taken in the August 2002 strike. The only difference between the two strikes was the occurrence of violence in the 2003 strike and its exhaustingly lengthy duration. While payment through banks was the main issue in the August 2002 strike, the trade unions united to agitate on reversing the so-called privatisation process in the company in 2003. They launched a frontal attack on the very process of reform and restructuring which was in motion since January 1997. They opposed mechanisation in mines, outsourcing of certain departmental activities and declared that this would be the 'mother of all strikes'.

The famous historian, Arnold Toynbee had once stated that when human beings are confronted with big challenges they are spurred into big responses. If their response is inadequate, they fail. Toynbee made these observations when studying the great civilisations. His theory is called, 'Challenge and Response'. We faced a similar situation in Singareni in January 2003. We were confronted by a massive strike. This time, trade unions managed to secure support of Naxalite elements. We received intelligence reports that violence was very much on the cards. Stung by their failure in August 2002, the trade unions had done their homework and were confident that they would prevail this time. They had launched a prolonged misinformation campaign by spreading stories that this was a life and death situation for the workers. They painted a grim picture of the company's future. They alleged that the company would drastically reduce its workforce and would soon be privatised. These false rumours did succeed in creating some panic amongst the workforce. We got reports that this time there was some support for the strike call.

We revived our 'War Council'. We went through our case study of August 2002 strike in great detail. We plugged whatever loopholes we found in our strategy and tactics, and launched extensive and intensive communication campaigns to counter the false propaganda of the trade unions. I must mention an interesting aspect here. Our efforts to reach out to the spouses and families of the workers started yielding very positive results, as the large number of welfare measures adopted had greatly benefited workers families and had created a receptive and favourable mindset. During the period of strike, the spouses and workers families acted as great motivators in persuading their husbands/parents not to support the strike. This is an example of success of the 'soft track' of management techniques. Often the unseen and intangible factors influence the course of events in unexpected ways. After all, human nature is complex and unpredictable. The challenge lies in harnessing silent goodwill for a good cause.

I must mention here about the role of N. Chandra Babu Naidu, who was then the Chief Minister (CM) of Andhra Pradesh. I had detailed briefing sessions with him regarding our strategy to face the strike. It was our good fortune that S.V. Prasad was working as Principal Secretary to the CM. Prasad had an extremely good understanding of the SCCL affairs. He was quite supportive. Known for his masterful understanding of situations, he played a pivotal role in explaining our viewpoint to the CM. Both of us made it very clear to the CM that if the government forced the management to cave into unreasonable demands, then it would irrevocably damage the company. All the good work done over long years would be demolished if this strike succeeded. To his great credit, Naidu promised to give his full support to the management in their fight against vested interests who were bent upon damaging SCCL seriously. I recall telling our senior management team that how lucky Singareni was to have secured the unstinted support of the CM largely due to the constructive, balanced and pragmatic advice given by S.V. Prasad to the CM.

The general strike commenced on 22 January 2003. It was finally called off on 7 February 2003. The Memorandum of Settlement (MoS) was a signal of victory for the principled stand taken by the management. I have deliberately not mentioned the momentous events that took place during the 17 days of strike. I would only like to mention some lessons which we learnt and how they helped in refining our management strategies.

We knew about the possibility of violence because of extremists' influence. We executed some novel measures to counter the threat of violence. Special camps were organised for the loyal workers. Full police protection was provided to the workers' families in the housing colonies. This was done to prevent extremists' elements from harming them. The spouses were kept informed about the welfare of their husbands who were staying in our special camps. Apart from providing good quality food, doctors were posted in these special camps to take care of their health and any stress-related problems. The morale of the loyal workers was maintained by constant motivation and keeping them informed about the safety and well-being of their children. The police personnel deployed for duty were treated as part of the Singareni family and the best of facilities were extended to them. The protection given by the police force was very crucial in our successful running of these special camps for a long period of 17 days.

Senior Singarenians marvelled at the high-quality coordination between company officials and district administration authorities. The district collectors and the superintendents of police of all four districts worked in complete harmony with the general managers and senior company officers of the respective area. I recall the comment made by J.V. Dattatreyulu who was then General Manager in Manuguru. He said that never before in living memory such flawless and smooth coordination was witnessed between company officials and district officials. There were some stray incidents of violence in different areas. Thanks to the timely intervention of police, stringent action was taken against the lawbreakers. In one particular case, when seven people assaulted an officer in Yellandu area, the trade union was shocked when all seven were arrested and booked by the police on criminal offence. This sent a clear message that violence and intimidation would not be tolerated under any circumstances.

Singareni Collieries Company Limited is a government company and its destiny is ultimately shaped by the political executive of the state. In earlier years when prolonged general strikes were witnessed, the government in power would give in when faced with severe political pressure on certain vital issues. This led to demoralisation of the management team. It used to be a case of so near and yet so far. In a democratic set-up the civil servants are subordinates to their political masters; hence, the management is helpless. In the case of SCCL, there were some moments when lack of government support at crucial times had weakened the management and strengthened the trade unions.

The February 2003 situation was dramatically different. Unlike in the past, this time the state government stood firm and fully backed the management. N. Chandra Babu Naidu made it very clear in his press statement that he would not succumb to the unreasonable demands of the trade unions. His strong support to the management was the turning point in the ultimate victory of principles. S.V. Prasad played a vital role in constantly briefing and updating the CM about the correct ground realities. This is yet another example of how 'political will', in the Indian context, is the single most important factor in fashioning and shaping events.

The success of 'team Singareni' in the most adverse and testing conditions proved to be a great inspirational and motivational source. It seemed almost unreal that for the first time in many decades a major general strike had failed in disrupting the company. The officers and workmen realised the power of bonding and working together. Self-belief was reinforced and cynicism took a beating. There was an air of optimism that even in *Kalyug* it was possible for truth and morality to triumph. Without an iota of doubt, the failure of the strike is one of the key moments in the recent history of the company. Had the strike succeeded, I am absolutely convinced that it would have done irreparable damage to the turnaround process of the company. It would have led to the possible revival of Singareni Karmika Samakya (SIKASA) and would have definitely led to the company becoming sick again.

Many Singarenians suggested to me that we should write a book on how 'The Mother Strike 2003' was tackled. We did not find the time to write a book, but we have written a case study for our internal consumption. Maybe one day somebody will write a book on it.

The greatest teacher in life is adversity. Human nature realises the unseen hand of destiny only when severe disasters take place. The test of true leadership manifests itself when faced by unexpected disasters. Singareni is no exception to this general rule. We had our share of 'Twin Disaster 2003'. Perhaps we became a little complacent and were basking in the aftermath of our glorious success in handling the 17-day strike earlier in the year. Or, perhaps we were coming face-to-face with the law of nature, and it was our destiny to taste the depths of despair very soon after enjoying the heights of euphoria. Who knows?

Early on 16 June 2003, a terrible disaster took place in an underground mine in Godavarikhani area. Seventeen workers perished due to water inundation in 7-LEP mine. This was one of the worst accidents in the company's history in nearly 50 years. Personally, it came as a great blow to me. Being the head of the Singareni family my conscience severely rebuked me. Somehow, I felt responsible for this accident. What caused me anguish was the fact that right from day one, I was emphasising the importance of safety in all our operations, and more so in underground mining. Yet, I had to face such a worst situation! I had launched a special campaign to enhance safe working practices. I had removed all budgetary limits for safety expenditure. I had given the inspirational slogan, 'Safety First. Safety Always. Safety for Ever'. I never ceased to highlight the fact that our safety record had lot of scope for further improvement.

My first response on learning about this accident was, why did it happen to me? I used all my willpower to control my emotions and plunged myself into organising rescue and relief measures. I would not like to recount the detailed steps taken by us in organising rescue, relief and rehabilitation measures. It would be suffice to say that team Singareni made sincere and sustained efforts to learn lessons from that disaster. We exercised clinical impartiality in fixing responsibility on the persons responsible for causing the accident. We avoided the common tendency of blaming junior-level employees and protecting the seniors in the hierarchy. The state government ordered a court of enquiry by a sitting judge of Andhra Pradesh High Court. The accident brought adverse publicity to the company and was a severe blow to the morale of the mining community.

We had hardly recovered from this tragedy when, on 17 October 2003, a second disaster struck us. A massive fall of the roof caused the death of 10 people in GDK–8A mine in Godavarikhani area hardly 5 kilometres away from 7-LEP mine. This blow utterly crippled our morale. We were still reeling under the impact of the first disaster and this second fatal blow totally devastated us. Once again we launched clinically effective rescue, relief and rehabilitation measures. Once again we took firm action against the senior managers, who in the preliminary enquiries itself were held responsible for this accident.

The role played by our mine rescue teams on both occasions was simply marvellous. Led by the redoubtable D. Baidya, Superintendent of mine services, our rescue teams undertook the gravest possible risks in retrieving the bodies of their colleagues who had perished in the tragedies. The officers of the Director General of Mine Safety (DGMS) who supervised rescue operations were lavish and generous in their appreciation of our rescue team's outstanding work. If the dead bodies were not quickly retrieved serious law and order problems would have taken place.

It seemed that my moment of reckoning was at hand. I got information from reliable quarters that some influential politicians told N. Chandra Babu Naidu, CM of Andhra Pradesh, to relieve me immediately from the post of CMD, SCCL. They argued that I was bringing 'bad luck' to the company and to counter criticism the best option would be to remove the CMD. I was personally feeling at my lowest ebb as I had publicly owned moral responsibility for the accidents. I was prepared to depart from SCCL if the government too felt the same.

I sent a message to the CM that I was willing to proceed on leave and that he could post another officer if he so desired. I clarified that while my conscience was crystal clear and I had in no manner whatsoever, directly or indirectly, contributed to the accidents, but being the head of the Singareni family I owned full moral responsibility. The response of the CM was that he did not hold me responsible for the accidents. He expressed his pain and anguish over the occurrence of the two disasters in quick succession, despite a track record of safety. He advised us to take all possible measures to prevent recurrence of accidents and to promote safety in every possible way.

The confidence reposed by Naidu in me and in the senior management of team Singareni was a flashpoint in motivating and inspiring us to repay in full, the trust reposed by the CM. I later learnt that Naidu's decision not to transfer me was based on the feedback he obtained from different quarters. He was fully convinced that the accidents took place despite the great emphasis laid on safety and professionalism by me. I goaded my management team to draw sustenance from the support extended to us by Naidu. I urged them to draw immediate safety enhancement management plans. We took a large number of measures to sensitise our workforce to adopt higher quality safety measures and to restore our badly mauled reputation.

I will not give the details of the large number of management decisions we implemented in the following months to improve our safety record. All I want to say is that we took action swiftly whenever we came across any instance or violation of good practices irrespective of the seniority of the officer. We strengthened our training machinery with special emphasis at the cutting-edge levels of functioning being exposed to modern technologies by subject matter experts. We substantially strengthened our mine rescue machinery. The content of training was enhanced and some of our officers were sent abroad to learn the state-of-the-art technologies in rescue and relief operations. The mechanisation in underground mining operations was stepped up. The unions were taken into confidence in all important policy decisions.

It must be said to their credit that they displayed maturity and were generally cooperative by not opposing the semi-mechanisation of the underground mines. It gives me some satisfaction to record that we did not have any major accidents during my remaining 35 months of stay in the company.

As I have noted earlier, the true test of leadership is when faced by calamities and adversities. The twin disasters of 2003 were a sobering experience for the senior management team of SCCL. Some strands of complacency which inevitably creep into organisations that experience good times had unobtrusively entered SCCL. I urged my senior management team to identify our weaknesses and to rectify them within the shortest possible time span. Our technical directors were badly shattered by the accidents. As mining professionals they felt dejected with the recent turn of events. My task was to keep up their morale. I did not indulge in a blame game. I did not berate them. We held some serious introspection sessions in which honesty and transparency were our mantras.

Slowly but steadily we overcame our recent trauma. I must give full credit to P. Vasudeva Rao, G.N. Sarma, J.V. Dattatreyulu, D.L.R. Prasad and S. Chandrasekhar in the revival of the spirit of Singareni within a relatively short time of three months. It is a great tribute to the Singarenian family that despite the setbacks we achieved 100 per cent production in our annual target for 2003–2004. This boosted our confidence enormously and put us back on the track to progress. We proved to ourselves and to the world that nothing could break our resilience and our strong determination to emerge as the best coal mining company in the country. In retrospect, the pain and sorrow, and the sacrifices made by the 27 Singarenians who perished in the twin disasters did not go in vain. As human beings we have to be eternal optimists. We have to face pain and sorrow and take disasters in our stride. What is important is not to repeat our mistakes; to be honest and truthful in accepting our mistakes and to take immediate and effective steps to reform all systems and procedures, which are found lacking.

The twin disasters of 2003 left an indelible imprint on me. I abandoned some ambitious ideas that I had been entertaining at the back of my mind. I decided to drop the project of establishing a coal museum in SCCL. I dropped the idea of constructing a new corporate office building in Kothagudem. Instead, I decided to lay greatest possible emphasis on enhancing safe functioning of the company. Our vocational training centres (VTCs) were strengthened and upgraded. The quality and content of training programmes for field-level officers and junior-level supervisory staff were enhanced. The numerical coverage of workers for training was increased and officers who had interest in imparting training were posted in VTCs. We intensified the system of surprise inspections in the underground mines during night shifts. Any slackness was severely dealt with.

I increased the frequency of my surprise checks in underground coal mines. I resolved field-level problems with greater promptitude. I started addressing workers in order to motivate them to follow safe practices. We instituted special awards to encourage safety in all our departments. Workers were encouraged to give suggestions for enhancing safety measures. All senior officers in the company significantly increased their frequency of interaction with the workers and tried to immediately rectify problems encountered in the field. Our combined efforts at different levels contributed to a heightened level of bonding and a sense of appreciation that each individual was responsible in contributing his mite in ensuring the welfare of our company.

As I look back now, I can discern three distinct phases in the evolution of my leadership style in SCCL. In the initial phase, I wanted to build upon the principles of professionalism, self-belief, self-respect, transparency and fair play. I am a passionate believer and practitioner of these principles. From the beginning, I made it very clear that I would not accept non-professionalism, dishonesty and indiscipline. I took strong action against persons who displayed any of these negative characteristics and I constantly harped on the concept of 'team Singareni', 'team spirit' and 'Singarenism'. I adopted a low-key profile and avoided unnecessary publicity. I resisted the temptation of playing to the gallery and becoming popular with the media. Instead, I focused on emphasising my transparent and impartial approach in dealing with men and matters. With the passage of time the Singareni family accepted my tough but humane management approach. The introduction of the concept of Singarenism started taking roots and it got constantly reinforced as time passed.

I got rude shocks when the two disasters took place in 2003. It dawned on me that there were serious infirmities in our systems and our organisation was found lacking. We then focused on redefining our professional benchmarks. Greater emphasis was paid to vigorous training and in enhancing skill levels. Good performances were rewarded. Encouragement and publicity were given to high achievers. Simultaneously lack of professionalism, indiscipline and carelessness were punished. It was made clear that the CMD would not lower his personal benchmarks no matter what the consequences were. With greater exposure to my management style the majority of our employees were willing to focus on self-improvements.

It is interesting to note that since the formation of the state of Andhra Pradesh on 1 November 1956, there have been only three CMDs of SCCL whose tenure has exceeded four years. I consider myself very fortunate to have served SCCL for nearly five full years. The length of my tenure gave me a unique opportunity of providing stability at the top. It helped me evolve into a more mature and balanced individual. It is impossible for any individual to make a mark in a huge organisation like SCCL unless he is given a minimum stay of three years at the top.

I consider myself a good learner, and as I travelled along I kept improving my communications at all levels. By the time I completed three years, it was generally acknowledged that I was honest and impartial in my approach to issues. I now started giving even greater emphasis to workers welfare. I was receiving unalloyed warmth and support from almost all officers and workers. Some of the most important welfare-centric policies implemented by us included introduction of man-riding systems in underground mines on a massive scale; construction of new quarters and repairs to over 20,000 houses belonging to workers; significant strengthening of medical infrastructure facilities in the company; and constant encouragement given to Singareni Seva Samithi (SSS), Singareni Employees Wives Association (SEWA) and Manochaitanya (Welfare Centre for mentally challenged children). These measures greatly consolidated my image of being a very caring CEO. I was perceived as being strict with non-performing officers while being extremely caring with workers. The trade unions, to their credit, generally supported me throughout my stay. The failure of the great strike of 2003 had a telling affect on trade unions. They realised that they could no longer mislead the workers. Moreover, they could not deny the significant and visible changes sweeping the company enhancing the quality of life of the workers.

Some of my very senior colleagues in the company remarked towards the end of my stay that I was a very different person then as compared to my initial days in the organisation. They said I was extremely soft then as contrasted to my being very tough in the beginning. I fully agreed with their observations. I could sense that I had changed, as I learnt more and more about the great traditions of Singareni, and as I was privileged to receive enormous affection from all Singarenians. In a lighter vein, I reminded some of my directors that I had always claimed, 'I am a temporary chairman, but a permanent worker.' I think my innate sense of detachment with the post of CMD was the basic reason for maintaining my sense of proportion and not getting blown away by a misplaced sense of self-achievement. I have always been a critic of individuals who are high consumers of what I call 'Vitamin I'. In my view nothing can be more self-destructive than being lulled into a false sense of megalomania. Indians in general thrive on lavish doses of false praise. This is one of the fundamental reasons that give rise to the culture of *chamchagiri* (sycophancy culture). This culture is anathema to me. In all humility, I can assert that my style of management is the very opposite to that of *chamchagiri*. I believe in building systems and in strengthening institutions. As an old saying goes, 'People come and people go. But the world goes on.' I adopted this approach in respect of SCCL where we have temporary chairpersons coming and going, but Singareni goes on and on.

I would like to conclude my observations on leadership by asserting that we can have brilliant individuals who may raise organisations to great heights of achievement with their personal qualities. But what happens when such individuals leave? If such brilliant individuals have not contributed to institution building, very often their organisations regress when they leave. I do not believe in promoting individuals. I believe in teamwork and team spirit. The story of SCCL is all about teamwork. It is about acknowledging and rewarding creativity, sincerity, dedication and innovative thinking. It is the story of adopting a transparent management system firmly embedded in ethical principles. And above all, it is the story of adhering to high moral principles with a humane and caring approach to a huge workforce.

Nobody can be successful unless he loves his work.

—David Sarnoff

(CEO, Radio Corporation of America)

Source: The above famous sentence is quoted by Eugene Lyons in his book *David Sarnoff: A Biography*

17 The Lovebird—In the Green Pastures of Singareni

It has been my personal mission in life to contribute in whatever ways I can to preserve the ecological balance of planet earth. Since childhood, I have always been in love with Mother Nature. I consider it a privilege to have worked as member secretary of the Andhra Pradesh Pollution Control Board for two years (1993–1995) and even more luckier to have worked as joint secretary in the Union Ministry of Environment and Forests for five years (1996–2001). I consider these two prestigious assignments as the best I have had in my career of over 31 years in the Indian Administrative Service (IAS).

When I joined as chairman and managing director (CMD) of Singareni Collieries Company Limited (SCCL) some of my friends and well-wishers jokingly remarked, 'Rajen, you will be a great misfit in SCCL. Coal mining savagely degrades mother earth. How will you resolve the dilemma of being a green person in a black environment?' There is undeniable truth in these humorous and candid observations of my friends. Coal mining is an inherently polluting and environmentally degrading activity. It has become an inevitable and necessary evil in humankind's quest for unceasing and boundless materialistic development.

I was determined to prove that where there is a will, there is a way. My inner self was clear in its mission statement. I was committed to evolving policies that would contribute to environmentally sustainable coal mining. The underlying principle was to give back in some measure to Mother Earth what coal mining was destructively extracting from it.

In my very first interaction with the senior management team of our company, I shared my vision of making SCCL an eco-friendly coal mining company. Understandably, there was scepticism from the vast majority of hard-headed mining engineers. They thought that the new CMD is soft-hearted and a romantic sort of person. He has fancy ideas of promoting his personal value system of environmental protection. I was conscious of the initial lack of response to my passionate exposition of integrating environmental concerns with coal mining. But I was encouraged in my mission by G. Srinivas Ayyangar (director, Personnel and Administration), J.V. Dattatreyulu (then working as staff officer to CMD) and a few others in the company who were responsive to my mission.

One of the first initiatives we took was to create an integrated environment and forest department in the company. The department was earlier known as plantation and timber management department. Later we created a horticulture department which was given the task of creating green pastures. Armed with my experience of five years in the Union Ministry of Environment and Forests, I began identifying priority areas where there was need for maximum intervention in containing environmental degradation.

New initiatives always require committed team leaders. The turning point in our attempts to bring about a complete change in the mindset of mining practices was the joining of Surendra Pandey in June 2002 as executive director (Forestry) in SCCL. In Surendra, we found an exceptionally dynamic, sincere and hard-working forester. During his stay of about three years in the company, Pandey succeeded in bringing about a virtual revolution in adoption of eco-friendly coal mining practices. It was a great source of strength and inspiration for me to have Pandey heading the forestry department of the company. He was ably assisted by a small group of committed foresters. I must mention B. Sridevi who along with K.N. Sekhar formed a great team in greening of the dry lands of SCCL into what my distinguished co-author, Moid Siddiqui, describes as 'green pastures'.

In order to have a sharply focused strategy we first produced a policy document clearly spelling out our mission statement. Subgroups were constituted and time milestoning was done. We tried to involve all departments in the exercise so that there was coordination and harmony in our efforts. Some key areas identified for attention included biological engineering in opencast mines, environmental awareness education in SCCL schools, energy conservation measures, water conservation measures, creation of green belts and parks, utilisation of fly ash, promoting innovative forestry practices, construction of effluent treatment plants (ETPs) and sewerage treatment plants (STPs), and launching a special environment awareness programme for company workers and their families.

Those who underestimate the unknown power of human passion and creativity do so at their own peril. Psychologists have never failed to emphasise the power of the subconscious mind over the conscious mind.

Most of us are unaware about our true potential and the virtual boundless limits of our creativity. All human beings possess in substantial measure positive qualities, which are unique to them. It is a great tragedy of our times that we do not use our positive qualities for promoting the welfare of the human race and the ecological sustenance of planet earth.

What we did in SCCL was to tap and channelise the subconscious love for Mother Earth and Mother Nature, which all of us possess, into some concrete actions. Looking back at the dramatic changes that occurred in our company within a relatively short period of five years appears to be a fairy tale. Let me share some facts to give a sense of perspective to what I am writing here.

Singareni Collieries Company Limited became the first coal mining company in the country to receive the prestigious 'Golden

Peacock Environment Management Award 2005'. The award was received on 11 June 2005 in the Seventh World Congress on Environment Management. The award is instituted by the World Environment Foundation.

On 26 June 2006 His Excellency, the President of India, gave the prestigious TERI Corporate Environmental Award 2004–2005 (First Prize) to SCCL. This was the crowning moment of glory, acknowledging the fact that SCCL had stolen the limelight from companies like TATA Industries and others, to emerge as the greenest and most eco-friendly company in the country. The Energy Resources Institute (TERI) award is the most coveted recognition in the country, which acknowledges corporate excellence in environmental conservation.

The Green Tech Foundation of India bestowed Environment Excellence Award 2006 (Gold Medal) in metal and mining sector for outstanding achievement in environment management to SCCL on 30 August 2006.

In December 2005, SCCL got the National Award for fly ash utilisation. This award is jointly instituted by the Union Ministry of Environment and Forests, Union Ministry of Power, and Union Ministry of Science and Technology. Singareni Collieries Company Limited became the first coal mining company in the country to bag this award, which was given for maximum utilisation of fly ash in construction activity.

I am not saying that winning awards by itself is a great achievement. To us it is a process. It is not an end in itself instead it is a means in working towards an unending process. The key concerns are sustainability of activities within an environmental framework. Nevertheless, if awards are given on merit and by institutions which have credibility, then they have great value. Awards then symbolise recognition of outstanding work done by our organisation. For us in Singareni, every award acted as a great motivator which continually reinforced the company's unswerving and unflinching resolve to practice environmentally sustainable coal mining. In particular, the TERI award was special. This world-renowned institution follows a rigorous and highly objective methodology in its evaluation process.

There are detailed field visits made by subject matter specialists. What gave us greatest satisfaction was the fact that we successfully competed against world famous industrial giants like TATA Steel and Reliance Industries. The award ceremony was in itself inspirational as it was Dr A.P.J. Abdul Kalam, the most respected president of India, who did the honours.

In June 2005, we did a stocktaking exercise to evaluate how our efforts in promoting green mining were succeeding. I thought it would be a good idea to document our efforts for sharing them with other coal mining companies in the country. We constituted a small group comprising T.R.K. Rao (executive director, Marketing & Movement), Surendra Pandey (ED, Forestry), Dr J. Usha Kumari (SC Women's College, Kothagudem), A.V.K. Sagar (mining engineer) and Y. Srinivasa Rao (mining engineer). I chaired the group. We decided that we would publish a book documenting our efforts. Within a short time of five months we brought out a book entitled, *Eco-friendly Coal Mining: The Singareni Approach*. When the group was working on writing this book we realised the incredible positive power which human beings possess. We could hardly believe that teamwork and team spirit had helped us in achieving something which looked unachievable. The book has 124 pages divided into nine chapters. It has beautiful photographs backed with technical data on the subjects of biological engineering, energy conservation, fly ash utilisation, innovative forestry practices and environmental awareness education in SCCL schools. I would like to share some of our achievements which are covered in detail in the book. I think it is important to generate positive energy which is urgently required by the human race for saving planet earth from extinction.

It is said that all revolutions first begin in the human mind. It is a human tragedy that most of us fail to utilise even a small proportion of our potential. The green revolution in SCCL is an apt example of unleashing the creative energy of 100,000 Singarenians. After an initial period of doubt and sluggishness, almost all Singarenians enthusiastically became a part of the green revolution. A key factor in this rapid change was our success in involving the families of workers in the green movement. The work done by the spouses of the workers through the aegis of Singareni Employees Wives Association (SEWA) and Singareni Seva Samithi (SSS) is really incredible.

I have always believed that no society can progress unless it fully involves 'women power' in all developmental activities. Singareni Collieries Company Limited is lucky to have extremely dedicated, highly motivated and innovative persons like V.S.R. Murthy (deputy personnel manager) in its fold. Known for his exemplary hard work, sincerity and unbridled energy, Murthy along with other associates such as Pitchaiah and Krishna Kumar worked unceasingly in promoting positive human values among Singarenian families. They found tremendous response from SEWA and SSS. It is to their full credit that they were able to effectively channelise this positive energy in raising awareness levels on societal issues and in promoting environmental values. It is well known that 'the hand that rocks the cradle, rules the throne.' I would like to add that if women are enlightened and empowered then they can revolutionalise societal values in a surprisingly quick time.

We focused on women empowerment in SCCL. We started getting encouraging results sooner than expected. This was because of another unique initiative which was reinforcing women empowerment in the households. This initiative commenced in June 2003 with the introduction of environmental studies as a compulsory subject from class six to nine in all the 21 schools and two colleges administered by the company. Within a period of two years 'young Singarenians', as I call them, became the pioneers of the Green Revolution in our company. The enthusiasm, energy and creativity of youth is unparalleled as it is highly contagious and spreads like a viral fever. The only difference is that this fever is marked by the fervour of doing good for the society. Our school children started silently and deeply influencing their parents in promoting good societal values along with environmental values.

I am reminded of the experience of the Scandinavian countries in the mid-1970s when they pioneered introduction of environmental education in their educational institutions. By the late 1980s, Scandinavian countries had emerged as leaders in promoting sustainable environmental development. We were witnessing a similar phenomenon in SCCL where young Singarenians were inspiring the older generation to become more conscious of the duties that they owed to Mother Earth. Naturally, we found the womenfolk in the households more receptive and sensitive to their concerns and duties. This synergy resulted in ushering in what I have called the 'Green Revolution'.

Let me give an example of the creative genius of a young Singareni student of Women's Degree college of Kothagudem. I quote translation of a Telugu poem written by her, which was published in the book *Eco-friendly Coal Mining: The Singareni Approach* (p. 85). The poem goes as follows:

Entreaty of a Tree

O Man! My Friend!!
In those cold bitter winter nights,
burning in the flames of your fire-place,
I embrace you with my warm, balmy hug.

In those blistering sweaty summer evenings,
I grant you the ultimate harmony
with my cool gentle breeze.

My slashed body parts deliver you,
your doors, windows and roofs.
My hacked branches become
sleeping beds and floating boats for you.

From match stick to field plough;
from your daily bread to cattle food,
I give you everything.

I am the capital for your trade;
I am the paper for your lyric parade.

I am the unending inspiration
in your paintings and poetry.

After your birth, I am the carrycot.
After your death, I am the casket.

I am the ready-made answer for your every appeal;
And my only appeal to you is—Save me …
… Save me from yourself.

I am sure the readers will feel as moved and inspired as I feel whenever I read these magical and lyrical lines. To me this is a perfect example of the change in the mindset which human beings are capable of achieving, but rarely attempt. I have supreme confidence that in the coming years the young Singarenians will carry the green movement in the company to greater heights. I am equally confident of their evolving into sensitive and eco-responsible citizens of the country.

The joint success of introducing environmental education in our schools and utilising SEWA and SSS as agents of change is, to my mind, instrumental in sensitising every Singarenian to the sacred duty he owes to Mother Earth. There has been a rapid and remarkable change in the mindset of Singarenians. Today, all officers and workers are conscious about the imperatives of water conservation, maintaining green cover and contributing their mite for promoting a cleaner and healthier environment. After the release of our book in October 2005, I sent the copies to the same friends who had indirectly motivated me by their comment on being 'a green person in a black environment'. To their credit they were generous in their appreciation of our efforts. Most of them paid glowing compliments to the high production quality of *Eco-friendly Coal Mining: The Singareni Approach*. These were enormously satisfying moments for me. It is rare for a person to see positive outcomes of his passionate efforts within a short time period of three to five years. Yet I had this privilege, due to the unbounded affection I received from virtually all members of the Singareni family. I must share the incisive and insightful comment of my good friend, P. Vasudeva Rao (former director, SCCL), on the Singareni culture. He said, 'We have a unique quality. Once we are convinced about something, then we adopt it with great dedication. The green movement in Singareni will henceforth only be further strengthened'. The encouraging words of P.V. Rao are a constant source of inspiration to me. I tend to agree with his observations as I notice no let-up in this aspect after departing from the company. Over the years, this has been one of the great strengths of Singarenians. Once they are convinced about something then they always work with great determination for the cause. Tenacity of purpose and sustained hard work are prerequisites for maintaining the momentum of any project.

It is said that seeing is believing. Theoretical concepts and powerful words are poor substitutes for physical achievements on the ground. One cannot bring about major changes merely by using attractive phrases for motivating people. The reason for the rapid transformation in the attitude and thinking of Singarenians was the fact that solid work was being done on the ground for practising environmentally sustainable mining systems. Concerted efforts were being taken to involve people at all levels in the company. This generated initial interest in the approach and soon the interest was transformed into enthusiasm. Once there was a visible transformation in the physical environment, the process of attitudinal change got speeded up. I would like to mention two or three major initiatives taken by our engineers which really revolutionalised the way in which the company functioned.

Opencast mining operations create huge overburden dumps (OB dumps). The challenges in opencast mining include containing damages on account of drilling and blasting operations, coal excavation, and transportation and dumping OB material. Being site specific, coal deposits are often found in forests and other ecologically fragile areas. The issues of environmental degradation are further compounded when green field projects are promoted in virgin areas. Unscientific exploitation of surface water and ground water creates serious challenges in mining operations.

Environmental management plans (EMPs) are formulated considering all pre-operational, operational and post-operational aspects of mining. Land management and reclamation of land become vital issues. Surface mining operations have the potential to destroy in situ flora and fauna, pollute ambient air quality, adversely affect ground water, degrade soil resources, accelerate soil erosion by damaging vegetation and generally degrade the area. Overburden dumps have very little organic matter and have unfavourable pH, which hinders plant growth.

We decided that reclamation of OB dumps by adopting biological engineering methods would be our top-most priority. An extremely detailed project was launched for reclamation of OB dumps under the dynamic and inspirational leadership of Surendra Pandey. Without going into the technical details, I will succulently summarise the objectives of biological engineering:

1. Early establishment of soil and biomass
2. Successful early plant growth
3. Minimising topsoil loss
4. Reducing adverse impact on the local ecosystem
5. Providing better ground for natural regeneration of the flora and early start of natural succession
6. Creating conditions congenial to local fauna
7. Preventing damage to water bodies
8. Reducing impact on fauna, flora and people
9. Increasing aesthetic look

The biological methods used included macro-level treatments involving closure of the area from biotic interference, introduction of pioneers, and covering the entire area with grass and legume species to give early restoration effects.

Engineering methods included stopping soil erosion, fixing soil and establishing slopes. The grading–regrading of the OB was done as per angle of repose to reduce the velocity of falling soil and run off. Rock-lined drains were constructed for carrying water into garland canals which were in turn connected to natural water bodies in the area. Toe walls were constructed at the bottom of the slopes to prevent erosion. Waste materials including barrels, jute matting and discarded wooden stakes were used for making cribs. This encouraged reuse and recycling of waste material.

Within a short span of three years, our bioengineering initiative yielded spectacular results. All 11 OB mines in the company were transformed from ugly looking, dusty and barren slopes into greener areas. The enthusiasm of our engineering colleagues was superb. There was healthy competition between general managers of different areas for doing better than their colleagues. We instituted some awards which acted as an added incentive. The TERI award for corporate environmental excellence in 2006 took into consideration the fantastic work done in biological engineering in our company. Gautam Khani Opencast Mine was selected for random evaluation by the TERI team. Impressed by the work done, they recommended the award for us. To me the success of bio-engineering in SCCL was a dream come true. It rejuvenated my inner self. It reinforced my belief and faith in the great potential of human beings for doing constructive and positive work if they are encouraged and guided correctly.

Another facet of our holistic approach to environmental management is the initiatives taken to conserve energy in all forms. Great credit must be given to G. Srinivas Ayyangar (former director, Personnel and Administration) who took extremely tough measures for curbing power pilferage. Although this work had started during the time of A.P.V.N. Sarma and Heeralal Samariya, it was Ayyangar who provided a hard thrust for installation of pole mounted transformers, installation of transformer protection devices, handing over private colonies to Northern Power Distribution Company (NPDISCOM), promoting use of compact fluorescent lamps and using fluorescent tube light fittings with electronic ballast for saving energy. These measures coupled with use of energy-efficient appliances; re-organisation of haulage; introduction of energy-efficient motors and re-organisation of ventilation circuits; introduction of variable frequency variable voltage drives and improvement in lighting systems gave phenomenal results. Some figures are necessary to convey the positive impact on the company finances and efficiency.

1. Colony consumption reduced from 230 million units in 1998–1999 to 115 million units by 2003–2004.

2. The average power consumption per residential quarter was 500–600 units per month during 1997–1998. This was reduced to 160 units per month during 2003–2004.
3. The specific energy consumption reduced from 25 kWh/tonne in 1998–1999 to 17.77 kWh/tonne by 2003–2004.
4. There was a reduction of about 105 million units in the overall energy consumption in 2003–2004 as compared to 1997–1998.
5. The power bills paid to Andhra Pradesh Transmission Corporation Limited (APTRANSCO) came down from ₹247 crore in 2000–2001 to ₹210 crore in 2003–2004 resulting in a reduction of ₹37 crore in three years.

Singareni Collieries Company Limited has the distinction of being the first coal company in the country which has undertaken path-breaking initiative in implementation of fly ash utilisation. In collaboration with the Department of Atomic Energy, Government of India, Heavy Water Plant (HWP) at Manuguru and Directorate General of Mine Safety, a pilot project was initiated for using fly ash in underground mines as a stowing material. PK 1 Incline was the mine chosen. Trials were launched in May 2002. After two years of dedicated efforts positive results emerged from this experiment. This is an ongoing project, and it is hoped that the lessons learned will be extended to underground operations in Coal India Limited (CIL) in the near future.

The mining operations of SCCL span a huge geographical area covering four districts of Andhra Pradesh. The company constructs houses, maintains roads, provides water supply, has its own power stations and looks after its gigantic infrastructure. Singareni Collieries Company Limited was the first major company in the country which decided to use fly ash bricks for all its construction work. Commencing use of fly ash bricks in a big way in 2001, we shifted to 100 per cent use of fly ash in all construction works by 2003–2004. This included construction of drains, sanitation works, compound walls, office buildings and residential quarters. Our phenomenal efforts were recognised when we received the National

Award in December 2005 for largest utilisation of fly ash in the country. The award is jointly instituted by the Union Ministries of Power, Environment and Forests, and Science and Technology.

It is an unfortunate fact that Indians have not realised the gravity of environmental degradation that is taking place in our country. In our insatiable thirst for more material comforts we are ignoring the nourishment of Mother Earth. We are indulging in self-deception by arguing that the imperatives of development are compelling us to overlook the massive ecological destruction which is taking place. While it is absolutely correct that the developed countries are the biggest global polluters and that we have to improve our material standard of living, this does not necessarily mean that we emulate them in their destructive practices.

Our attempt should be to evolve developmental policies which can be sustained on a long-term basis. This is possible only when the carrying capacity of areas is assessed when environmental management plans are formulated.

Our mission in SCCL is to realise our environmental, social and moral responsibilities, and promote environmentally sustainable mining. All our efforts are a living testimony that it is possible to limit environmental degradation by adopting policies and practices that reduce damage to nature while being sustainable on a long-term basis. There has to be a vision–mission approach based on long-term planning. There are no easy quick-fix solutions for repairing nature. We have strongly demonstrated that even a highly polluting activity like coal mining can contribute to greening of the mind, provided there is strong determination and will. It is necessary to briefly mention some other major initiatives which powerfully contributed to the greening of the mind in SCCL.

We undertook construction of ETPs and STPs on a big scale. Within five years, fourteen ETPs and five STPs were taken up. The demonstration effect of these plants has been substantial. Our officers and workers have realised that their responsibilities do not end in coal mining operations alone. They have been exposed to a wide range of possibilities in implementation of environmental protection measures. The company has a large number of workshops.

We could discern a sea of changes in the attitudes of workers manning our workshops after oil and grease taps were constructed. Not only did they reduce polluting activities but also actively improved their housekeeping practices. We instituted competitions for best maintained workshops. Some workers suggested that there should be a competition for green workshops as well. We accepted the suggestion. The response was staggering. Within two years, our workshops changed completely. Now, most of them have well laid out gardens in which the workers take great pride. This is a concrete example of attitudinal change driven by a clear mission approach. I have always believed that positive strokes and encouragement are great motivators in unleashing human goodness.

For the first time, we encouraged development of medicinal plantations in nurseries. Wastelands in the company were converted into industrial plantations. Bamboosetums were established in different areas. Improving the adjoining reserve projects habitats was taken up in cooperation with the state forest department. We actively worked with the forest department for protection of forest cover. Our attempt was to restore the natural ecology of the area. For this an ecosystem approach was implemented. This covered protection of biodiversity and microclimatic zones.

Water resource management was given top priority. We tried to take up rainwater harvesting in a scientific manner. Water conservation measures were encouraged in all establishments. Vermicomposting of biodegradable waste was a good practice which became widespread throughout the company. All employees were encouraged to promote cultivation of greenery. Competition was instituted for clean and green colonies and for the most eco-friendly house. Some unique measures were taken for utilisation of waste material. Kodepaka Mallesham, an SCCL employee in Manugur area, converted waste material into visual delight by making models of animals, which have been installed in company parks in different areas. Mallesham's quality of workmanship is outstanding. I recall giving him an award as a token of recognition and appreciation of his unbounded talent. I was very particular that wide publicity be given to individual acts of brilliance by our employees as this has a cascading effect in encouraging greater creativity.

Intellects Biz, the business consultancy headed by Moid Siddiqui, my respected management guru, carried out a survey on the 'Pygmalion Effect in SCCL' towards the end of 2006. Moid and his team has conducted studies on 'Pygmalion effects' and he has also been conducting workshops on this virgin theme with focus on—how your expectations get you the desired results! In early January 2006, Moid communicated his findings to the SCCL management. I have gone through his report and I am thrilled beyond words to write that our 'eco-friendly approach' was rated very highly in the survey as one of the crucial factors of turnaround. The report says that creation of 'green pastures' in the barren land created a unique impact on the morale of the people. It created inner joy in them and their families. The inner joy was reflected in high productivity. Some of the findings of his report, strongly supported by the vast majority of Singarenians interviewed, included the following:

1. There is some invisible relationship between 'creating green pastures' and 'turnaround'.
2. Mining creates an imbalance in ecology which has been successfully brought to balance by plantations, greenery, flowering plants and creating green pastures, which has become a major cause of the success.
3. The 'greenery' all around soothes the heart, which, in turn, creates inner happiness and good feelings that led to higher output in SCCL, and stands as one of the causes for its success.
4. 'Barrenness', or what we call 'sand traps', all around create bad inner feelings, which, in turn, affect the output adversely. Thus, we gained through greenery.
5. Singareni Collieries Company Limited's mines are 'eco-friendly' mines.

These clear statements are an irrevocable testimony to the success of the green revolution in SCCL within a short period of five years. They reflect what our sages and *yogis* have known since time immemorial—nature soothes the soul. It is a balm for troubled hearts. Our *yogis* would go to mountains, forests and caves for meditation. They would commune with nature in complete tranquillity and peace. After all, Mother Nature in all her pristine glory is a manifestation of the Supreme Being. According to Moid's findings, the greening of the barren pastures of Singareni was one of the fundamental reasons for the 'Pygmalion effect', which transformed the company almost miraculously.

As I have repeatedly asserted, our motto in Singareni was teamwork. The success that we achieved was a result of team spirit. Today as I look back with nostalgia, I am reminded of what wise men have said, 'Life is a mysterious journey. We human beings cannot fathom the mysteries of our existence'. As Lord Krishna had said to Arjuna, 'Do your duty with sincerity: Do not bother for results.' Let us hope that we all work together in the true spirit of this inspiring message and continue to give back to Mother Earth in a small measure what we are extracting from her.

I conclude this chapter with the poetic words of Moid, which he had written to me:

> Create a green pasture in your heart and you will see the lovebirds visit you more often. There is no other way to create a loving place for humanity. And when you create a green pastures in the barren land drying up bit-by-bit with the global warming, you create a place in the heart of God for He loves those who love and work for humanity.

Good character is more to be praised than outstanding talent. Most talents are to some extent a gift. Good character, by contrast, is not given to us. We have to build it piece by piece—by thought, choice, courage and determination.

—John Luther

(An author)

Source: http://www.google.com/search?hl=en&q=John+Luther&btnG=Search

18 Pygmalion Singarenians—Some Profiles of Courage

Intellects Biz, explains what 'Pygmalion effect' means. Psychologists and management experts have conducted thousands of experiments to prove the phenomenon, 'what you expect you get'. The Pygmalion legend tells us how the power of expectations and passion of Pygmalion brought Galatea to life. The pith and substance of Pygmalion effect is how to get the best from your people. The 'Galatea effect' explains how best people give to the management.

Moid Siddiqui, in his study on factors causing the turnaround of Singareni from the viewpoint of leadership, has focused on six parameters for his detailed evaluation. These factors are listed as follows:

1. *Bonding*: one for all and all for one.
2. *Eco-friendly strategies*: creating green pastures.
3. *Self-worth of employees*: recognising the worth of people so that they will contribute their best potential and capabilities.
4. *Effective communication*: clarity and transparency about the company's status.

5. *Power of positive*: positive attitudes from the management and people alike—focus on good things happening, neglecting the negative aspects.
6. *Power of expectations (Pygmalion effect)*: people give what you expect from them—higher expectations get you the best from your people.

In his findings, Moid compliments the leadership of Singareni Collieries Company Limited (SCCL) for unwittingly using the technique of 'Pygmalion Effect' in the turnaround of SCCL. The most encouraging part of his findings is that 'the power of expectations' was the prime cause for motivating people and getting the best from them. The power of positive, effective communications and eco-friendly strategies were also rated higher on the scale.

Human nature innately craves for recognition and rewards. Only supreme hypocrites will deny that lack of recognition does not bother them in the least. History is full of stories where superb talent which when neglected and suppressed had in frustration become destructive. On the other hand, there are innumerable instances of persons possessing average abilities outperforming themselves and scaling the peaks of glory and success. I consider myself a balanced and pragmatic person. I will, therefore, accept the highly encouraging findings of Moid in complete humility. I can say with total conviction that my 'love story with Singareni' is an eternal source of strength and inspiration to me. Leadership cannot function in a void. Individual efforts cannot bring about monumental changes. But leadership can always motivate people to dream, and it can then guide them on the path that fulfils and realises their dreams. The top management of SCCL, perhaps, was successful in discharging this leadership role. The credit for unwittingly using 'Pygmalion effect' in our management approach goes to all members of team Singareni. After all, the essence of our bonding is rooted in our motto 'One Family, One Vision, One Mission—The Spirit of Singareni'.

It is impossible for me to mention the innumerable instances of exceptionally good work done by a large number of Singarenians. As I was privileged to have a long stay of almost five years, I went through some sublimely satisfying moments interspersed with darkness and despair. It was the incredible acts of courage and bravery displayed by some Singarenians that kept me going when everything was engulfed in gloom. My story would be incomplete if I do not pay a tribute to whom I call, 'Pygmalion Singarenians'. I am mentioning only a few instances where individual acts deeply impacted in generating positivity in the company. These brief capsules of narration underline the themes of self-worth, power of positive, power of expectation and bonding.

J. Tulasi is a middle-aged lady and wife of an SCCL officer residing in Manugur area. In 1994, doctors diagnosed her with breast cancer. She was subjected to the usual tests including radiotherapy and chemotherapy. One can well imagine the excruciating trauma of having cancer and its highly painful treatment. Instead of falling into the deep abyss of depression, Tulasi took inspiration from the advice of her doctor who said:

> The best life amongst the living beings is living a life of a 'Loving Being'. As a human being we have lots of difficulties, hardships, sorrows as well as happiness. You get what you focus on—sorrows or happiness. So, keep focus on happiness and develop your willpower, get involved in doing something for the Nature.

This incredibly inspiring advice metamorphosed Tulasi. She plunged herself enthusiastically in nurturing nature. Her house became a beautiful garden. She started cultivating medicinal plants. In 2005–2006, she won the 'Best Eco-friendly House' prize from the Environment Department of SCCL. Apart from her green activity, Tulasi learnt painting and other handicrafts. I visited her house in May 2006. She presented a beautiful papier mâché vase to me. This vase occupies a place of pride in the official residence of the CMD in Kothagudem. Not content with creativity, Tulasi is also an active counsellor for people suffering from terminal diseases. Her example is the greatest motivator for people with whom she interacts. Her case is a classic example of the 'placebo effect'. According to psychology our mind creates the chemistry of our body. Medical science has given this the name placebo effect. There are documented stories where deadly diseases have been cured through the placebo effect. Tulasi is a living example of the power of positive where the subconscious mind creates miracles for the conscious mind. I consider it a great privilege to have met Tulasi in her beautiful house at Manugur.

D. Baidya is superintendent of Mine Rescue Services in SCCL. He and his dedicated team of rescue personnel have constantly displayed courage and skill of an exceptionally high order. During the twin disasters of 2003, Baidya and his team performed incredible acts of bravery in retrieving bodies of employees who had perished in the accident. On 16 September 2006, Baidya and his team won laurels for the company when participating in the Fifth International Mining Rescue Competition in China, their team won the prize as the second best team in first-aid. They were placed at the fifth position in the rescue and recovery event, and secured the seventh place in the breathing apparatus test. This was the first time ever that the rescue team of SCCL participated in an international competition. And to SCCL also goes the unique distinction of becoming the first coal company in the country to win prizes in an international event. No greater evidence is required to acknowledge the greatness of Baidya and his team.

Some Singarenians have excelled in the realm of creativity. Kodepaka Mallesham, of Manugur area, has crafted really beautiful models of animals from waste materials. Visitors who see these models of dinosaurs, giraffes, deers and other animals are left speechless when they are told that these have been moulded from scrap material lying uselessly in workshops. They cannot believe their eyes. The unlocking of the creative genius of Mallesham is symptomatic, and so is the power of positive and the power of bonding. It is such individuals who have silently contributed in the transformation of SCCL.

Iqbal Pasha works as a clerk in SCCL. He and his talented group of singers have composed a beautiful *qawali* (musical song). The *qawali* is entitled, *Mera Koyla Kala Hai to Kya Hua, Bade Daam Wala Hai*, which means 'so what if my coal is black, it is invaluable'. The *qawali* is tuned to a popular Hindi film song. It never ceases to entertain, educate and inspire the audience as it is extremely melodious. Iqbal and his group won the first prize in singing in the Annual All India Coalfields Meet organised by Coal India Limited (CIL).

There are other equally heart-warming and inspiring stories. One cannot overlook Rekha, wife of a Singarenian worker, who is doing fantastic work in spreading literacy amongst women in the coal belt. Then there is Kavya, another worker's wife, who is an active member of Singareni Employees Wives Association (SEWA). She teaches the skills of stitching, embroidery and fabric painting to spouses of Singarenians. P. Saroja is a counsellor who motivates the wives of the employees to prevent their husbands from falling into bad habits like gambling, drinking and heavy smoking. She has made a great impact in de-addiction of nearly 1,000 workers. She works to prevent women from becoming victims of middlemen who exploit them for prostitution. G. Uma Devi is a yoga master in Srirampur area who has motivated a large number of Singarenians to practise yoga and improve their health. And who can forget K. Radha Hima Bindu whose husband is a senior technical inspector in Manugur area. Radha is an authoress who has penned more than 100 literary compositions including articles, stories and dramas. Some of her writings have been broadcasted in All India Radio (AIR) by the Kothagudem and Vijayawada stations.

It is virtually impossible for me to go on writing about many other nameless 'Pygmalion Singarenians' about whom I did not get an opportunity to know or interact with. I consider myself privileged to have interacted with some of the Pygmalion Singarenians mentioned in this chapter. But I know with full conviction that there are hundreds of individuals who have silently transformed the psyche of Singarenian workers from negative to positive. The team of Intellects Biz, which did extensive research in the districts of Karimnagar, Khammam and Adilabad, has documented several case studies of spouses of the workers who continue to do yeomen service in raising levels of awareness on important issues like health care, inculcating savings habit, adult literacy, imparting high-quality education to children and in curbing wasteful expenditure. Inspired by the great work that SEWA and SSS are doing, I decided to dedicate 2006–2007 as 'Mahila Shakthi Samvatsaram' (Year of Women Empowerment). Special schemes have been launched and initial reports indicated tremendous response to these new schemes. The fundamental focus of the new schemes is on generating employment for all ladies possessing skills like tailoring, stitching, painting and others which promote traditional handicrafts. There has been steep increase in the literacy levels of spouses. Craft bazaars are being regularly organised in coal belts where items manufactured by Singarenian ladies are sold. We have taken the innovative initiative of opening SEWA stall in the annual All India Exhibition held in Hyderabad. Our stalls have proved to be very popular and the participants have earned handsome profits.

An old saying goes, 'The child is the father of the man.' I would say that, 'The mother is the creator and cherisher of good societal values.' Great achievers throughout history have never failed to acknowledge the powerful role their mothers played in shaping their destiny. In Singareni, it is the women power (*stree shakti*) that has been the silent force in the revolutionary change in the mindset of Singarenians. This is nothing unusual. Sociologists have always stressed that any society that does not respect women and fails to utilise their enormous creative potential is less successful compared to a society that fully utilises the talent and potential of 50 per cent of humanity (i.e., women).

The highly creditable work being done in rehabilitation of physically and mentally challenged children of Singarenians in institutions like Manochaitanya in Ramagundam, Manovikas in Srirampur and Manoteja in Manugur deserves special mention. We have been the prime financers, organisers and sustainers of these institutions in the coal belt. Krishna Kumar, a Singareni employee, has been relentlessly toiling to raise Manochaitanya to great heights of achievement. This institution has received numerous prizes at the national level for the excellent work it is doing.

I always felt deeply humbled whenever I visited Manochaitanya and saw the hard work being done there. I felt that whatever I did in encouraging and sustaining this institution, and the two other sister institutions was inadequate given the magnitude of the task. It gave me immeasurable satisfaction when, in my own way, I did whatever best I could to strengthen these institutions by improving their infrastructure in a significant manner. This included construction of a new hostel building in Ramagundam. We also sought expert advice from national level institutions like National Institute of Mental Health (NIMH) for improving the content and quality of our rehabilitation programme.

It is my firm belief that our positive interventions in improving the functioning of Manochaitanya and its sister institutions played a silent but significant role in promoting bonding and the spirit of Singarenism. Service to mankind and to those who need it the most is the crux of humanism. All officers and workers were deeply moved when they saw the heightened concern of the top management in alleviating suffering. They were very appreciative of the touch of sensitivity and sincerity, which characterised the efforts made in helping their children in leading meaningful and productive lives despite some cruel handicaps.

There are two other vital ingredients that contributed to the Pygmalion effect. These were identified by the Intellects Biz's team as enhancing 'self-worth of employees' and the 'power of positive expectations'. The assessment was based on the following parameters:

1. Although many initiatives were taken during the past 10 years as 'turnaround strategies', one of the most important strategy was 'corporate bonding'—a deep level of relationship between management, people and their families.
2. There is some invisible relationship between 'creating green pastures' and 'turning around'.
3. During our bad times, the Singarenians were looked down upon by society but today the people of SCCL, by and large, feel proud to be known as 'Singarenians'.
4. Attempts have been made to improve the quality of training by providing opportunities for learning, which in turn, has become one of the major causes of turnaround.
5. Change of focus from 'negative strategies' like disciplinary actions, punishment, and so on to 'positive approach' with words of praise, appreciation, rewards and recognition has brought about the success.

6. The top leadership has inspired, motivated and raised the expectations from the people, and people in-turn, tried to give their best, matching those expectations and finally 'turning around'.
7. The involvement of families (in some of the initiatives) strengthened the quality of participation of people, which in turn, has created good impact on productivity, production and overall improvement.
8. Mining creates an imbalance in ecology which has been successfully brought to balance by plantations, greenery, flowering plants and creating green pastures, which has also become a major cause of the success.
9. During the past few years, the efforts of the people of SCCL in various areas were recognised in many forums and trophies, certificates, and so on were awarded. This has boosted the morale of the people and energised them with a higher level of commitment.
10. Effective communication through films, *burrakatthas*, cultural programmes, programmes aired on Mana TV channel, and so on is one of the major causes of SCCL's success.
11. When you keep your focus on 'avoiding failures' you get failures, and when you keep your focus on 'success' you get success. This is relevant to the success story of Singarenians.
12. The Singarenians gave their best because high expectations from them were created, which were followed by strong persuasion by the leadership.
13. The slogan 'One for All and All for One' has created an impact and has been the cause of 'corporate bonding'.
14. The greenery all around, soothes the heart, which, in turn, creates inner happiness and good feelings that led to higher output in SCCL and stands as one of the causes for its success.
15. People give their best when they are treated with a 'human face'—this reflects in the success story of SCCL.
16. The top leadership has proved that they talk and sermonise through their actions—walking the talk—that is one of the reasons of the success.

17. Singarenians have turned the threats into opportunities, following a positive approach by concentrating on opportunities rather than on the threats thereby getting positive results.
18. SCCL's subordinates are like soldiers: they obey and do what they are expected to do.
19. 'One Family, One Vision, One Mission', is not a mere slogan but an existing reality in SCCL that boosted the morale of the Singarenians.
20. Barrenness, what we call as sand traps, all around creates bad inner feelings, which, in turn, affects the output adversely. Thus, we gained through greenery.
21. People behave in the manner in which they are treated, good or bad. The good results of SCCL are reflective of better treatment of the juniors by the seniors.
22. Karmikamitra—the high-tech mobile van—has created the desired positive impact.
23. We find a *Mein Hoon Na* ('I am there to support you' type of leadership) spirit in the top leadership.
24. High expectations lead to high performance; low expectations lead to low performance. The 'turnaround' of SCCL proves this.
25. Singareni *padayatra*s by the complex's leaders have created a feeling of involvement, mutual respect and harmony.
26. SCCL's mines are eco-friendly mines.
27. When Singarenians were considered third grade, they gave low output and when they were considered first grade they gave their best.
28. The Mana TV channel is an effective communication process and has created the desired positive impact.
29. 'Kind words do not cost much—yet they accomplish much.' This statement is relevant to the success of SCCL.
30. When the leadership has strived for 'what best can be got from Singarenians?' people tried to give their best, matching the high expectations of leadership.

The parameters taken into consideration by Intellects Biz team very explicitly bring out the reasons that have contributed to the successful turnaround of SCCL. I drew enormous strength from the findings of this team. It was highly satisfying to realise that a completely detached and independent observation and evaluation process had vindicated my personal belief system in the innate goodness of human behaviour. I will always carry with me the strengths derived from my stay in Singareni when I deal with complex human behaviour and gigantic challenges.

Trust is the cornerstone of the edifice of human relations. One cannot win trust through hypocrisy. One has got to take the difficult and less travelled road paved with high moral values and ethical principles. Building trust was one of the significant features that got me success.

I have learnt many lessons from the turnaround of SCCL. Though many factors contributed success, to my mind, it was power of Bonding that created miracle. 'Bonding' calls for *trust* and *credibility* in leadership. I trusted the Singarenians and they returned the trust by trusting my leadership. This created, what I would call, *Synergy Spark*—a spark that flashes from the combination of psychological and emotional feelings. When you join your heart with your mind it creates the synergy spark. I have seen this happening not once but many times.

Management cannot force people to 'feel good'. The leader must cultivate the culture of care and create an environment where people start trusting each other. 'Feel-good' is the by-product of 'culture of care and trust'.

The leader must understand the ground realities—*all human situations are inherently dynamic*. What works at a given point in time, may not work at another time even though the group is same. Therefore, the leader must take steps understanding the ground realities. Effective communication is very important. Grapevines are scotched only when communication fails. Never allow the resentment to brood. Act speedily and resolve the issues. Relationships are built through trust. It takes time to cultivate the culture of trust. But a single wrong step can destroy the environment of trust.

19 The Journey Continues—Some Key Milestones Post 2006

My passionate and vibrant bonding with Singareni is unaffected by the passage of time. I have kept myself updated on a regular basis about Singareni. I have been a vicarious partner as the company continues its journey notching successful key milestones post 2006 since my departure. Perhaps Singarenism is in my blood. I am immensely humbled with the realisation that the majority of institutional reforms attempted during my tenure have not only survived, but have been enriched and strengthened by my distinguished successors Mr S. Narsing Rao (2006–2012), and Mr Suthirtho Bhattacharya (in office since May 2012 onwards).

When entrusted with the responsibility of adding an additional chapter to the revised edition of this book, I obtained details from SCCL Management on the current status of some key initiatives, schemes and projects post 2006. I would like to share with readers certain aspects which reinforce the inherent strength of institutional reforms and the power of Singarenism. I have tried to remain as objective as humanely possible in essaying this attempt.

I have focused on significant achievements in social and environmental areas. The management has provided me with a report submitted in October 2009, which it commissioned to the Centre for Economic and Social Studies, Hyderabad. They undertook an Impact Study on Singareni Sewa Samity (SSS) activities. This report focused on concrete achievements made by SSS in training and skill upgradation of employees, spouses and their children.

The report is well researched and scientifically designed. The results are heart warming. The study found that 70 per cent trainees have succeeded in either establishing their own independent units in different trades or in securing employment in the private sector. The monumental progress of adult literacy efforts is reflected in the fact that over 50,000 employees, spouses and children have been successfully enrolled and taught.

I requested Mr Rao (former CMD of SCCL) to share his thoughts on his over five and half years stay in the company, who mentioned that the emotional bonding of the employees with Singareni, their concern with its future welfare and their consistent desire to take the company to greater heights are unparalleled. He particularly highlighted the positive aspects of Singarenism and emotional bonding.

Great credit goes to Mr Rao for sustaining the reforms' process initiated by his predecessors. He provided continuity with unrelenting commitment and intensity. During his stay the company increased its production dramatically and achieved many records in productivity and profitability. Perhaps the biggest achievement was in 2007 when not even a single strike took place for the first time ever in the entire history of the company! Mr Rao focused on pioneering advanced Underground Mining Technologies, including Continuous Mining Systems, Short Wall Mining and Long Wall Bulk Production. These efforts won SCCL the INFRATECH 2006 award by the Union Ministry of Environment and Forests.

Unique developmental programmes were undertaken in the coal belt areas in 2003–2004 by commencing Surrounding Habitat Assistance Programme (SHAPE) with great enthusiasm. Nearly

₹100 crore has been spent by the company under its corporate social responsibility for SHAPE.

Both Mr N. Rao and his able and competent successor Mr S. Bhattacharya strongly affirm that SHAPE has been instrumental in enabling SCCL in maintaining its excellent relationships with all stakeholders in the coal belt areas. I am unaware of any other PSUs in the country successfully executing a programme like SHAPE. The uniqueness of this programme lies in complete integration of the 3Cs—Coordination, Collaboration and Cooperation. SHAPE was launched in 2003 during my tenure. Its distinctive features include implementing the 3Cs with the three main stakeholders: District Administration represented by District Magistrate; Local Gram Sabha represented by the Sarpanch; and the Company represented by its Area Manager. Together these three partners identify projects for developing socio and human infrastructure in coal mining areas. SCCL gives a one-time non-recurring 'GRANT' for creation of durable assets. These include school buildings, medical centres, drinking water facilities, roads, drainage facilities and community activity centres. These are the key 'felt needs' of persons residing in these areas. I am convinced that if SHAPE is implemented in its true spirit it can serve as a role model for other corporate sector entities in the country for emulation. Credit goes both to Mr Rao and Mr Bhattacharya for boldly and tenaciously strengthening SHAPE.

SCCL is continuing some very important initiatives which are yielding excellent results. The company continues to be a national leader in Mine Rescue Systems. It has successfully participated in International Mine Rescue contests since 2006 in China, United States, Australia and Ukraine. It is rare for public sector undertakings in India to win international awards competing against the very best in their respective fields. I am unaware of any mining company in India winning international awards in Mine Rescue work.

A key initiative of Mr Rao was starting SPANDANA Mobile Hospital Services. This is a reinforcement of a glorious Singareni tradition of providing medical diagnostic facilities to population affected by coal mines. The essence of this partnership is embedded genuine concern for stakeholders and not in mere tokenism for achieving short-term goals. It comes as no surprise that with its cordial relationship with local stakeholders, the company has succeeded in obtaining 17 environmental clearances in recent years enabling it to nearly double its mining production within a short span of 7 years. Fifty-one villages and thirty thousand persons have benefited from the medical initiatives of the company. This is a significant factor contributing to SCCL retaining its leadership status as the best administered and professionally managed coal company in the country.

I have unflinching belief in the boundless power of communication initiatives which form the bedrock of Singareni philosophy. With its large workforce and troubled history of labour relations, effective communications constantly dispel false propaganda of vested interests. The great popularity of audio–visual communications is reflected in efforts like Singareni Video Programme through Doordarshan and Singareni Kala Tarang. Regular production of high-quality cultural programmes rooted in local folk culture continues to flourish. It is to the credit of Mr Rao and Mr Bhattacharya that they have constantly innovated in their communication strategies.

I am very appreciative of the efforts of Mr Bhattacharya, the current CMD who is giving high priority to customer satisfaction. This is a hallmark of professionalism in promoting customer satisfaction. In recent times, the company has signed long-time Fuel Supply Agreements with its key customers including National Thermal Power Corporation (NTPC), and Andhra Pradesh Generation Company (APGENCO). I am confident that Mr Bhattacharya's emphasis on technology upgradation in brown field areas will continue to yield rich dividends in the coming years.

I am a passionate lover of nature. I continue to be the love bird in the green pastures of the mind. I am delighted that both Mr Rao and Mr Bhattacharya have placed high emphasis in promoting safe, scientific and sustainable mining practices. Despite its challenging and difficult geo-mining conditions the flag of green mining continues to fly high in the Singareni skies. Environmental education is still taught in SCCL schools in association with World Wide Fund India (WWF). Recently, I was overwhelmed when informed that the Government of Andhra Pradesh has included a chapter on SCCL in its social studies text book for class VIII. Can there be a greater tribute to the triumph of environmentalism in Singareni? Nothing gives me greater happiness than the realisation that the green seeds planted in young minds are strong and healthy trees today. 'This Green Revolution' of Singareni will continue to inspire me for the remaining days I am destined to spend on planet earth.

I have attempted a brief summary of some key milestones post 2006 in this chapter. The continuing success of the Singareni story is the greatest source of strength to me. My conviction in ethical and moral values to bring about revolutionary changes is constantly strengthened and reinforced by the lessons learnt from Singareni.

Life is a constant journey. It has only milestones. There is only one final common destination for all humanity. The Singareni story demonstrates that there is no substitute for Team Work and Team Spirit. The head and heart must pulsate to a common rhythm. Since no success is forever, it is imperative that we constantly introspect and review, adapt, renew and make appropriate mid-course corrections. Change is constant. It is inherent in the nature of the universe. When we abuse nature, nature destroys us. It is my fond hope and conviction that so long as Singareni continues its commitment to safe, scientific and environmentally sustainable mining, it will continue to prosper. I fervently prayer that may Singareni never abandon Singarenism. Long live Singareni!

I conclude my love story with Singareni and Singarenians by quoting the lyrics of the Singareni song—the poetic composition communicates the depths of Singarenism:

Jai Singareni
Jai Singareni
Jai Singareni
Hail to you a Giver of life
Hail to you a Giver of life!

We salute you; Singareni
you were born in Telangana
Near the Godavari
Singareni, your benevolent presence is everywhere…
In Khammam, Karimnagar, Warangal and Adilabad
Singareni!
Singareni, you unearth precious Black Gold
And make us shine!
We salute you, O! Giver of Life (protector of the Telugu people)

Energy is the foundation of progress,
And coal fuels this progress;
It's the core of this coal, the ore
That Singareni unearths!
The ore that is boon to South India,
The ore that fuels India's onward journey…
Ours is a rich legacy of over hundred years.

Through the ups and downs
Singareni overcomes by its own will
Marching ahead, united, in an unbreakable bond
As one family.
These are the fruits of tireless efforts
An inspiration for a bright tomorrow
We shall continue onward on this inspired path.

There are miles to go, to achieve milestones
Through discipline and fortitude;
We have to make way for a golden future
From the wealth of values and our earnings;
We will reach our goals, confident that our efforts
Will benefit us all.

Victory will be ours!
Triumphant will be our efforts!

Annexures

Supportive Data of SCCL Turnaround

ANNEXURE I: PROFILE OF SINGARENI COLLIERIES COMPANY LIMITED (SCCL)

Year of establishment	1886 Hyderabad Deccan Coal Company
Commencement of mining operations	1889 (Stocks quoted in London Stock Exchange)
Number of opencast and underground mines	Opencast: 11 Underground mines: 47
Total manpower as on 31 March 2001	105,627
Total manpower as on 31 March 2006	86,025
Total manpower as on 31 March 2013	64,600
Accumulated losses as on 31 March 1997	₹1,219 crore
Accumulated losses as on 31 March 2013	Nil
Accumulated profit as on 31 March 2006	₹176.42 crore
Accumulated profit as on 31 March 2013	₹738.90 crore
Gross turnover as on 31 March 1997	₹2,114 crore
Gross turnover as on 31 March 2006	₹4,209 crore
Gross turnover as on 31 March 2013	₹12,354.33 crore
Net worth as on 31 March 1997	(–) ₹11.20 crore
Net worth as on 31 March 2006	₹2,084 crore
Net worth as on 31 March 2013	₹3,432.50 crore

Accumulated debts as on 31 March 1997	₹1,109.54 crore
Accumulated debts as on 31 March 2007	Nil (accumulated debts were cleared by August 2004)
Accumulated debts as on 31 March 2013	829.48 crore (The loan has been obtained for Power Project from Power Finance Corporation as part of debited equity)

Source: Official records of SCCL.

ANNEXURE II: PERFORMANCE INDICATORS OF SCCL DURING PRE AND POST REFORMS

Sl No.	*Particulars*	*Units*	*Pre-Reforms (1996–97)*	*Post-Reforms (2005–2006)*	*Remarks*
1.	Coal production	Million tonnes	28.73	36.14	Increased by 26%
2.	Coal despatches	Million tonnes	28.83	35.32	Increased by 23%
3.	Overall output per manshift (OMS)	Tonnes	0.98	1.73	Increased by 78%
4.	Manpower	Nos	114,486	86,025	Decreased by 25% due to natural attrition and VRS packages offered 8 times
5.	Number of strikes	Nos	310	11	2005–06 is significant as it recorded lowest number of strikes, i.e., 11, in the history of the company after nationalisation of coal industry in 1973–74
6.	Gross turnover	₹ crore	2,114	4,209	Increased by 99%
7.	Gross investment	₹ crore	3,339	4,691	Increased by 41%

Source: Official records of SCCL.

ANNEXURE III: WELFARE MEASURES IN SCCL (BEFORE AND AFTER REFORMS)

The *Post-Reform Era* in SCCL is characterised by innovative, humane and courageous welfare measures undertaken for promoting the spirit of *Singarenism*. The statement given below clearly and sharply brings out the tremendous improvements in the quality of life of the company's employees by a series of novel welfare measures.

Particulars	*Pre-Reform Period (1996–97)*	*Post-Reform Period (2005–2006)*	*Remarks*
Earnings per manshift (₹)	346	833*	Increased by 121%
Welfare expenditure per employee (₹)	14,402	54,403	Increased by 278%
Welfare expenditure (₹ crore)	165	468	Increased by 184%

Source: Official records of SCCL.
Note: *Includes NCWA VII arrears of ₹110 per EMS.

ANNEXURE IV: GREAT READINGS

1.	*The Dance of Change*	Peter Senge	NB Publishing London
2.	*The Fifth Discipline*	Peter Senge	Century Business
3.	*A Whack on the Side of Head*	Roger von Oech	Warner Books
4.	*Change without Pain (Article)*	Eric Abrahamson	HBR
5.	*Change Management*	V. Nilakant and S. Ramnarayan	SAGE (Response Books)
6.	*Corporate Soul*	Moid Siddiqui	SAGE (Response Books)
7.	*Soul Inc.*	Moid Siddiqui	Wisdom Tree
8.	*Tao Te Ching*	Lao Tzu	Vintage Books
9.	*The Greatest Works of Kahlil Gibran*	Kahlil Gibran	Jaico Publishing House
10.	*Built to Last*	James C. Collins and Jerry I. Porras	Century Business
11.	*Good to Great*	Jim Collins	Harper Business
12.	*Blue Ocean Strategy*	W. Chan Kim and Renee Mauborgne	Harvard Business School Press
13.	*The Borderless World*	Kenichi Ohmae	Fontana
14.	*Future Shock*	Alvin Toffler	Bantam Book
15.	*Eco-friendly Coal Mining—The Singareni Approach*		SCCL Publication
16.	*Twenty-five Years with HMT*	S.M. Patil	Bhavan's Book University

Note: These books are great readings and are inspiring. No book can be written without having been inspired. We, Moid Siddiqui and R.H. Khwaja, acknowledge our gratitude to these authors.

About the Authors

Moid Siddiqui was the Managing Director (MD) of Intellects Biz, a firm which is highly regarded for its innovative training and consulting outlooks. He is a new-age corporate professional with interests ranging from developing human potential to scripting and directing business management films.

Moid Siddiqui has served Corporate India in senior and board level positions with premier, public sector and private sector organisations, including Bharat Heavy Electricals Ltd (BHEL), National Hydroelectric Power Corporation (NHPC) Limited, Cement Corporation of India (CCI), Hindustan Machine Tools (HMT), Bharat Earth Movers Limited (BEML) and Nagarjuna Group. He has also been a senior professor at the Centre for Organizational Development, Hyderabad. He is the author of 17 books on management themes and articles in international training journals of repute, including American Society for Training & Development's professional journal *Training & Development*. He is the recipient of several awards including the All India Management Association's 'Best Management Book Award of 1995–96' for his book, *The Brave New Manager*. *Corporate Soul* was adjudged the best book (third position) of the year 2005–2006 by Indian Society for Training and Development (ISTD). The same Society awarded the 'Commendation Award' for the year 2012 for his book *Enrich Your Personality*.

He has also carried out a research study on 'Performance Management Systems' at the International Resource Centre, United Kingdom, and participated in the Global Convention organised by the State of the World Forum at San Francisco, California, in October 1999, on 'Envisioning and Creating a Sustained Compassionate Society'.

His current areas of interest include 'soft skills', spirituality in business management, exploring values, human potential development, and 'creativity and innovation'.

R.H. Khwaja has served as Secretary, Ministry of Mines and Ministry of Tourism, Government of India. He belongs to the 1976 batch of the Indian Administrative Service (IAS). He completed his graduation in 1974 from St Stephen's College, Delhi. His postgraduation in history is from Aligarh Muslim University.

During his tenure in IAS, he has served with distinction in many key assignments in the Union Government and State Government. Some of his important assignments include (a) Collector and District Magistrate, Khammam, (b) Commissioner, Municipal Corporation of Hyderabad, (c) Joint Secretary to Government of India in the Ministry of Environment and Forest and (d) Chairman and Managing Director (CMD), Singareni Collieries Company Limited (SCCL).

Mr Khwaja has served as Special Secretary, Government of India, Ministry of Environment and Forests, New Delhi. He later worked as Union Tourism Secretary.

In recognition of the outstanding leadership during his tenure as CMD in SCCL, Khwaja received three national-level awards including 'Manager of the Year Award 2005' by Hyderabad Management Association.

The Government of Andhra Pradesh bestowed the prestigious 'Telugu Uttama Seva Pathakam' on him for outstanding work done during river Godavari floods in 1986 while serving as collector and district magistrate, Khammam.

He has visited many countries as an expert under the aegis of Convention on Biological Diversity Programme. Khwaja was in United States from 1989 to 1990 as a Hubert Humphrey North–South Fellow in University of Minnesota.

Khwaja is a committed environmentalist with special interest in the conservation of biological diversity. He is fond of trekking, reading and photography.